THE TRUTH ABOUT THE UFO CRASH AT ROSWELL

THE TRUTH ABOUT THE UFO CRASH AT ROSWELL

KEVIN D. RANDLE, CAPTAIN, U.S. AIR FORCE RESERVE &
DONALD R. SCHMITT, DIRECTOR OF SPECIAL INVESTIGATIONS,
CENTER FOR UFO STUDIES

M. Evans and Company, Inc.
New York

To Deborah:
In searching for the truth,
she presented me with the greatest gift of all
—her hand
—DRS

M. Evans and Company, Inc.
216 East 49th Street
New York, New York 10017

Library of Congress Cataloging-in-Publication Data

Randle, Kevin D., 1948–
    The truth about the UFO crash at Roswell / Kevin D. Randle and
Donald R. Schmitt. — 1st ed.
        p.   cm.
    Includes bibliographical references and index.
    ISBN 0-87131-761-3 : $19.95
        1. Unidentified flying objects—Sightings and encounters—New Mexico—
Roswell.   I. Schmitt, Donald R.   II. Title.
TL789.3.R343   1994
                                                                94-779
                                                                CIP

Design by Charles A. de Kay

Typesetting by AeroType, Inc.

Manufactured in the United States of America

9   8   7   6   5   4   3   2

Acknowledgments

I N ANY WORK of this sort, dozens of people assisted in putting it together. A special thanks must be given to Tom Carey for his help in tracking down the archaeologists. Without Tom, that aspect of the case might still be shrouded in mystery. Our deepest gratitude to both Brad Radcliffe and Richard Heiden for playing important roles in this investigation. Thanks are due to the members of the J. Allen Hynek Center for UFO Studies, including Mark Rodeghier, Jerome Clark, Jennie Ziedman, George Eberhart, and Dr. Michael Swords. UFO researchers Robert Hastings, Mark Chesney, Barry Greenwood, Joe Stefula, Clifford Stone, Ralph Heick, and, of course, Leonard Stringfield provided valuable assistance. Also our good friends, George Vogen, Carrie Wallace, and Jane Kilbolarn. Thanks are also due to the Fund for UFO Research.

More important are the witnesses, such as Walter Haut, Glenn Dennis, Frankie Rowe, Jim Ragsdale, Ruben and Pete Anaya, Jesse Marcel, Jr., Edwin Easley, Bill Rickett, Frank Joyce, the Wilcox family of Phyllis McGuire, Elizabeth Tulk, Barbara Dugger, and Christine Tulk, Arthur Exon, Jason Kellahin, Robin Adair, Bill Brazel, Jr., and many more too numerous to mention.

And, finally, the many friends we have made in Roswell, including Max Littell, Frank Kaufmann, John Price, and professional photographer Jack Rodden. There was Robert Pratt, who provided us with a transcript of his interview with Jesse Marcel, Sr., and kindly allowed us to quote from it; Paul Davids and Chester Lytle, Sr., who supported our work with their enthusiasm; Sheridan and Mary Cavitt, who invited us into their home on several occasions.

Unfortunately there is always someone left off such a list. To those we should have named and overlooked, an apology. There were so many helpful people.

Contents

8. KGFL, Walt Whitmore, and Frank Joyce   53

While the world waited for more information, army officers in Roswell were trying desperately to shut off the flow of data. Using intimidation and lies, they were able to stop the reports that something unusual had happened. One of the areas attacked was radio station KGFL. Frank Joyce, the reporter, was able to shed light on this. Teletype messages are used to reconstruct the reports. Joyce, the only person who interviewed Mac Brazel before he spoke to the army and after, provided a unique insight to what happened during those few days.

Part III

AFTERMATH

9. The Wright Field Connection   61

If there was a crash of an alien spacecraft at Roswell, then a committee to reverse-engineer it would have been created. Although the name of the committee isn't known, its existence is. Through eyewitness testimony, a portrait of that committee is presented.

10. The Autopsy Reports   67

The bodies recovered were, quite naturally, studied by a variety of experts. Access to the doctors who conducted the autopsies has been limited. Len Stringfield has provided some interesting data and shared it. And one doctor provided information about her research on the spinal cord. The bodies contained fewer vertebrae than a human spine.

11. The Threats   72

The army and the government wanted nothing said about the crash near Roswell. They moved quickly to suppress the information. While the military men and women could be sworn to secrecy, the civilians were another matter. A number of them, including Glenn Dennis, Frankie Rowe, Ruben Anaya, and the family of George Wilcox, explained how they had been threatened by officials of the government. Had this been the crash of an experimental balloon, they might have requested those involved to remain silent. But the threats went beyond that. Glenn

Dennis "would be picking his bones out of the sand." Frankie Rowe was going to "be taken out into the desert." There was nothing subtle about the attempts to silence the civilians, including several children.

12. Anatomy of an Investigation   77

The Associated Press sent two representatives into the Roswell area. Their stories had never been reviewed. Now, with their first-hand reports, and the documentation available, it is possible to learn exactly how human memory works, how two people can tell what they believe to be the truth, and how all of that fits into a complex whole.

13. The Twining Letter, Project Moon Dust, and a History of Deception   85

On September 23, 1947, Lieutenant General Nathan F. Twining, the commander of the Air Materiel Command, announced that "the phenomenon reported is something real and not visionary or fictitious." Twining was telling his subordinates that flying saucers existed. Unfortunately, in the text of that same letter, he claimed that there had been no proof "in the shape of crash recovered exhibits." An examination of that letter, of the attitudes of the time, and the circumstances of the creation of the letter provide us with a better understanding of both those statements. Coupled with a handwritten note by J. Edgar Hoover that said, ". . . We must insist upon full access to discs recovered," that suggests that something real was going on, and a study of that tells us exactly what was happening.

After Twining's suggestion for a priority investigation was made, the government responded with Project Moon Dust. Documents obtained through Freedom of Information reveal that Moon Dust was a real project that was charged with the retrieval of space debris.

14. The Search for the Archaeologists   102

Barney Barnett suggested that archaeologists had been on the impact site with him. For the first time those people have been located and their stories are incorporated into the Roswell case. First-hand testimony from one of the archaeologists brings this aspect of the Roswell case into sharper focus. No longer is it necessary to speculate about them, because they have been identified.

PART IV

THE EXPLANATIONS

15. Alternative Explanation Number One: A Japanese Balloon Bomb?   113

One researcher has claimed that Roswell can be explained by a balloon bomb. There is very good evidence to refute that claim, including the testimony of more than a dozen people in Roswell who were in a position to know.

16. Alternative Explanation Number Two: A V-2 Rocket?   120

There are those who have claimed that Roswell can be explained by the wreckage of a V-2. Notwithstanding the fact that many of the men at Roswell had served in Europe and a few even had wreckage from a V-2, there is a better case to be made. Evidence collected from the White Sands Missile Range as well as various archives shows that a V-2, or any other rocket, will not account for the wreckage found.

17. Balloons, Bombs, and Experimental Aircraft   124

All the other explanations for the wreckage will be explored, showing that there is not a shred of evidence that can explain the Roswell case in the mundane. A careful examination of the facts reveals little room for any other explanation.

18. A Complete Examination of the Evidence   134

Looking at the case from the point of view of a lawyer building a closing argument shows no room for any explanation other than extraterrestrial. By looking at a small portion of the case, an alternative can be found. But when all the facts are brought into play, the alternatives fall away.

B. The Witnesses   192

A comprehensive listing of the witnesses involved in the Roswell case broken down into first- and second-hand sources.

C. The Documentation   199

REFERENCES

Glossary   215

A short list of some of the words and phrases that aren't found in everyday use.

Notes   217

The endnotes from the first fourteen chapters, providing a comprehensive list for the sources used.

Bibliography   232

Includes a list of organizations and agencies that provided assistance and a list of the various periodicals used.

Index   245

PART I

IMPACT

1

On the Impact Site

H ISTORY IS OFTEN observed at the strangest times by those least prepared to witness it. Historic events are not always planned so that a corps of observers can be present. Today there are legions of video camcorder operators who seem to be everywhere recording everything, but in July 1947 that wasn't the case. And in New Mexico, where the population is still sparse, it is fortunate that there was anyone around to see what might be considered the major event of the last one thousand years.

It was Friday, the Fourth of July, and the beginning of a rare three-day weekend for James Ragsdale and his female companion, Trudy Truelove.* They had driven north from Roswell, New Mexico, using old Highway 48 (now Pine Lodge Road), turned off it, and continued on the back roads until they were far from the city and civilization. The night was anything but quiet, as lightning flashed and thunder boomed. A wind, blowing at thirty or forty miles an hour, whipped across the bleak desert landscape, driving dust and dirt. Rain came, briefly, roaring for a moment, hiding everything, and then evaporating in minutes. About 11:30 P.M., brightness flashed as an object roared overhead.[1]

Ragsdale said that it was a flaring bright light, blue-gray like that from an arc welder. At first he thought that it was a lightning strike not far from him, but then he saw the object as it roared over his campsite. Seconds later it slammed into the ground about a mile or so from the camp.[2]

South of Roswell, William Woody was watching the night sky with his father when he spotted a white light with red streaks in it. It glowed brilliantly and, unlike the many meteors he had seen in the past, took a long time to fall. It was brighter than any of those other meteors, and according to Woody, the wrong color.[3]

---

* The story told by Jim Ragsdale has been well corroborated by various family members, including Clint Brazeal, Wendelle and Willard Ragsdale, his wife Mary, and his mother-in-law, "Grandma Lucky."

In Roswell proper at Saint Mary's Hospital, Franciscan Catholic nuns Mother Superior Mary Bernadette and Sister Capistrano making routine night observations, saw a brilliant light plunge to earth, due north of their location. They believed it was a disabled aircraft of some kind and recorded its passage in their logbook. The entry noted the sighting was late on the night of July 4, between 11:00 and 11:30 P.M.[4]

A group of archaeologists in the Roswell area on site surveys also saw the strange blue-white object in the sky. They watched it fall to the ground, believing that it struck north of Roswell, not far from them. They made plans to search for it the next morning.[5]

Fifteen miles southwest of the base, Corporal E. L. Pyles, on a detached facility, looked up to see what he thought at first was a shooting star, but larger. It moved across the sky and then arced downward. There seemed to be an orange glow around it, a halo near the front. Pyles believed that the event took place between 11:00 P.M. and midnight because the lights at the facility were turned out after 10:30, and he would normally retire before midnight. He thought it was near the weekend, but couldn't be sure of the exact day.

When the rain ended, just moments after it had started, Ragsdale convinced Truelove they should go look for the thing that crashed. They drove across the rocky terrain and stopped at the edge of a short cliff. Using a flashlight with weak batteries, they explored the area. They saw the remains of the ship stuck in the side of the cliff but could see no movement around it. It was late, and the flashlight was failing. They returned to their Jeep and drove back to the campsite. There was nothing they could do that night. Besides, they had been drinking and neither was supposed to be out there. They decided they would return in the morning.[6]

It was not only civilians from the Roswell area that knew something strange had happened. Military officials, both officers and the enlisted technicians had been tracking, on their radar, an unidentified object in flight over southern New Mexico since July 1. The object had first appeared over the highly restricted areas near the White Sands Proving Ground (later the White Sands Missile Range) about one hundred miles from Roswell. This was the site of the first atomic bomb detonation in 1945 and currently the home of sensitive rocket and missile research being conducted by members of various components of the United States military.

On July 2, Steve MacKenzie,[7]* stationed at Roswell Army Air Field, had received a call from Brigadier General Martin F. Scanlon of the Air Defense Command, ordering him to report to the radar sites at White Sands. MacKenzie

---

* Sworn affidavit on file.

was to monitor the object's movements and report them directly to the general. MacKenzie could not leave the scope unattended for even the shortest of times. In fact, once he had his watch established, he set up a system of mirrors so that he could see the screen even when he needed to use the latrine.

No one at White Sands doubted that this was a real object. When it first appeared, radar operators at White Sands had considered the possibility of a malfunction, but a check with a second set, as well as coordination with other sites, including those at Roswell and in Albuquerque, established that the target was real, and solid.

MacKenzie stayed at his post for twenty-four hours straight, but nothing changed. The object appeared periodically over southern New Mexico, but usually just "flitting from one location to another."

When MacKenzie reported that nothing had changed significantly during his twenty-four-hour watch, Scanlon decided to end MacKenzie's part of the operation. Although MacKenzie was ordered back to Roswell, the operators at White Sands were told to continue to monitor the object, as were the radarmen at Roswell and Albuquerque.

MacKenzie was in contact with Robert Thomas, an officer stationed in Washington, D.C., all during this time. Thomas asked on several occasions if he should head out to New Mexico, but MacKenzie told him not to bother for the time being. The situation was still fluid, and he didn't know what would happen. At two or three in the morning on July 4, however, Thomas called to inform MacKenzie he was on the way, explaining that he wanted to be on the scene in case something happened.

Thomas's special flight from Washington, D.C., arrived early on the afternoon of July 4. He had requested some special equipment and arranged for transportation for himself and for the small party of experts he had brought with him. He held a quick briefing with the men stationed at Roswell and then settled in to wait.

That evening the situation changed radically. The object, as displayed on the radar, seemed to pulsate, the blip growing larger and brightening before shrinking to its original size and dimming. This activity kept up for a short time and then the object blossomed into a sunburst and disappeared from the screen at about 11:20 P.M. Because there were three sites tracking the object, the army technicians were able to plot, within vague parameters, the location of the crash or landing.

But the radar coverage in that section of New Mexico was not as complete as the military would have liked. The Capitan Mountains sit between the impact site and the radar sets of White Sands and Alamogordo. Other mountains rest between Albuquerque and Roswell. Coverage in some places did not extend below eight or nine thousand feet. That meant that the army, based on what it had learned while tracking the object at Roswell, knew that the object was down north of town. They just didn't have a precise location. A comprehensive search would be launched at sunrise.[8]

The military wouldn't be the first to arrive, however. An archaeological team lead by Dr. W. Curry Holden from Texas Tech University stumbled upon the site about dawn on the morning of July 5.[9] The craft, according to one of the archaeologists with Holden, was "a crashed airplane without wings," and it had a "fat fuselage."[10]

As they approached, they saw three bodies. Two were outside the craft, and one was visible through the hole in the side. Like Ragsdale, who thought it might be some sort of government vehicle, they believed they were looking at an experimental aircraft.

Holden sent one of the students back to the main highway with orders to find a phone and alert the local authorities, either the sheriff or police, that they had found an aircraft accident.

Holden confirmed that the site was near Roswell, almost due north of the city limits. That would become important later when Mary Ann Gardner told of a female anthropologist she knew. A woman dying of cancer in the late 1970s told Gardner that she had seen a crashed spacecraft and the bodies of the alien crew. Gardner didn't believe the story at the time. Later, when she learned about the events around Roswell from a television report, she knew that the woman had been describing that field on that morning in July. The woman mentioned that one of the men had even tried to enter the craft, but the military had arrived too quickly and had sworn them all to secrecy.[11]

Tom Carey, a researcher living in Pennsylvania, confirmed the location through others. Carey found a student who had heard the story of the UFO crash from one of her professors. She confirmed that anthropologists had been on the scene and that the location was in southeastern New Mexico, near Roswell. He was able to confirm that the archaeologists were north of the town, not northwest near Corona.[12]

Under questioning by Carey, she also confirmed the date. It was the Fourth of July weekend. They remembered that because it was a long weekend. She was certain that it hadn't been during the week.[13]

Holden wasn't the only scientist in the area. Dr. C. Bertram Schultz, a vertebra paleontologist, was attending a conference in Roswell. He was also working in the mountainous areas south and east of the city. On the morning of July 5, while about fifteen to twenty miles north of Roswell,[14] he encountered the cordon thrown up by the military.[15] He hadn't planned to drive to the west of the highway, so he didn't have an opportunity to ask the military men what they were doing out there.

Later, in Roswell, he talked with Holden and a few of his students. He learned from them that there had been a crash of an extremely unusual craft.[16] He noted the event in his personal diary.

With the sun now up, Ragsdale and Truelove left their campsite in a Jeep, the windshield down, hoping to see more. They bounced across the open ground and drove up a gentle slope to a point where the ground dropped away and they could see out across the desert. They climbed from the Jeep and worked their way to the edge of the cliff. Now, in daylight, Ragsdale got his first good look at what had smashed into the ground. Although he was calm, Truelove was not. She wanted to "get the hell out of there." There was no telling what it was.

According to Ragsdale, in an interview conducted more than forty years later, it had hit the ground, sticking in the cliff at an angle. The front of the craft was crumpled. It looked like part of an aircraft with narrow wings. Ragsdale said, "You could still see where it hit. . . . One part was buried in the ground, and part of it was sticking out of the ground." He indicated an angle of about thirty degrees.

Ragsdale and Truelove moved around so that they could get a better look at the craft, though Truelove was insisting that they should get out of there. She was frightened by the object and the events of the night before.

Debris was scattered across the crash site, and both Ragsdale and Truelove picked up a few of the pieces. According to him, "You could take that stuff and wad it up and it would straighten itself out."

Of one piece, he said, "You could take it and put it into any form you wanted, and it would stay there. You could bend it in any form, and it would stay. It wouldn't straighten out."

But that wasn't the most amazing thing about the wreckage. Near the craft, Ragsdale saw "bodies or something laying there. They looked like bodies. They weren't very long . . . four or five foot long at the most." According to Ragsdale, they looked like midgets. He didn't know what to think. Truelove was tugging at him, trying to get out of there. She was scared of the craft and the bodies. Had they seen the bodies the night before, Ragsdale said they wouldn't have camped out there. They would have left for Roswell.

As they threw some of the wreckage into their Jeep, they "heard all of them coming. . . . It was two or three six-by-six army trucks, a wrecker and everything.

Leading the pack was a '47 Ford car with guys in it, MPs in it." He said that one vehicle had a siren, and that was what had first drawn his attention.[17]

While they watched, the trucks fanned out and parked. MPs climbed out and began to surround the crash site. The man in charge of the MPs, Major Edwin Easley,[18] ordered them to the top of the cliff where they could watch the surrounding territory. Now Ragsdale began to worry, too. Ducking low, he and Truelove ran back to their Jeep. As Ragsdale started the engine, Truelove tried to throw all the debris they had collected clear. She was afraid they would be arrested for taking it.

Ragsdale drove into a concealing copse of trees and bushes. He crouched in the weeds to watch as the military police, concerned with the wreckage and bodies, began to cordon the immediate area. Truelove still wanted to get clear. Before the MPs began a search, Ragsdale and Truelove returned to their campsite.[19]

At the Roswell Army Air Field, MacKenzie and the special Washington team received word that they had to get out to the crash site immediately. "There are civilians on the site," he was warned.

They headed out along Highway 285, which in 1947 was a twenty-foot-wide paved road. According to him, "We went in in three Jeeps [and] then four trucks, one truck with a crane. [There were] MPs, but I don't know how many trucks were with them."

Once they left the main road, they "cut across-country. . . . We cut straight across. We cut some fences. We went over some terrain . . . rocks, cactus, everything." They continued straight, until "we came to the top . . . and saw the damned ravine dropped off, and we backed off and circled around. As we were coming down that ravine . . . we could see the glisten from the metal and we knew right away where we were. This was the area."

Complete access to the impact site, the immediate area where the object had crashed, was restricted to those with the highest clearance and a real need to know. There were nine such men, at least three of whom (Thomas, Howard Fletcher, and a man identified only as Lucas) had come from Washington, D.C. Other men, including Adair[20] and Harris, came in from the West Coast, as well as a special unit from White Sands.* A few assigned to the 509th Bomb Group in Roswell, including William Blanchard, Easley, and W. O. "Pappy" Henderson, were also heavily involved.[21] Blanchard's involvement would be particularly significant in the next few days.

---

* In addition to MacKenzie, Lieutenant Colonel Albert Lovejoy Duran, a member of that unit, has confirmed their assignment and acknowledges witnessing the "bodies."

The impact site, about thirty-five miles to the north-northwest of the front gate of the Roswell Army Air Field, was heavily guarded, with MPs stationed around the perimeter and facing away from it.[22] Louis Rickett, a counterintelligence corps agent who would not arrive at the scene for three more days, said that the craft had a curved front and a wide wing with a batlike trailing edge.[23] [24] There was a rip or hole in the left side. The craft had slammed into the ground, crumpling the front of it. It had impacted in the side of the cliff, sticking out at an angle of about thirty or forty degrees. Debris was scattered around it.

Easley's MPs wasted no time in rounding up the archaeologists. They were asked to give their names, their school affiliation,[25] and then were taken into Roswell for further interrogation. They were escorted to the base and not allowed to leave for the moment.[26]

The main group, the nine men with the highest clearances, covered the center of what MacKenzie called the impact site. According to MacKenzie, when they first saw the craft, they were stunned. They stood, transfixed, staring at the object, momentarily unable to move.[27] Because they had watched it on radar, they knew that something strange had crashed, but they were not prepared for what they saw. In the first moments, as the MPs scattered across the fields, taking up positions on the top of the cliff, at the access points to the area and along the roads, the men stood staring at the ship.[28]

The trucks and jeeps were pulled up closer and parked, setting a partial screen around the impact site. No one approached at first. One man, dressed in a protective suit and carrying a Geiger counter, advanced, checking the area for signs of radiation. MacKenzie said, "He went in there and made a number of tests. It took about fifteen minutes. . . . We were all smoking cigarettes and talking about how in the hell we were going to handle this thing. We were all concerned and a little scared."

When the preliminary examination was finished, the men moved over the site. Easley ordered the MPs to face away from the ship and to watch the surrounding terrain. No one was to approach without being identified and properly cleared.

Easley continued, saying, "The second group scanned quite a large area looking for debris. . . . It was loaded onto a truck and then onto a plane [in Roswell], and it took off. Whatever they found [in the outside area] . . . was just odds and ends."

The main part of the craft, about twenty-five to thirty feet long and twelve to fifteen feet wide, had forcibly crashed into the arroyo at the base of a tall cliff. The nine men approached it, but the others were held back, used as guards to screen the impact site. They made a careful examination of the ground around the point of impact, searching for additional debris.

MacKenzie said there was a major in from Washington with the special group who took care of the remains. He had ordered in the man in the special suit and rubber gloves, and he was the one to order lead-lined body bags.[29]

The bodies, five in number[30] and obviously not human, were not all within the ship. The ship's crew were small, about five feet tall and slender, and had heads that seemed too big for their bodies. The eyes were only slightly larger than human eyes, and they had pupils.

Two of them were found outside the craft, one sprawled on the ground and the other sitting next to a cliff. Both were dead. Looking through the hole in the fuselage, MacKenzie saw another inside the craft. It was in a chair, slumped to one side. He could see the legs of a fourth. The fifth, inside the craft, was not immediately visible. It was later that MacKenzie learned about it.

MacKenzie's attention was drawn to the being sitting near the cliff. "That's the one that I cannot forget. It had that damned serene look on its face . . . like it was at peace with the world. . . . I [was] amazed at that."

Two photographers on the site had come from Washington on the flight with Thomas. Neither was on the special nine-man team, but they were given full access to the impact site so that they could record the scene before everything was moved out. According to Easley, "One was a tech sergeant and the other a master sergeant. . . . [They were] real pros [who] knew their business. They came out with Thomas. . . . [They] took stills and they took movies of the area."

They had set up a grid, and according to Easley, "Each group took a certain section and recorded everything they saw, anything unusual . . . marked it on the grid."[31]

Small planes flew overhead,[32] "flying low and taking photographs. . . . They had a grid map they worked from. . . . [They] then examined everything very carefully to see if they had overlooked anything."[33]

Easley's MPs cordoned the whole area, not only surrounding the impact site, but blocking all the roads leading into the area. William Woody would later confirm this when he said that his father had decided to try to find the spot where the object they'd seen the night before had hit the ground. They had driven out on Highway 285, the road from Roswell to Vaughn, but they were prevented from leaving the main road by the military police. The Woodys couldn't get into the area. According to him, all the access roads throughout the area were blocked.[34] [35]

Ragsdale and Truelove watched long enough to know that "they cleaned everything all up. I mean they cleaned it. They raked the ground and everything." That was confirmed by MacKenzie's later statement that the retrieval crew had used industrial vacuums to clean the site.

To stay away from the military, Ragsdale and Truelove kept moving farther away from the impact site. Truelove was thoroughly frightened by the soldiers. She was afraid that she would be arrested if the military discovered them. They avoided the back trails and tracks, driving cross-country to get clear.

The trucks were pulled forward so that they were aimed at the craft. Military jeeps, used as the command posts, were parked outside the perimeter. MPs were stationed around, facing away from the craft. These men were rotated frequently, sent back into Roswell so that no one group would get a good long look at what was happening.[36]

With the site secured and photographed, the men moved in. Through a large hole in the side, part of the interior was visible. MacKenzie saw another two beings on the inside. The fifth was deeper in the craft, invisible to those outside it.

"We had a special group come in who were well covered," explained Mac-Kenzie. "[They wore] rubber gloves. . . . [They] put them in body bags."[37] The bodies were placed in the rear of old box-type ambulances to be driven to the base hospital. Sergeant Melvin E. Brown was ordered to climb into one of the ambulances but to leave the body bags alone.[38]

The phone calls to Ballard's Funeral Home in Roswell began about 1:30 P.M. The base mortuary officer was asking Glenn Dennis, a young mortician working at Ballard's, a series of strange questions. According to Dennis, "He was inquiring about what size, what type of caskets, and how small [were the] caskets that we could furnish that could be hermetically sealed."*

Thirty or forty minutes later, Dennis received another call from the mortuary officer. "He was asking me about our preparations . . . preparing a body that had been laying out in the elements . . . how we treated burnt bodies or the very traumatic cases. . . . I went through the steps on how we treated the bodies. . . ."

But the mortuary officer wasn't through yet. According to Dennis, "The next question was what would you do where you wouldn't change any of the chemical contents, you wouldn't destroy any blood, you wouldn't destroy anything that might be very important down the road. What would your process, the chemicals you use, [do that] would change the chemical contents [of the blood]."

Interviewed over forty years later, Dennis said, "I knew at the time that something had happened . . . something they probably weren't ready to release. It

---

* Former Roswell chief of police, E.M. Hall, has confirmed that days later Dennis discussed the request for such caskets for the "bodies from a flying saucer."

might be some VIP or something. . . . I told them at the time I could come out and help them, but he said no, this is for future reference."[39]

The bodies were taken into Roswell and kept in a hangar overnight. "Everything in the hangar was cleared out," according to Frank Kaufmann, a man assigned to the 509th Bomb Group staff, "and a single box was placed in the middle of the hangar, which had a great big double door. Guards were placed all the way around it. [They] were armed with carbines. You couldn't get near the place."

Kaufmann said, "There was nothing unusual about the crate itself. . . . it was maybe twenty by six . . . a large crate." Kaufmann said that he knew what was in the crate: the bodies recovered at the impact site.[40]

MacKenzie mentioned a photographer from Roswell, Woodrow Jack Rodden, was also deeply involved.[41] According to him, Rodden was brought into the hangar to photograph some of the strange debris stored inside. An enlisted man with Rodden handed him the photographic plate, let him expose it, and then took the plate back. When Rodden finished, they made a complete inventory of the photographic plates to ensure that nothing had disappeared. The photographer was then escorted to a car and driven home. He was, of course, sworn to secrecy.[42]

When Rodden was gone, everyone, except the guards, was ordered from the hangar. The crate was left in the center, illuminated by a spotlight shining down on it. Although there was a full complement of guards on the outside, MPs were stationed around the interior of the hangar to watch the crate. No one could enter the hangar or approach the crate without the proper clearances. According to MacKenzie, the guards had orders to shoot anyone who approached without authority.[43]

Brown, who had ridden with the bodies from the crash site, was added to the guard detail outside the hangar. While he was standing guard, the commanding officer of Squadron K, Captain John Martin, walked up and said, "Come on, Brownie, let's have a look inside."

There was nothing to see inside except the plain wooden crate. Brown said that it had been prepared for shipment out that night. Martin and Brown walked back outside.[44]

Interestingly, MacKenzie said that the crate was shipped to Andrews Army Air Field and then on to Patterson Army Air Field. It left Roswell at two or three in the morning. Other flights were ordered and then diverted, destinations changed in flight, while others had their paper records altered later. MacKenzie had never seen such a concerted effort to create diversions evidently intended to cover the trail just in case anyone ever tried to follow it.[45]

MacKenzie was sure of the destination of the crate with the bodies because he, along with Thomas, was aboard the aircraft, a C-54. Pappy Henderson, one of the most trusted members of the 1st Air Transport Unit, was the pilot in command.[46] The crate, kept in Hangar 84 on the eastern side of the flight line, was loaded onto the aircraft under conditions of maximum security at night. All the lights around the hangar area had been extinguished during the loading. The guards, along with the crews, used flashlights to see.[47]

The airplane flew from Roswell on to Andrews, where the crate was unloaded, again under the cover of darkness. For a short period, maybe as much as twenty-four or thirty-six hours, it sat in a guarded hangar at Andrews, apparently so that the army chief of staff, Dwight Eisenhower, and the secretary of war, Robert P. Patterson, would have an opportunity to see at least one of the bodies.

According to MacKenzie, all the bodies were not on that flight. They were split between two aircraft to ensure that the evidence would not be lost if one of the planes crashed. The second flight followed the first by about thirty minutes.[48]

Later, the bodies were again loaded on aircraft and sent on to Patterson Army Air Field in Dayton, Ohio. It should be pointed out that Wright Field and Patterson Field were close, but the more classified flights went into the second field. Later the two bases would be combined into the large, sprawling Wright-Patterson Air Force Base complex.

In the wake of all these events, according to MacKenzie, files were altered. So were personnel records, along with assignments and various codings and code words. Changing serial numbers ensured that those searching later would not be able to locate those who were involved in the recovery. The trail was being carefully altered.

MacKenzie said that there had been two Secret Service men dispatched to Roswell during that week in July. One man, named McCann, the president's personal representative, escorted the bodies from Roswell to Washington.[49] That left the second Secret Service agent, Devinnes, behind as the president's representative in Roswell.[50]

MacKenzie was unaware of a second crate shipped to Fort Worth a couple of days later. Nor did he know that a preliminary autopsy had been conducted at the base hospital. Yet two of the participating physicians had flown in from Washington, and a third, Sanford, was routed through Beaumont General Hospital in El Paso, Texas. He wasn't assigned to the base there, merely routed through it in an attempt to cover the trail.

MacKenzie was later warned not to talk about it or respond to any rumors he might hear. A lot of rumors and wild stories were sure to follow, but he should "let

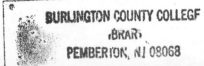

them fly. If they get close, keep your mouth shut . . . don't start a conversation, don't ask them how they knew. Just play dumb." Thomas said that if he tried to learn where someone heard a rumor, the very act would lend the rumor a degree of credibility.

Edwin Easley confirmed the secrecy more than forty years later. Repeatedly he said, "I can't talk about it. I was sworn to secrecy."[51] But more important, Easley told family members why he could not talk about the case. He'd promised the president that he would never reveal what he had seen.[52] But Easley knew what he had seen, confirming that the craft had been extraterrestrial in origin.[53]

MacKenzie also knew of individuals brought into Roswell from Alamogordo, Albuquerque, and Los Alamos. The MPs were a special unit constructed of military police elements from Kirtland, Alamogordo, and Roswell.[54] The reason was to help keep the secret. If the men didn't know one another, or were separated after the event, they would be unable to compare notes, and that would make the secret easier to keep.

After the impact site was cleaned, the soldiers debriefed, and the bodies and craft removed, silence fell. It would not be broken for almost forty-five years.

2

Glenn Dennis
and Ruben Anaya

THE FIRST-HAND WITNESSES, the men who had been on the impact site and seen both the bodies and the craft, disappeared for almost fifty years, sworn to secrecy, which most of them maintained. The first information about the bodies and the activities around them came from the second-hand sources.

After the phone calls of the early afternoon of July 5, 1947, Glenn Dennis, the mortician at Ballard's, returned to his daily routine, which included driving one of Roswell's ambulances. Late in the afternoon he was summoned to pick up an injured airman. Dennis put the soldier, suffering from minor head injuries and a broken nose, in the ambulance, and headed to the base. Once there, he was waved through the front gate, as was normal operating procedure.[1]

He drove to the rear of the hospital, where the emergency room was located. There he found three old boxy "field" ambulances parked near the ramp. Standing near each of the rear doors was an MP. Dennis escorted the injured airman to the ramp, and as they passed the ambulances, "naturally I noticed as I was passing the first ambulance, there was some wreckage. . . . Looked like some particles or pieces from a crashed airplane. In the second there looked to be some almost identical pieces. In the third ambulance, I don't believe there was any debris, but there was an MP by the door."

Dennis saw nothing unusual about any of this. When bodies were recovered at an aircraft accident site, Dennis explained, inevitably some of the debris was thrown into the rear of the ambulances. Because of that, he wasn't surprised to see the debris inside.

Dennis managed to get a fairly good look at some of the wreckage and was struck by its unusual appearance. He said, "What I saw reminded me of the front part of a canoe . . . about three feet long and lying up against the side . . . tipped [so that] the open part was against the floor. There were some inscriptions on [a] border around

15

part of it . . . three inches maybe . . . going along the contour of the wreckage. At the time . . . it reminded me of Egyptian inscriptions."[2]

As the airman was being treated in the emergency room, Dennis, who knew most of the medical staff from his experiences as an ambulance driver, stepped into the lounge for a Coke. As he walked down the corridor, one of the new nurses spotted him and, according to Dennis, was "very excited. . . . She said, 'How did you get in here? You're going to get into trouble. Get out of here as fast as you can.' Then she went through a door on the side. She disappeared immediately."

But Dennis didn't get out immediately. Instead he was spotted by an officer who was about forty-five or so and was, according to Dennis, turning prematurely gray. "He turned around and said, 'Who are you? What are you doing here?' "

Dennis replied that he "was with the Ballard Funeral Home and I just made an emergency run. [I said] I was going back to the lounge to get a Coke. But I said, 'Looks like you've had a crash. I see some debris in the ambulances there.'

"And that's probably where I got into trouble. He said, 'Just a moment.' He went to the door and motioned for somebody, and about that time . . . two MPs came out. He said, 'Get this man out of here. Get him out of here as fast as you can.' We were starting down the hall and we heard a voice say, 'I'm not through with that SOB yet. Bring him back.' "

Dennis turned and walked back a few steps, where he confronted a red-haired captain. "There was a sergeant [with him], a black man, holding a clipboard. The red-headed captain told me, 'There was no crash here. You did not see anything. You don't go into town. You don't tell anybody you saw anything. If you do, you'll get into serious trouble.' "

Furious at being called an SOB, Dennis informed the captain that he had no power over him because he, Dennis, was a civilian. Having established that, he then told the officer to go to hell. "Those were my exact words," said Dennis. "I remember it very clearly."

The red-haired officer said, "Don't kid yourself, young man. Somebody'll be picking your bones out of the sand."

"Or you'll make good dog food," added the black sergeant, staring at Dennis.

They escorted Dennis from the hospital and to his ambulance. They then followed him all the way into Roswell and on to the Ballard Funeral Home.[3]

Glenn Dennis wasn't the only civilian to learn a little of what was happening on that day in July. Frankie Rowe, whose father, Dan Dwyer, was a fire fighter with the Roswell Fire Department in July 1947, saw more than just a few fragments of debris. As she recalls, the fire department, or rather one of the trucks, responded to a call early on the morning of July 5, 1947. "Daddy was on the crew that went," she said. "He told us later that what he saw was the wreckage of some type of flying craft. He did not know what it looked like. He couldn't tell. He said they were very small pieces. A lot of it had been picked up."[4]

The military had already arrived, as had some of the city of Roswell police officers. There were also some state police at the site, but she didn't know the names of any of them. It wasn't clear whether they just guarded access to the site or helped clean the field. If there had been any large pieces, or the main body of a craft, all that was gone before the fire department arrived.

She said, "There were apparently three people in the craft, because he saw two body bags and he saw one live person . . . a very small being about the size of a ten-year-old child."

He could tell his daughter little more than that because "they put this being in a vehicle and took it away immediately. . . . They did take the two body bags away in a separate vehicle."

Dwyer had no doubt that these were not human beings. Rowe remembers his belief that "these were adults that were about the size of a ten-year-old child and they didn't have any hair. . . . He . . . only saw the one. The other two were in body bags. . . . He saw one person walking. He didn't think it suffered any injuries."

Frankie Rowe later heard rumors that the being was taken directly to the base hospital. Supposedly it walked into the building without assistance.

That night, when he got home, Dwyer told his wife a little about it but also mentioned there were many things that he couldn't say. Rowe didn't overhear all the conversation they held that night.

Later, according to Rowe, "The air force or the army or the military came up to our house and told us we could never talk about this. As far as we were concerned, the whole incident never happened. If we talked about it . . . we were threatened."[5]

Other members of Rowe's family confirm her father's involvement and the later threats. Helen Cahill, who was married and living in California in 1947, was told a little about the events. Her father told her that something important had happened but refused to say any more about it because of his concern for the safety of the family. He would tell her nothing else and refused to answer questions, though he said that he wished he could.

Her mother told Helen Cahill more, explaining about the threats made against the family. Her mother said that her father was afraid that someone would find out. Like so many others, Cahill was told, "You are better off if you don't know."[6]

Frankie told her of the threats made by the military. Cahill confirmed that they had been sitting around the table when the military had told Frankie that she would disappear into the desert. According to Cahill, she learned of this aspect in the early 1960s, long before any UFO researchers were interested in the events in Roswell.[7]

Roy Musser happened to be at the base that afternoon. He was a civilian contractor, painting part of the hospital. Working in the rear, he saw the one creature arrive. Apparently uninjured, it walked under its own power into the hospital. It looked like a child and was very slender.

The military warned Musser that he was to never mention what he had seen to anyone or both he and his family would be in jeopardy. Musser kept quiet for a few years before relating the experience to Dan Dwyer.[8]

Other people knew of the beings that had been taken to the base hospital. In July 1947 Mary Bush was the secretary to the hospital administrator. Her brother George would vividly recall the day she came home extremely agitated. She sat in the kitchen that evening, a cup of coffee in front of her, and told what she had seen. A creature from another world. She'd been with the administrator when she had seen the body in the base hospital. It was a horrible sight, something that she would never forget.

Seeing how badly shaken she was, the family didn't press her for more details. No one questioned her truthfulness, and she never mentioned it again. It made such an impression on her brother that he didn't forget it either.[9]

Another witness to the bizarre events of July 1947 was New Mexico Lieutenant Governor Joseph Montoya,[10] according to his lifelong friend Ruben Anaya. In 1947 Anaya was a cook at the Roswell officers' club.

Few people had phones in those days, especially young Hispanics. Because of that, Montoya had to call Anaya's father, telling him to get Ruben to come out to the base. Anaya returned the call, and the base operator had to track down Montoya and pass a message along to him. Anaya finally managed to locate Montoya, who told him, "Get your car, Ruben, and pick me up. Get me the hell out of here."[11]

Anaya went to his brother Pete's house to pass on Montoya's messages. Three of them went, the two Anayas and Moses Burrola. They had no trouble entering the base because Anaya worked there and had an official sticker for his car. Montoya had told Anaya that he would be waiting near the water tower on the east side of the base near several of the hangars. Montoya cautioned Anaya not to go near the headquarters because there were too many people there. He gave directions that took them past the commissary and toward the hangars.

They found him, as promised, near the water tower. According to Anaya, "He [Montoya] got in the car and said, 'Get me the hell out of here. I want to go.' "

Anaya noticed that Montoya was very pale, almost white, and he was shaking. Something had frightened him severely. Recalling the event years later, Anaya repeated, over and over, "He was very, very scared."[12]

Pete Anaya would also remember Montoya's frightened demeanor. Montoya had sat quietly, glumly staring out the window during the ride back into town.[13]

Once inside the house, Montoya began to talk. He said, "You all are not going to believe what I've seen. If you ever tell anyone, I'll call you a damned liar. We don't know what it is. . . . They say it moves like a platter. It's a plane without wings. . . . It's not a helicopter. . . . I don't know where it's from. . . . It could be from the moon. . . . We don't know what it is."

Montoya collapsed on the couch, and Anaya handed him a scotch, but it had no apparent effect. Montoya wanted something else, and Anaya gave him some Jim Beam. According to Anaya, "The man took half a quart just boom, boom, boom. He was very scared."

Montoya then told them that he had seen "four little men." He described how small they were and that, according to Anaya, "one was alive."[14]

Pete Anaya confirmed his brother's belief that Montoya had mentioned there were four little men,[15] but Pete's wife, Mary, thought that Montoya had mentioned just two.[16] She admitted that she had not been involved in the discussions.

According to Ruben Anaya, Montoya described the beings as "short . . . skinny-like with big eyes. . . . [The] mouth was real small, like a cut across a piece of wood."[17]

Pete Anaya, who heard less of the description of the bodies, recalled only that they were small, with big heads. That was the thing he remembered the most, the oversize heads.[18]

All had been stretched out on mess hall tables set up in the hangar. Montoya said that he knew one of them was alive because it was moaning. It was moving and had its knees up, which were moving slightly. They were so skinny that they didn't look human. And one hand was moving, though barely.

There were doctors pressed around the table, so that Montoya couldn't get very close. He did see that they had no hair, that their skin was white, and that each wore a tight-fitting one-piece suit that Anaya described as similar to those worn by navy divers. From what Montoya could see, they had four long, thin fingers. They were bald, and Montoya had no opportunity to see an eye color. The eyes were larger than normal.

After a short period, the beings were taken over to the hospital. Montoya said military personnel brought in some of the debris about that time. There was nothing that resembled a large ship, just pieces of metal. He didn't get close enough to it to examine it.

Anaya kept asking questions until Montoya snapped at him, "I tell you that they're not from this world."

Once he heard that, Anaya said, "That's when I shut up."

Montoya finally began to relax slightly. He lay back on the couch and, according to Anaya, said, "I want to go back to Albuquerque. If I sleep too long, wake me." There was a military plane scheduled to return to Kirtland Army Air Field, and Montoya wanted to be on it.

Montoya did sleep, but he kept jerking himself awake, as if he was under a great deal of stress. Anaya said that when he was in the infantry during World War II, he had seen the same thing in combat veterans. He described it as being like battle fatigue.

When Montoya woke, the four drove back to the base. The gate had been blocked, but since Anaya worked on the base, his car was waved on through. Anaya said there was above normal activity on the base, especially around the headquarters, the hospital, and the hangar areas. But Montoya was a public official, so he was allowed to pass.

Before he left, Montoya told them to keep their mouths shut. He told them that even if they did talk about it, no one would believe them.[19]

Moses Burrola died several years ago, but before he did, he told his wife of Montoya's strange account. She confirmed that her husband knew Montoya, and that he was good friends with the Anayas. She remembered little about the event, only that something very unusual had happened.[20]

Anaya said that he, his brother, Burrola, and Montoya did discuss the episode on several subsequent occasions, but Montoya was always cautious. He told them that it was too dangerous and that if they talked about it, the FBI would do away with them. Anaya wasn't sure what that meant, but the warning was clear. Later still, Montoya told them that someone would get them if they talked about it—not necessarily the FBI but someone in the government.[21]

Others were more directly involved than Anaya and his friends. Some of the people were on the site when the bodies were discovered. One man was there when the living being was found. He confirmed a number of things, including the impressions of Frankie Rowe, who thought that the crash had taken place near Roswell, about thirty to thirty-five miles northwest of the city. The new source said the exact distance was thirty-six miles.

This individual confirmed that one of the beings had survived the crash and had walked under its own power to one of the military vehicles. He knew that it had been taken into Roswell, to the base, but didn't know what happened to it once it got there. He knew it because he had been there when the creature arrived and watched as it walked into the base hospital.[22]

A day or so later, Chaves County Sheriff George Wilcox drove to Glenn Dennis's father's house and spoke to the older Dennis. Wilcox said that Glenn had gotten himself into trouble out at the base. Wilcox told the older Dennis that he didn't know what Glenn had done but that a black sergeant had informed him, at the sheriff's office, that Wilcox should encourage the older Dennis to have a talk with his son. Glenn would be well advised to keep his mouth shut other than to say that he didn't see anything at the base.

When his father asked him about it, Glenn said that he wasn't in any trouble and that he hadn't done anything wrong. Glenn's father said, "I can't do anything to help you if you don't tell me what's going on." Glenn then explained the situation.

Dennis also said that the military, either the black sergeant or the red-haired captain, later had been asking about any brothers and sisters. Dennis had a brother, Robert, who was still in the army as a fighter pilot, and he had three sisters, but the family refused to volunteer any information.[23]

The same day that the sheriff was visiting Dennis's father, Dennis himself was trying to learn more about the situation at the base. He contacted the nurse he knew and asked "if it would be all right if I could drive out because I would like to know more about the incident. . . . I didn't make contact for two or three hours. . . . She called me back and said, 'I understand you've been trying to call me.' She said, 'I don't want you coming to the hospital. I would rather see you at the officers' club.' This was around eleven-thirty so I got in my car and went to the officers' club."

He met her at the club, found a table, and ordered Cokes and lunch. Finally she got to the point. "I want to tell you what this is all about, but you have to give me a sacred oath that you won't ever mention this or my name and get me into trouble."

She continued, "I can't believe what I've just seen. This is the most horrible thing I've ever seen in my life."

She then drew a sketch on a small prescription pad that she normally carried. As Dennis remembered it, "I don't think she said alien bodies, I think she said foreign bodies. . . . Then she described to me what happened when she got involved in it."

According to Dennis, she told him she was performing her normal duties at the hospital when she entered an examination room that was across the hall to obtain some supplies. She saw two doctors whom she'd never seen at the base hospital. One told her, "You stay here. We've got to have you."

A horrible odor filled the room. The doctors were examining three bodies; "foreign bodies" was the term she used. Two were badly mutilated, but one looked as if it might have survived the crash and was mostly in one piece. It had apparently died of exposure some time after the crash. She said that the doctors believed the other two might have been mutilated by predators and that they looked as if they had been exposed to the elements on the high desert.

The overpowering odor made it almost impossible to stay in the room. The doctors worked on the bodies, with her assistance, but finally, feeling sick, she was forced to leave. The doctors gave up as well, sealing the bodies in mortuary bags to be taken to the hospital's morgue.

She later told Dennis that the anatomy of the beings' arms was different from that of human arms. The distance between the wrist and the elbow was longer than the distance between the elbow and the shoulder.

She believed there were only four fingers on the hands which were long, slender, and fragile. The hands themselves were very small and very narrow. When they turned one of the hands over, they noticed that the thumb was missing. They also noticed that the ends of the fingers had little hollowed pads looking like suction cups.

The bones were no larger than a medium-sized human finger and didn't feel like the bone structure of a human. These bones were brittle and felt, more or less, "like real thick cartilage."

The head was larger than the human head. The eyes were sunken. The nose wasn't convex but markedly concave, with two little orifices. There was no ear, but two little orifices on the side of the head, with two small lobes that might have folded in to protect the ear.

The mouth was a very thin line "very thin. . . . [It] didn't have a full lip . . . hardly any lip at all. In place of teeth, it looked like a piece of rawhide. The doctors said it was even harder than the bone structure."

The bones of the head "were very pliable. It was like a newborn baby. . . . You could push the sides and it would be movable."

When Dennis asked if she could tell if they were male or female, she replied, "I didn't pay any attention and was so sick." The doctors, according to her, might have known something about the sex, but she didn't.

Dennis tried to learn more, but she didn't have any answers for his questions. She hadn't seen any clothes and didn't know if they had been dressed. Her nausea and desire to get out of the room overwhelmed her curiosity.

"She was in a state of shock," according to Dennis. "She said it was so gruesome and so horrible. . . . She looked like she was going into total shock. She never touched her food."

They talked for a few more minutes. Before she left, she provided him with a sketch of the beings. Finally, saying that she was sick, she excused herself. She just wanted to go back to the barracks to lie down. She didn't even touch her Coke, according to Dennis.[24]

He walked her out of the club and watched as she headed back to the barracks. That was the last time that he saw her. She then seemed to have disappeared from the face of the earth.

PART II

DEBRIS

3

Mac Brazel
and the Debris Field

I F MAC BRAZEL hadn't been in his field on the morning of July 5, 1947, the story might never have reached the public. The strange, metallic debris that was scattered over one of his pastures southeast of Corona, New Mexico, might never have been discussed publicly. Had it not been for Mac Brazel, the entire story of the crash near Roswell might have remained a military secret.

Brazel heard a loud crashing sound late on the evening of July 4. It came during an electrical storm that raced across Lincoln County, New Mexico, but it did not sound like thunder.[1] It was strange enough that other ranchers would later remember it. Early the next morning, as Brazel and a young neighbor boy, William D. Proctor, rode the range, they discovered the source of that crash.[2] A field south of the ranch headquarters was filled with metallic debris. It extended from near the top of a small arroyo, up another hill, and disappeared on the reverse side.[3] There was quite a bit of debris—some of it shiny, but most looked like dull metal. There were big chunks and little pieces.[4] The material was so densely packed that the sheep refused to cross it.[5]

A closer examination produced no clear evidence of an aircraft accident. There was no indication of passengers in whatever had crashed. The debris was so thin and so light that it stirred in the wind, but it was so strong that most pieces wouldn't even flex.[6] Brazel couldn't cut it with his knife and he couldn't burn it with matches.[7]

Taking some of the smaller samples with him, Brazel headed off to see his nearest neighbors, Floyd and Loretta Proctor (William's parents), who lived about ten miles from the ranch headquarters and twenty from the debris field. When Brazel showed his neighbors a sliver of the metal-like material, they were as puzzled by it as he was. Loretta Proctor later said she "didn't know what the stuff was." Floyd tried to whittle on it with his knife but couldn't make a mark. Brazel held a match up to it to show that not only wouldn't it burn, it wouldn't even blacken.[8]

27

Brazel suggested they drive down to look at the debris field, but the Proctors, busy with their own ranch, declined. Today Loretta says, "We should have gone, but gas and tires were expensive then. We had our own chores, and it would have been twenty miles."[9]

Brazel didn't know what to do about the material, which was causing him practical problems. Because the sheep wouldn't cross the field, Brazel had to drive them the long way around to get them to water. Somebody, possibly whoever was responsible for it, was going to have to clean up the mess. He was too busy to take time to do it. And there was so much of it that it would take days for him to complete the task.

Someone also suggested that Brazel should try to claim the various rewards being offered for proof that "flying disks" were real. Others suggested he notify the sheriff or the government, assuming that the debris was from a classified military experimental project. Reluctantly Brazel decided that he would have to drive to Roswell, because neither he nor his neighbors had a phone.

The next day, July 6, Brazel drove to Roswell to see the Chaves County sheriff, George A. Wilcox. Wilcox let one of the deputies handle Brazel at first. According to Jay Tulk, son-in-law of the sheriff, Brazel was an old cowboy in old clothes and scuffed boots. But when Brazel showed a small piece of the debris to Wilcox, the sheriff suggested that he call the local air base.[10]

Before that call was made, Frank Joyce, an announcer and reporter for Roswell radio station KGFL, phoned looking for anything new. Wilcox put Brazel on the line, and Joyce, while he was changing records and running the control board, interviewed Brazel over the phone. Today Joyce is specific about what Brazel said, saying that his story told on Sunday was significantly different from that told by Brazel later, on Wednesday evening, July 9.[11]

Major Jesse A. Marcel was eating lunch in the officers' club when, as he would recall, "I got a call from the sheriff from Roswell and he wanted to talk to me. He said, 'There's a man here, and he told me something weird.' . . . I said, 'Well, I'm all ears,' and he said . . . he found something on his ranch that crashed, either the day before or a few days before, and he doesn't know what it is."[12]

Marcel drove immediately to the sheriff's office, questioned Brazel, and then returned to the base. Because Brazel had described a field filled with strange metallic debris, Marcel realized he would have to make a trip to the ranch. And he would need some help.

Marcel and a plainclothes counterintelligence officer later identified as Captain Sheridan Cavitt departed in separate cars, with Brazel in the lead. According to

Marcel, "He [Cavitt] drove a jeep carryall. I drove my staff car. . . . We took off cross-country behind this pickup truck this rancher [Brazel] had. He didn't follow any roads going out there. We got to his place about dusk. It was too late to do anything, so we spent the night there in that little shack." They spent the night at the Hineses' house just three or four miles north of the debris field.[13]

As they waited for daybreak, Marcel inspected a large piece of debris that Brazel had dragged from the field. Using a Geiger counter, he could find no trace of radioactivity.[14]

Early the next morning, July 7, Brazel took the two military officers out to the crash site. Brazel, in preparation to lead the military men to the debris field, had saddled two horses, but Marcel had never ridden a horse. Marcel said, "You two ride the horses. . . . So they took off. . . . We went up there."

Marcel drove the jeep carryall, following Brazel and Cavitt. They came over a slight ridgeline and saw the debris field spread out in front of them. Brazel and Cavitt dismounted, and Marcel stopped the Jeep. They slowly moved down into the field. Marcel said that the debris was scattered "over a wide area, I guess maybe three-quarters of a mile long and a few hundred feet wide. . . . I'd never seen anything like that. I didn't know what we were picking up."

Later he would describe some of the material as being as thin as newsprint and yet so strong that even a sledgehammer couldn't dent it. There was thin, foil-like material, small I beams, "other stuff there that looked very much like parchment that didn't burn" and something later described as Bakelite™ or plastic.[15]

After watching the two officers for a short time, Brazel rode off to complete his duties. Marcel and Cavitt spent the day examining the field, walking the perimeters of it, and then picking up the debris.

"We loaded up all this stuff in the carryall and we got through kind of late," Marcel said, "but I wasn't satisfied. I went back. I told Cavitt, you drive this vehicle back to the base, and I'll go back out there and pick up as much as I can put in the car."[16]

In Roswell, Joyce told KGFL owner Walt Whitmore about Brazel's strange claims. Intrigued, Whitmore decided to pursue the story further. He drove out to the Brazel ranch, picked him up, and returned to Roswell. George "Jud" Roberts, minority owner of the radio station, later said, "They hid him out at Whit's [Walt Whitmore, Sr.'s] house. Kept him there overnight."[17]

They made a wire recording about Brazel's find, but it was too late to air it that night. According to the "Radio Log—KGFL-1400" as published in the *Roswell Daily Record*, KGFL signed off at 10:00 P.M. on July 7. The interview would never be aired, on direct orders of both the Federal Communications Commission and part of the New Mexico congressional delegation. Roberts later said, "We were told that we would have twenty-four hours to find something else to do, because we would no longer be in the radio business."[18]

The military, with the assistance of Walt Whitmore, Sr., picked up Brazel at KGFL early on the morning of July 8. He was taken out to the base, and according to Major Edwin Easley, provost marshal, Brazel was kept under guard in the guest house for a number of days.[19]

Mac's son, Bill Brazel, learned of his father's ordeal when he saw his picture in the Albuquerque newspaper. Bill Brazel said, "I was living in Albuquerque at the time. . . . I said to Shirley [Brazel], 'What the hell did he do now?' I read about it, and they said that he wasn't being held but they had asked him to stay in Roswell for a few days, and I told Shirley, 'Dad needs help.' So I proceeded out to the ranch. I think it was two or three days before Dad showed up."[20]

On the evening of July 8 military officers escorted Brazel into downtown Roswell to talk to reporters at the offices of the *Roswell Daily Record*. Two reporters from Albuquerque, Jason Kellahin and R. A. Adair, had brought a portable wire photo transmitter with them so they could transmit pictures over the telephone lines. The Associated Press in New York had ordered them to Roswell to obtain and transmit pictures of Brazel and Sheriff Wilcox.[21]

Brazel told the reporters that he had found the debris on June 14, while inspecting ranch pastures with his wife, daughter Bessie, and his son Vernon. In that interview, published in the July 9 edition of the *Daily Record* and picked up by the wire services, Brazel now claimed the object was smoky gray rubber and that it was confined to an area of about two hundred yards in diameter. While no words were visible on any of the wreckage, there were letters on part of it, along with a little Scotch™ tape and some tape with flowers on it. Although no strings or wires were fastened to it, a few eyelets in the paper indicated an attachment might have been used.

The new story ended with Brazel saying he had found weather observation devices on two other occasions, but this object didn't resemble those. "I am sure what I found was not any weather observation balloon," he said.[22]

The military escort officers, reported by *Record* editor Paul McEvoy, then led Brazel out of the newspaper offices. While they were walking toward the car, two of Brazel's neighbors, Floyd Proctor and Lyman Strickland, happened to pass by. Both were surprised that Brazel didn't say a word to them. Proctor said later that the military was keeping Brazel on a very short leash.

Two other neighbors, Leonard Porter, who lived on the ranch south of Brazel's, and Bill Jenkins, another rancher, reported they saw Brazel surrounded by the military in downtown Roswell. Brazel kept his eyes down, pretending that he couldn't see anyone.[23]

Brazel got into the car and was taken to radio station KGFL, where he went inside alone. According to Frank Joyce, Brazel stood against the wall and told the cover story the army had given him earlier that day. The strange object was nothing more than a balloon.

Joyce bluntly told Brazel that he knew the story wasn't true. He listened to it and then pointed out it was not the same story that Brazel had told a couple of days earlier, before the "army had gotten to him." Specifically, Brazel had said nothing about his family being with him on the ranch, and he had described a debris field considerably larger than two hundred feet in diameter.

Joyce said, however, that Brazel stuck with the new story while growing more agitated. Finally he said, "It'll go hard on me." Presumably he had been warned of the consequences if he said anything else.

Joyce remained at the radio station control board throughout the discussion, glancing occasionally at the rancher. At the end of the interview, Brazel turned and walked out of the building.[24] The military officers were waiting for him outside to take him back to the base, where he was held incommunicado.[25]

Three weeks later, speaking to neighbors Lyman and Marian Strickland, Brazel complained bitterly about his treatment by military officers. He said he had been refused permission even to call home, to Tularosa where the family lived, to tell his wife where he was.[26]

To protect young William Proctor, Brazel lied to the army officers, telling them he had been alone on the ranch when he found the debris. Proctor apparently returned to the field at some point before the retrieval was completed, with a number of his friends. Proctor showed them the debris field. One of the boys picked up some of the debris and took it home to show his father. They later hid the material in the barn.[27]

Before long the military knew everything, including the facts that Dee had been with Brazel and that and some friends had been to the site. Within days, military personnel visited the boys who had taken some samples home, demanding that the material be turned over immediately. The officers obtained all the pieces that had been taken from the field.[28]

Brazel remained in custody in Roswell for approximately eight days.[29] After his return to the ranch, he would say little about what had happened to him in Roswell.

Some of his neighbors reported that he now talked about finding a weather balloon.[30] Tommy Tyree, a ranch hand hired two months after the incident, said it had been one of the Japanese balloon bombs launched during World War II.[31]

But privately, to his family and to his closest friends, Brazel told a slightly different story, all the while remembering the security oath the army had insisted he take. Bill Brazel said, "My dad found this thing and told me a little bit about it. Not much, because the air force asked him to take an oath that he wouldn't tell anybody in detail about it. And my dad was such a guy that he went to his grave and he *never* told anybody."

All Mac Brazel would say was that whatever it was, it wasn't any type of balloon. He told his son Bill that he was better off not knowing a thing about it.

By the time Brazel returned to the ranch, all signs of the debris were gone. The military had packed the wreckage into trucks and taken it away.[32]

Months later, while riding the range, Brazel spotted a piece of the debris in a sinkhole. He pointed it out to Tommy Tyree, but neither man climbed down to retrieve it. At that time it seemed to be more trouble than it was worth.[33] But even had Brazel picked it up, he would never have been able to hold on to it. The military was still watching.

4

Sheriff George Wilcox

Y EARS LATER, GEORGE A. Wilcox, the Chaves County sheriff in July 1947, would complain about the way the military handled the retrieval of the flying saucer. He was angry with himself for bringing the military into it, because they claimed jurisdiction and completely cut him out of it. And there were the threats made by the military in the days that followed. If he'd had it to do over again, he said, he would have notified the press first, and let the reporters get to the crash site before he told the army a thing about it.

Brazel arrived at the jail sometime on the afternoon of Sunday, July 6, according to the witnesses. Deputy B. A. Clark took the initial report and then turned it over to Sheriff Wilcox.[1] Because Brazel was an old-time cowboy, dressed in old clothes and scuffed boots, Wilcox didn't pay much attention when Brazel walked in. But Brazel not only brought a story of a crashed flying saucer with him, he brought in some of the material.

Although Brazel's ranch was in Lincoln County, Roswell is in Chaves County. Roswell is the hub of that area in New Mexico. The local ranchers don't pay much attention to the fine lines between counties. Roswell is the place where business is conducted, and it would have been natural for Brazel to go there rather than Carrizozo.[2]

Wilcox decided that the best thing to do was call the military at the base. Military representatives, one of them Major Marcel, arrived at the office almost as soon as the sheriff got off the phone. No one had questioned Brazel's sanity or doubted the sheriff's judgment about the material. The military officers came as soon as they were notified.

They met with the sheriff, his deputies, and Brazel in a small room off the main office, where they examined the contents of a box that Brazel had brought with him.[3] At one point Wilcox sent two deputies out to the ranch.[4]

The two deputies headed for the Corona area, leaving Brazel behind. Although the military officers might not be familiar with the ranches outside Roswell, the sheriff's deputies were. Brazel had described the location of the debris field, and they felt confident that they could find it based solely on Brazel's directions.

When they returned later in the afternoon, they said that although they had seen no debris, they did find an area of blackened ground. It looked as if something large and circular had touched down. The ground had been baked to a hardness that surprised them both.[5]

Jay Tulk, husband of Wilcox's daughter Elizabeth, arrived at the jail shortly after the military. He asked the sheriff what was going on with all the military vehicles parked outside. Tulk and Wilcox retreated to the small room where the debris was stored and talked about it there.[6]

The soldiers and Brazel left the office before the deputies returned. Wilcox called the air base, but no one there had any new information for him. Things settled down temporarily, as it turned out.

On Tuesday the situation changed radically. Wilcox, wondering what was happening, dispatched another two deputies to the ranch. No one could get close to the site. The army, which had cordoned off the roads, was stopping and turning back all traffic, even deputy sheriffs.[7] Because they were lawmen from Chaves County, they had no real legal status in Lincoln County, and in this case, the U.S. Army was in control.

Wilcox then tried to get more answers from the military at the base, but again, no one had much to say. But the word was leaking out. Just after noon on July 8 the sheriff and his deputies began fielding phone calls from around the world. Wilcox sat up all night taking calls from Germany, England, France, and Italy, as well as every state in the union.[8]

Soon afterward, on July 9 or 10, Wilcox was again visited by military officers. They wanted to retrieve the box of debris that Brazel had left in the small locked room in the sheriff's office. The sheriff had made sure that the box had been guarded. The soldiers directed the sheriff to say as little as possible about the recent events, and to refer all calls about it to the base. And if the sheriff had other ideas, there would be grave consequences.[9]

At first, Phyllis McGuire, one of the sheriff's daughters, understood none of this. She pestered her father, asking questions about what the rancher had seen and what the military had been doing at the jailhouse. Finally her mother, Inez, who knew exactly what the military had said to the sheriff, told McGuire to stop asking questions.[10]

Years later, Barbara Dugger, then living with her grandmother Inez, learned more about the events of July 1947. Inez, known as Big Mom by the family, told her that a flying saucer had crashed near Roswell. She made Dugger promise never to say anything about it because the military had sworn her and her husband to secrecy.

According to Dugger, the sheriff knew more about the crash than he would ever let on. Inez told her granddaughter that there had been bodies found, little men with big heads wearing gray, silklike suits. There had been a burned area and metallic debris.

Naturally Dugger wanted to know more, but Inez was hesitant to talk about it. She had not spoken of it since that week in July 1947. She'd kept the story buried inside so long that she now had to tell someone. She cautioned Dugger a number of times, telling her that she could never tell anyone what she was about to hear.

According to Dugger, the sheriff had gone out to some site, not far to the north of town, where he saw a big area of metallic debris. He had also learned of a number of small beings, three of them dead and one still alive. Inez was not sure that her husband had actually seen the beings.

Inez's story was based on what the sheriff had told her after he had returned that evening. Apparently Wilcox and/or his deputies were somehow aware of the impact site just north of the city before the rancher, Brazel, reported his find. Their independent inquiry led him to the impact site, not the debris field near Corona. Inez indicated that the location her husband found was only about thirty miles from Roswell.

According to Inez, these events so upset Sheriff Wilcox that he lost interest in being the county sheriff. He refused to run for reelection when his term expired. Inez ran for sheriff, but in the late 1940s, Chaves County wasn't ready for a female sheriff and she lost.

One of Wilcox's deputies, Tommy Thompson, later told various researchers that Wilcox had been "destroyed" by the events. Thompson would claim that he knew nothing about the crash or the flying saucer, but he was clear about the sheriff's attitude.

Wilcox's demoralization had as much to do with the military's behavior as with the extraordinary nature of the secret the military was trying to keep. Once the initial flap was over, and the Roswell military authorities had recovered the box of debris, Wilcox received a second visit from them. Dugger, repeating what Inez had told her, said, "When the incident happened, the military police came into the jailhouse and told George and I [that] if [we] ever told anything about this incident, talked about it in any way, not only would we be killed, but they would get the rest of the family."

Dugger asked, "Did you hear them say that, Big Mom?" and she said, "Yes, I did."[11]

Wilcox played a huge, if unwitting, role in the story. Without that initial contact from some civilian witness just a short distance from Roswell, the information might have spread farther and faster so that the army and local authorities would not have been able to contain it. With that one phone call, Wilcox became a major player in one of the most successful military disinformation operations of all time.

5

Major Jesse Marcel and the Debris Field

W HEN JESSE MARCEL first saw the debris field on Monday morning, July 7, it was clear to him that "something . . . must have exploded above the ground and fell."[1] With Captain Sheridan Cavitt and Mac Brazel, he inspected the area and was able to "determine which direction it came from and which direction it was heading. It was in that pattern. . . . You could tell where it started and where it ended by how it was thinned out. . . . I could tell that it was thicker where we first started looking and it was thinning out as we went southwest."

Marcel said, "We found some metal, small bits of metal. We picked it up." According to Marcel, it was something that had been manufactured. "I wanted to see some of the stuff burn, but all I had was a cigarette lighter. . . . I lit the cigarette lighter to some of this stuff and it didn't burn."

He also described I-beam-like structures. Though unbendable or breakable, they did not look metallic. According to Marcel, "They were, as I recall, perhaps three-eighths of an inch by one quarter of an inch thick, and [came] in just about all sizes, none of them very long." The biggest was, "I would say, about three or four feet long [and] weightless. You couldn't even tell you had it in your hands."

He also noticed "undecipherable" two-color markings along the length of some of the I beams. "I've never seen anything like that myself. . . . I don't know if they were ever deciphered or not. . . . Along the length of some of those [I-beam-like members], they had little markings. Two-color markings . . . like Chinese writing. Nothing you could make any sense out of."

Marcel said that they had "picked up as much as we could carry, and some was left there." Marcel then sent Cavitt back to the base and returned to the debris field to collect more of the wreckage. Marcel picked up as much as he could, loading his staff car. According to Marcel, "We picked up a very minor portion of it."[2]

His car full, Marcel headed toward the base, but on the way, he stopped at his house. He said later that he was so impressed with the debris, he wanted his wife and son to see the extraordinary material, even if he had to wake them.[3]

37

Clearly the debris was not that of an aircraft, missile, or weather balloon. "I'd never seen anything like that. I didn't know what we were picking up. I still don't know. As of this day, I still don't know what it was. . . . [I]t could not have been part of an aircraft, not part of any kind of weather balloon or experimental balloon. . . . For one thing, if it had been a balloon . . . it would not have been porous. It was porous. . . . I've seen rockets . . . sent up at the White Sands Testing Grounds. It definitely was not part of an aircraft nor a missile or rocket."[4]

Jesse Marcel, Jr., age eleven, remembered being awakened with his father standing over him and asking him to accompany him to the car to retrieve one of several boxes of metallic debris.

Inside the house, they spread the debris over the kitchen floor, trying to fit pieces of it together like a giant jigsaw puzzle. It filled most of the kitchen floor from the back door to the door that led into the living room. It was spread from the stove on the left, across the floor to the sink and refrigerator.

Besides the lead foil and I beams, Jesse, Jr., described some small, black, plasticlike material thicker than the foil and much stronger. Years later he said that it resembled Bakelite.

While Marcel and his son were trying to put together the debris, Marcel's wife, Viaud, picked up one of the I beams and said, "There's writing on this."

Jesse, Jr., described it as "different geometric shapes, leaves, and circles." Under questioning, Jesse, Jr., said that the symbols were a shiny purple and they were small, less than a fingernail wide. There were many separate figures.

Marcel, Sr., said the pieces were from a flying saucer. His son asked him what a flying saucer was, and his father had to explain it to him.

When they finished examining the material, Jesse, Jr., helped his father put it back in the box and then carried it out to the car. Marcel resumed his trip to the air base then.[5]

When Marcel met with Blanchard early the next morning, he showed the colonel some of the debris that they had picked up and explained that it was nothing that he recognized.

Later that morning, according to Marcel, Colonel Blanchard "sent me to Carswell [Fort Worth Army Air Field] to stop over and talk to General Roger Ramey. My CO told me, 'Go ahead and fly it to Wright–Patterson Air Field [Wright Field] in Ohio,' but when I got to Carswell, General Ramey wasn't there."[6]

After the aircrew made the preflight check of the aircraft, a B-29, a staff car from Building 1034 brought out the material in four small packages. One of the crew members, Sergeant Robert Porter, would recall that they handed the packages up to him, through the hatch. The largest of the pieces was two and a half to three feet across, three to four inches thick, and triangular. The other three packages were about the size of shoe boxes. All felt as if they were empty.

Once the packages were inside the plane, they were passed to the rear of the forward compartment. Porter said that he could no longer see them.

When the plane arrived at the Fort Worth Army Air Field, Porter and the other enlisted men were ordered to stay with the aircraft until a guard was posted. When that was done, the flight crew was allowed to go to the mess hall to eat. According to Porter, the material was transferred to a B-25 and flown on to Wright Field. When Porter and the others returned to the aircraft, they were told that the debris had been nothing more than a weather balloon.[7]

Marcel took pieces of the debris into Ramey's office after the general returned to show him what had been found, placing the material on Ramey's desk. Ramey said he wanted to know the exact location of the recovery site, and the two of them ducked into the map room. When they returned to Ramey's office, the wreckage was gone. In its place was a weather balloon, spread out on the floor.[8]

At that point, Major Charles A. Cashon, the Fort Worth Public Information Officer (PIO), took two photos of Marcel crouched near the remains of the weather balloon.

Later in the evening Ramey held a press conference in his office. Although Marcel was there, he'd been ordered to keep silent. According to Marcel, "[T]hey had a lot of news reporters there and a slew of microphones. . . . [They] wanted to interview me, but I couldn't say anything . . . until I talked to the general. I had to go under his orders."[9]

Also at that press conference was Warrant Officer (later major) Irving Newton, a weather officer stationed at Fort Worth. He was called in to identify the debris on the floor. Newton arrived to find a rawin-type weather balloon spread out on the floor that was, according to him, in a "degraded state." It was torn up, in pieces and displayed on brown paper. "The general was asking me," said Newton, "what I thought. . . . I told him what I thought. . . . It appeared to me that the general was sort of ridiculing him [Marcel] for being such an ass for bringing that weather balloon all the way over from Roswell."[10] Once he'd identified the debris as a balloon, Ramey canceled the special flight that was to take the debris on to Wright Field.[11]

With the press conference over, Marcel said, "The general told me, you go back to Roswell. You're more needed there."[12] Marcel remained overnight in Fort Worth and returned to Roswell the next day.[13]

Robert Slusher, an aircrewman from Roswell, brought another special flight into Fort Worth on July 9. According to Slusher, when they arrived at Fort Worth, there was a reception committee at the airfield, including many of the top people of the Eighth Air Force.

Once the crate they had brought from Roswell was unloaded and taken away, Marcel came from the Operations Building. According to Slusher, Marcel returned to Roswell with them that evening.[14]

On his arrival home, Marcel told both his wife and son that they were not supposed to mention what they had seen. He told them "to forget it."[15]

But Marcel wasn't finished with the crash at Roswell. He knew that what he'd found on the ranch was no weather balloon. Years later he would remark, "I was pretty acquainted with most things that were in the air at the time, not only from my own military aircraft but also a lot of foreign countries, and I still believe it was nothing that came from earth. It came to earth but not from earth."[16]

Marcel drove out to the base and found Cavitt and Master Sergeant Lewis Rickett at the Intelligence Office. Marcel approached Cavitt and asked if he had prepared a written report. Cavitt said that he had but that Marcel couldn't see it. According to Rickett, this angered Marcel, and given his treatment and humiliation in Fort Worth the day before, it was not surprising.

Marcel snapped, "I outrank you and I want to see that report."

Cavitt responded that his orders came from Washington, and if Marcel didn't like it, he could take it up with them. Marcel was unable to force the issue.[17]

That was the last official thing that Marcel heard about the debris. He never heard anything more from Ramey or from Wright Field. If Blanchard ever learned anything more, he never mentioned it to Marcel.

Jesse, Jr., discussed the events with his father periodically over the years. Each time he did, the senior Marcel always emphasized that he saw nothing that he recognized. Had it been a radar-reflecting balloon, there was no reason for Marcel not to have recognized it. According to his son, he had been trained in radar operations during World War II. There was a radar interpretation officer assigned to his staff, and there were, naturally, several weather officers assigned to the base at Roswell who launched various types of weather balloons.[18]

As Marcel said, "As of this day, I still don't know what it was."[19]

6

The Press Accounts

WHILE THE PRESS was being silenced in Roswell, Brigadier General Roger Ramey, commander of the Eighth Air Force, was doing everything he could to stop the story in Fort Worth. The plane from Roswell had already been dispatched, and there were people in Fort Worth who were interested in its arrival.

As he walked into the office at the *Fort Worth Star-Telegram* that day in July 1947, staff reporter J. Bond Johnson[1] heard an incredible story. The AP wire signaled that an airplane was on the way with the wreckage of a flying saucer found outside of Roswell.

City editor Cullen Greene asked Johnson, normally the police beat reporter and a backup photographer, if he had his camera, a Speed-Graphic. When he said he did, the editor told him to get out to General Ramey's office.

Johnson arrived at the base late in the afternoon. The guard at the gate was ready for him, knew that he was coming, and directed him toward Ramey's office. This was not the normal procedure. Normally Johnson went to the Public Information Office.

In Ramey's office, Johnson saw the wreckage scattered on the floor. It wasn't an impressive sight, just some aluminumlike foil, balsa wood sticks, and some foul-smelling burnt rubber. Johnson said, "It was just a bunch of garbage anyway."

Describing the scene, Johnson said, "He had a big office, as most of them [generals] do. And he walked over, and I posed him looking at it, squatting down, holding on to the stuff. . . . At that time I was briefed on the idea that it was not a flying disk as first reported but in fact was a weather balloon that had crashed. . . . Almost the first thing that Ramey had said was, 'Oh, we've found out what it is, and you know, it's a weather balloon.' "

Johnson took four pictures.[2] Two showed Ramey by himself, and another two with Colonel Thomas J. DuBose, chief of staff of the Eighth Air Force. Johnson had only brought two holders, so he could only take the four pictures. According to him, he talked to Ramey about fifteen minutes before returning to the newspaper

41

office. This was a couple of hours before the stage-managed press conference that would be held in Ramey's office.

Johnson was sent into the darkroom immediately to develop the film and make the prints. The editor was so excited about it that he made Johnson bring the dripping prints into the city-room.

Technicians from the AP were already waiting for him. Johnson mentioned that they, along with a portable wire photo transmitter, had been brought by bus from Dallas.

The phones in the press room were ringing, too. Johnson said that had he taken more pictures, he might have become rich. "Everyone wanted an exclusive, and I'd only taken two [*sic*] pieces of film."[3]

Later that same day, Ramey called a press conference. This was in addition to the discussion that he'd held with Johnson earlier in the afternoon. Johnson was clear that he was the only reporter there when he'd interviewed and photographed Ramey. He said that no one else was in the office at the time, and that it was his idea to bring Colonel DuBose over to be in two of the photos.[4]

While Johnson was at the *Star-Telegram*, writing his story explaining that the debris was nothing more than a weather balloon, other reporters were calling the base. The *Dallas Morning News* learned at five-thirty, according to their story, that the officers at Roswell had mistaken the balloon wreckage for that of a flying disk. The reporter spoke to Major Edwin M. Kirton, an air intelligence officer at the base.[5]

Later that same afternoon, Irving Newton, one of the weather officers attached to the Eighth Air Force, was sitting alone in his office when a colonel on Ramey's staff called. Newton was ordered to report to headquarters, but he refused, explaining that he couldn't leave the office vacant. General Ramey then called him, ordering Newton to "get your ass over here now. Use a car and if you have to, take the first one with keys in it."

When Newton arrived, a colonel briefed him quickly in the hallway, away from the reporters. Newton couldn't remember who it had been, but did say the message had been clear. "These officers from Roswell think they found a flying saucer, but the general thinks it's a weather balloon. He wants you to take a look at it."

Inside Ramey's office, Newton saw the balloon lying on the floor. According to Newton, there was no question about what he was seeing. It was a rawin target balloon.

Five or six reporters were in the room, according to Newton. They were standing back, out of the way, listening to what was happening in front of them.

Ramey, a couple of colonels, and the major who was supposed to be the one who had flown up from Roswell were also there.

According to Newton, the reporters didn't ask questions, and Marcel had said that he was not allowed to speak with the reporters. But according to Newton, "The major kept pointing to portions of the balloon to ask if I thought it would be found on a regular balloon." Newton said he had the impression the major was trying to save face and not appear to be a fool who couldn't tell the difference between a normal balloon and something from outer space.[6]

It is not clear if this major was Marcel or Major Charles Cashon, the PIO. Newton knew neither man. Cashon, as part of his job, might have been trying to sell the balloon explanation to the press.[7] Marcel, as an officer trained in radar operations, and the group air intelligence officer, should have been able to identify a balloon, even one as ripped up as the one in Ramey's office. In fact, forty years after the report, weathercasters at various TV stations were able to identify the wreckage of the balloon from the photos taken in Ramey's office.[8]

After Ramey had identified the balloon, he told his aide, Captain Roy Showalter,[9] to cancel the special flight. Newton left as quickly as he could, because there was no one in the weather office.

Years later DuBose acknowledged that the weather balloon story was designed to get the reporters "off the general's back." And although Ramey, with the reporters watching, ordered the special flight canceled, it was not. According to DuBose, Major General Clements McMullen, deputy commander of the Strategic Air Command, ordered Ramey to cover up the whole thing. They wanted to "put out the fire" as quickly as they could.

DuBose knew even more about it. According to DuBose, some wreckage from Roswell had been taken to Fort Worth "two or three days earlier." DuBose was the officer who alerted the men in Washington that something had been found near Roswell. And it was DuBose who received orders from McMullen about the debris sometime later on Sunday, July 6.

According to DuBose, "He [McMullen] called me and said that I was . . . there was talk of some elements that had been found on the ground outside Roswell, New Mexico, . . . that the debris or elements were to be placed in a suitable container, and Blanchard was to see that they were delivered. . . . They were placed in a suitable container, and Al Clark, the base commander at Carswell [Fort Worth Army Air Field], would pick them up and hand deliver them to McMullen in Washington. Nobody, and I must stress this, no one was to discuss it with their wives, me with Ramey, with anyone. The matter as far as we're concerned was closed as of that moment."

DuBose then called Blanchard and relayed the instructions to him. At that moment, samples of the debris that Brazel had taken to the Chaves County sheriff were brought, under Blanchard's orders, to Roswell Army Air Field.

DuBose continued, saying, ". . . and told him that there is this material his S-2 [Marcel] found in the desert, and I said this is to be put in a suitable container by this major, and you are to see that it is sealed, put in your little command aircraft, and flown by a proper courier [meaning an officer or NCO who is cleared to carry classified material], flown to Carswell and delivered to Al Clark, who will then deliver it to McMullen."

Because it was hot that day, DuBose waited in his office until he was told that the aircraft from Roswell was in the traffic pattern. Once he had the word, he drove out onto the ramp and waited for the airplane to land. He couldn't remember whether it was a B-25 or a B-26, but did say he knew it wasn't a B-29. McMullen would not have approved of using one of the bombers in that way.[10]

As the plane rolled to a stop, Colonel Alan Clark[11] walked over and received the bag from the Roswell crew. DuBose said, "Clark took the package and got into the B-26 [the Fort Worth plane standing by] through the belly of it. . . . He handed it to somebody. . . . It was one of those things you tied to your wrist, and he handed it to somebody and climbed in there. And that's the last I saw of it. In a couple . . . three hours it was delivered to McMullen, and that's the last I heard of it."

Dubose wasn't sure of what happened to the debris after it got to Washington, because McMullen had told him not to talk about it. But he did say, "McMullen said to me, or someone . . . what we're going to do with this is send it out to Wright Field and have it analyzed. That's a capability they didn't have at Andrews [the base in Washington where Clark and the flight landed]."

According to DuBose, there were no guards on the flight from Roswell and none on the Fort Worth aircraft. He also said that he never had the opportunity to see the debris. "I only saw the container, and the container was a plastic bag that I would say weighed fifteen to twenty pounds. It was sealed . . . lead seal around the top. . . . The only way to get into it was to cut it."

That, according to DuBose, was the only package. He made it clear that the debris in the bag was different from the debris that would be displayed in Ramey's office two days later. The only flight with debris that DuBose knew about was the one made on Sunday, July 6.[12] There would be other flights, but by that time, everything would be highly classified. In fact, DuBose said that "McMullen told me you are not to discuss this, and this is a point at which this is more than top secret, beyond that. . . . This is the highest priority, and you will say nothing. That was the end of it."[13]

To the reporters in Fort Worth the weather balloon explanation seemed reasonable. After all, Ramey had been willing to show the wreckage, had brought in his local expert to identify it, and Marcel, the man who had started it all, did not appear to object to the explanation.[14]

Ramey also told his story to reporters outside Fort Worth. Joe Wilson of ABC News in Chicago interviewed Ramey. He got a description of the debris that matched the balloon on the floor in Ramey's office. The cover story was reported on the 10:00 P.M. "ABC Headline Edition" that night.[15]

It is possible that the weather balloon cover story was suggested by an event that had attracted national press coverage days earlier. Sherman Campbell of Circleville, Ohio, had gone to the local sheriff with what he thought was the solution to the mystery of the flying disks. The picture of Campbell's daughter Jean holding part of it had been published throughout the country on July 6, 1947. That photograph might have suggested the cover story to the military. In this case, however, everyone involved in Ohio knew it was a weather balloon when they saw it.[16]

Other reports seemed to underscore the balloon explanation. Weatherman L. J. Guthrie said that he was sure that the so-called disk found by Brazel belonged to the weather service. Based on the descriptions he had heard, he was sure it was one of "several styles [used] to measure wind velocities in the upper stretches, and that some of them had been designed in triangular shape, with a radar target disk attached."[17]

Newton, still in Fort Worth, was quoted as saying, "We use them because they go much higher than the eye can see."[18]

Attention shifted from Fort Worth back to Roswell. Reporters calling from around the world were told that Colonel Blanchard was now on leave.[19] Mac Brazel, in military custody, was unavailable for comment until July 9. Under military escort, he was taken to the offices of the *Roswell Daily Record*, where he was interviewed by reporters from that newspaper and by two men from Albuquerque, Jason Kellahin and R. A. Adair.[20]

The news media, then, was convinced by the evidence they were shown. They'd seen the balloon, they'd heard the explanation by the weather expert and the officers at Fort Worth. They had no reason to suspect that they hadn't seen or been told everything. It would be more than thirty years before anyone would discover that Ramey had not been telling the truth.

7

The Story of the Century

T HE STORY OF the century lasted for most of the afternoon on July 8, 1947. Newspapers, and later radio stations, around the country carried the report that the army had captured a flying saucer on a ranch near Roswell, New Mexico. For just over three hours, the press was in a panic, demanding to know if the army had used the term "flying disk," if it was at Alamogordo or White Sands, and pleading for additional details. For those three hours, the answers to the questions about the flying saucers were believed to be known.[1]

It started about noon in New Mexico (2:00 P.M. in Washington, D.C.) when First Lieutenant Walter Haut, the public information officer at the 509th Bomb Group, took a press release to the office of KGFL, one of the two radio stations in Roswell. He continued his rounds, providing KSWS with a copy, as well as the *Roswell Daily Record*, finally ending at the *Roswell Morning Dispatch*. Finished, he went home for lunch.[2]

Morning Dispatch editor Art McQuiddy would later remark, "I can remember quite a bit about what happened that day. It was about noon and Walter brought in a press release. He'd already been to one of the radio stations, and I raised hell with him about playing favorites.

"By the time Haut had gotten to me, it hadn't been ten minutes and the phones started ringing. I didn't get off the phone until late that afternoon. I had calls from London and Paris and Rome and Hong Kong that I can remember."

Unfortunately for McQuiddy, the *Dispatch* was a morning paper, and by the time they could get the next issue on the streets, interest was dead. "The story died, literally, as fast as it started."[3]

Others didn't have McQuiddy's problem. They had afternoon newspapers with deadlines that allowed them to print the information as it came from Roswell.

The excitement began at 4:26 P.M. (2:26 P.M. Roswell time) when the story went out over the wire. The first bulletin read:

Roswell, N.M.—The army air forces here today announced a flying disc had been found on a ranch near Roswell and is in army possession.

The Intelligence office reports that it gained possession of the 'Dis:' [*sic*] through the cooperation of a Roswell rancher and Sheriff George Wilson [*sic*] of Roswell.

The disc landed on a ranch near Roswell sometime last week. Not having phone facilities, the rancher, whose name has not yet been obtained, stored the disc until such time as he was able to contact the Roswell sheriff's office.

The sheriff's office in turn notified a major of the 509th Intelligence Office.

Action was taken immediately and the disc was picked up at the rancher's home and taken to the Roswell Air Base. Following examination, the disc was flown by intelligence officers in a superfortress (B-29) to an undisclosed "Higher Headquarters."

The air base has refused to give details of construction of the disc or its appearance.

Residents near the ranch on which the disc was found reported seeing a strange blue light several days ago about three o'clock in the morning.[4]

Four minutes later, at 4:30 P.M. Washington, D.C., time, there was the "first add," which was the first update on the story. According to that, "Lt. Warren Haught [*sic*; Walter Haut], public information officer of Roswell field, announced the object had been found 'sometime last week.' "[5] The report also indicated that the object was going to higher headquarters.

The many rumors regarding the flying discs became a reality yesterday when the intelligence office of the 509th Bomb Group of the Eighth Air Force, Roswell Army Air Field, was fortunate enough to gain possession of a disc through the cooperation of one of the local ranchers and the Sheriff's office of Chaves County.

The flying object landed on a ranch near Roswell sometime last week. Not having phone facilities, the rancher stored the disc until such time as he was able to contact the Sheriff's office, who in turn notified Major Jesse A. Marcel, of the 509th Bomb Group Intelligence office.

Action was immediately taken and the disc was picked up at the rancher's home. It was inspected and subsequently loaned by Major Marcel to higher headquarters."[6]

The Associated Press reported that Lieutenant General Hoyt S. Vandenberg, deputy chief of the army air forces, hurried to the AAF (army air force) press section in Washington to take active charge of the news about the find in New Mexico. General Carl Spaatz, commander of the army air forces, was in Washington state on vacation and was unavailable for comment.[7]

At 4:55 (Washington, D.C.) came a second add, but this one carried a "95" designation, which meant it was next in importance to a bulletin. This time they reported where the disk had been found. They repeated this once, and then at 5:08 they repeated the entire story.

Another "95" was sent at 5:10 (4:10 in Fort Worth, Texas, 3:10 in New Mexico) addressed to the various editors, telling them that the AP was now "going after the story."[8]

In Fort Worth, J. Bond Johnson, a reporter for the *Fort Worth Star-Telegram*, arrived at his office about four o'clock (five o'clock on the east coast), and was told by his editor, Cullen Greene, to get out to General Ramey's office because they had a flying saucer and were bringing it from Roswell. Johnson left the office to drive over to the Fort Worth Army Air Field.[9]

At 5:11 (4:11 in Fort Worth) the "third add" to the bulletin announced that "the War Department in Washington had nothing to say immediately about the reported find."[10]

About 4:30 (5:30 in Washington) Johnson arrived at the Fort Worth Army Air Field and was directed to Ramey's office. Johnson later said that this surprised him because normally he would have been required to report to the Public Information Office.

Johnson was invited into Ramey's office and saw the wreckage scattered on the floor . . . aluminum-like foil, balsa wood sticks, and some burnt rubber.[11]

Twenty minutes later, at 5:53 (4:53 in Fort Worth), there was another bulletin over the AP wire. Although it had a Washington dateline, it quoted Brigadier General Roger Ramey saying that the "disk" had been sent on to Wright Field near Dayton, Ohio.[12]

It should be noted that Ramey had already told Johnson that the device was a weather balloon and had shown him the debris spread out on the floor of his office. Later it would become clear that the debris on display by Ramey was not the same as that recovered at Roswell. It was also clear that a cover story had been created but that coordination with Washington had failed. Ramey is quoted in both places, saying things that are contradictory. The debris couldn't be on its way to Ohio if it was on the floor in his office.

At 5:56 and again at 5:59 (4:56 and 4:59 in Fort Worth), additional information was sent over the AP news wire. Just a minute later, at 6:00, there was a correction to a typographical error and then a continuation of the 5:59 information.[13]

Johnson returned to the offices of the *Star-Telegram* with the four photographs he had taken in Ramey's office. "I got back to the newspaper. The newspapers had gotten excited. The AP had sent over a portable wire photo transmitter. Everyone wanted an exclusive."

As Johnson emerged from the darkroom carrying the wet prints of his pictures, the phones in the newsroom were ringing. He said there were sixty or seventy messages waiting for him. Everyone wanted a picture.[14]

At 6:02 (5:02 in Fort Worth) the AP put together the whole story and started the transmission with "First Lead Disk." The new story was datelined from Albuquerque and said, "The army air forces has gained possession of a flying disk, Lt. Warren Haught [*sic*; Walter Haut], public information officer at Roswell army airfield, announced today." That new lead was to be integrated into the stories that had already been transmitted over the news wire to offices around the country.

Two minutes later there was another bulletin, this one coming from Oelwein, Iowa. A farmer had claimed that he had found a disk, but that story was ignored.[15] There was no official backing for it, unlike the reports coming from New Mexico and Texas.

Phone lines in Roswell were completely jammed. Colonel William Blanchard, commanding officer of the 509th Bomb Group, wanted to call off base but couldn't get a free line.[16] Reporters from around the world were trying to learn more. Sheriff Wilcox later reported that he received calls from London, Paris, and Rome.[17]

The *Dallas Morning News* reporters called the Fort Worth Army Air Field to interview officials about the flying disc. At 5:30 (6:30 in Washington) Major E. M. Kirton, an intelligence officer at Eighth Air Force Headquarters in Fort Worth, told the reporters that "there is nothing to it. . . . It is a rawin high altitude sounding device." Kirton said that the identification is final and that it wasn't necessary to send the device on to Wright Field in Ohio as originally planned. Kirton confirmed that the object had been flown from Roswell to Fort Worth on a B-29.[18]

Almost thirty minutes later, at 6:59 (5:59 in Fort Worth), there was more information from New Mexico, and four minutes later another "First Lead" story came from Washington. This was the first hint from the Associated Press that the disk wasn't anything spectacular but was only a meteorological device.

Then, at 7:15 (6:15 in Fort Worth), there was a new bulletin that said Ramey would speak over the National Broadcasting Company (NBC) network. The hookup was apparently arranged with the cooperation of WBAP, a radio station in the Dallas–Fort Worth area.[19]

Two minutes later (6:17 in Fort Worth, 7:17 in Washington), the FBI entered the picture. The FBI office in Dallas sent a message to the Cincinnati office about the crash. It was directed to the director (J. Edgar Hoover) and to the SAC (special agent in charge), and was labeled as "Flying Disc, Information Concerning."

The text said:

> Major Curtan [*sic*; Major Edwin Kirton], Headquarters Eighth Air Force, telephonically advised this office that an object purporting to be a flying disc was recovered near Roswell, New Mexico, this date [July 8, 1947]. The disc was hexagonal in shape and was suspended from a balloon by cable, which ballon [*sic*] was approximately twenty feet in diameter. Major Curtan [*sic*] further advised that the object found resembles a high altitude weather balloon with a radar reflector, but that telephonic conversation between their office and Wright Field had not borne out this belief. Disc and balloon being transported to Wright Field by special plane for examin [*sic*]. Information provided this office because of national interest in case and fact that National Broadcasting Company, Associated Press, and others attempting to break the story of location of the disc today. Major Curtan [*sic*] advised would request Wright Field to advise Cincinnati office results of examination. No further investigation being conducted.[20]

In General Ramey's office, a group of reporters had gathered. According to Colonel DuBose, there were three or four reporters, including the Fort Worth PIO, Major Charles A. Cashon, questioning the general and his weather officer, Warrant Officer Irving Newton.[21]

Newton, called in by the general, said that he knew what it was the instant he saw it. Newton had launched dozens of similar balloons during the invasion of Okinawa in 1945, and had since launched hundreds more. The debris displayed on the floor was "a deteriorated rawin target balloon."[22]

At 7:29 (6:29 in Fort Worth) another bulletin came through that said, "Precede Washington, Lead all disk." It meant that the new lead was to begin a "new" story that would contain all the material sent up to that time.

A minute later that "95" was broken by another bulletin. It said, "Fort Worth— Roswell's celebrated 'flying disk' was rudely stripped of its glamor by a Fort Worth army airfield [*sic*] weather officer who late today identified the object as a weather balloon."

After that bulletin, the rest of the story "limped through," but the story was already dead. With a solution presented to the press, one that labeled the disk as nothing more than a common weather observation device, there was no longer any interest in it.[23]

ABC News, in their 10:00 "Headline Edition" with Taylor Grant, reported, "The army air forces has announced that a flying disk has been found and is now in the possession of the army. Army officers say the missile, found sometime last week, has been inspected at Roswell, New Mexico, and sent to Wright Field, Ohio, for further inspection."[24]

After the commercial break, they continued the report, saying, "Late this afternoon a bulletin from New Mexico suggested that the widely publicized mystery of the flying saucers may soon be solved. Army air force officers reported that one of the strange disks had been found and inspected sometime last week. Our correspondents in Los Angeles and Chicago have been in contact with army officials endeavoring to obtain all possible late information. Joe Wilson reports to us now from Chicago."

Joe Wilson said, "The army may be getting to the bottom of all this talk about the so-called flying saucers. As a matter of fact, the five hundred and ninth atomic bomb group headquarters at Roswell, New Mexico, report that it has received one of the disks, which landed on a ranch outside of Roswell. The disk landed at a ranch at Corona, New Mexico, and the rancher turned it over to the air force. Rancher W. W. Brazel was the man who discovered the saucer. Colonel William Blanchard of the Roswell air base refuses to give details of what the flying disk looked like.

"In Fort Worth, Texas, where the object was first sent, Brigadier General Roger Ramey says that it is being shipped by air to the AAF research center at Wright Field, Ohio.

"A few moments ago I talked to officials at Wright Field, and they declared that they expect the so-called flying saucer to be delivered there but that it hasn't been delivered yet. In the meantime General Ramey described the object as being of flimsy construction, almost like a box kite. He says that it was so battered that he was unable to determine whether it had a disk form, and he does not indicate its size. Ramey says that so far as can be determined, no one saw the object in the air, and he describes it as being made of some sort of tinfoil. Other army officials say that further information indicates that the object had a diameter of twenty to twenty-five feet, and nothing in the apparent construction indicated any capacity for speed, and there was no evidence of a power plant. It also appeared too flimsy to carry a man. Now back to Taylor Grant in New York."[25]

At 11:59 one of the photos taken by Johnson earlier in the day was put on the AP news wire for newspapers around the country. The caption said, "Brigadier General Roger M. Ramey, Commanding General of 8th airforce [sic] and Col. Thomas J. DuBose, 8th airforce Chief of Staff, identify metallic fragments found near Roswell, N. Mex. as a raywin [sic] high altitude sounding device used by airforce and weather bureau to determine velocity and direction and not a flying disc. Photo by J. Bond Johnson."[26]

The next morning, newspapers reported that the disc found was not from another world. One of the headlines in *The New York Times* said, WARRANT OFFICER SOLVES A PUZZLE THAT BAFFLED HIS SUPERIORS—"FLYING SAUCER" TALES POUR IN FROM ROUND THE WORLD. The lead paragraph said, "Celestial Crockery had the Army up in the air for several hours yesterday before an Army officer explained that what a colleague thought was 'a flying disc' was nothing more than a battered Army weather balloon."[27]

On July 9 other explanations appeared in newspapers around the country. According to the Associated Press, "Reports of flying saucers whizzing through the sky fell off today as the Army and Navy began a concentrated campaign to stop the rumors." That marked the end of the story for more than thirty years.[28]

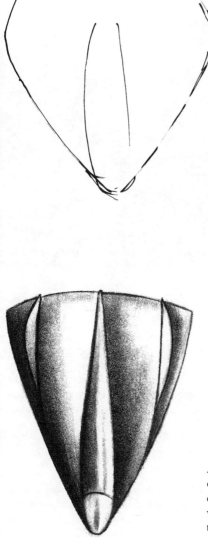

Above left: Original sketch of the top view of the unknown craft that crashed north of Roswell, New Mexico, by a first-hand witness, a high-ranking army officer stationed at Roswell.

Left: Co-author Don Schmitt's illustration of the craft, based on the original first-hand witness's drawing from July 26, 1947.

Above: An archaeological team lead by Dr. W. Curry Holden (far left) stumbled on the impact site about dawn on the morning of July 5. They saw a "crashed airplane without wings" and three bodies. The Texas Tech field staff is pictured here at the Arrowhead Ruin site near Glorietta, New Mexico, in 1938. *(Photo courtesy of Tom Carey)*

Right: George A. Wilcox, the Chaves County sheriff in July 1947, who notified the army of Mac Brazel's story of a crashed flying saucer. He later said, if he'd had it to do over again, he would have notified the press first, and let the reporters get to the crash site before he told the army anything. *(Photo courtesy of Phyllis McGuire)*

Above: The craft that crashed at Roswell was long and narrow; it was not a "flying saucer." Through a rip in the side of the craft, one man saw the symbols pictured. These were described by another witness as forming a border around part of the inside of the ship, reminding him of hieroglyphics. *(Illustration by Don Schmitt based on the first-hand testimony of three eyewitnesses)*

Below: The impact sight showing the terrain and the curve of the slope where the object struck the ground. *(Photo courtesy of Kevin Randle)*

Above: This side view of the craft shows the hole that might have caused the crash. When they cautiously approached, several military witnesses saw two bodies inside. *(Illustration by Don Schmitt based on first-hand testimony)*

Below: The appearance of the aliens found at Roswell differ from the conventional wisdom of what aliens look like: their eyes are small, they have slight noses, their features are fine—almost human in appearance—and they have individualized faces. (Illustrations by Don Schmitt based on first-hand testimony)

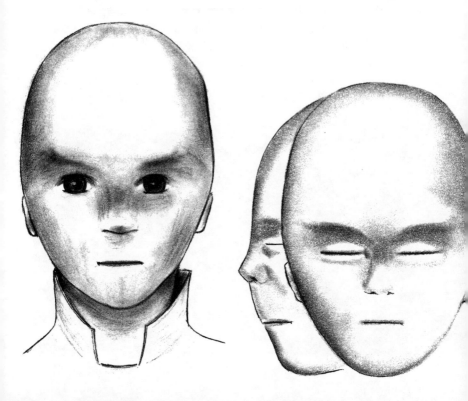

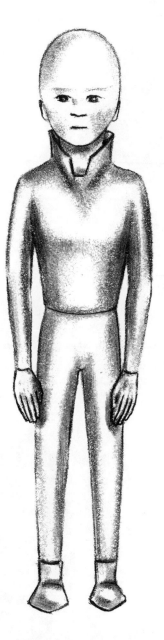

Above: A full-length drawing of one of the five beings found at the Roswell crash site. The clothing was described as gray and metallic-looking, yet as soft and yielding as cloth. *(Illustration by Don Schmitt based on first-hand testimony)*

Left: One of the men who saw the bodies said that he was struck by the serene attitude of the dead. *(Illustration by Don Schmitt based on first-hand testimony)*

Right: After decades of silence, provost marshal, Major Edwin Easley confirmed the bodies as well as the impact site north of Roswell just before his death in 1992. *(Photo courtesy of the RAAF Yearbook)*

Left: Lewis S. Rickett, NCOIC-CIC, pictured here in Germany, 1945. NCOIC of the counterintelligence office at Roswell, he arrived at the impact site on July 8. He described the debris as very thin, lightweight metal that didn't act like metal. *(Photo courtesy of Mrs. Lewis Rickett)*

Right: The debris field as it appeared in January 1990. If Mac Brazel hadn't been in his pasture on the morning of July 5, 1947, the Roswell story might have never reached the public at all. *(Photo courtesy of Paul Davids)*

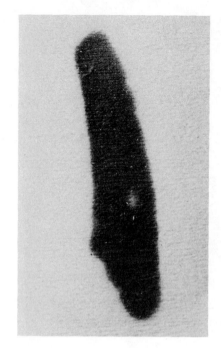

Photographs taken by William Rhodes over Phoenix, Arizona, on July 7, 1947, became important when the craft that crashed near Roswell was revealed to be crescent-shaped, not a "saucer."

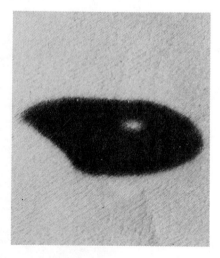

8

KGFL, Walt Whitmore, and Frank Joyce

FRANK JOYCE MIGHT have been the first newsman to learn of the flying saucer crash.[1] In 1947 Joyce was one of the few employees of radio station KGFL. During his Sunday afternoon radio show, he played records, read commercials, and operated as the engineer. More than once he had to quickly repair the "board" to keep the station on the air.

On Sunday, July 6, he called Sheriff George Wilcox looking for news. Wilcox said that he had something that might be of interest and handed the phone to Mac Brazel. As Joyce continued to spin records, he listened to Brazel tell about finding the strange metallic debris in one of his pastures. "I thought he was crazy," Joyce recalled.

Today Joyce reveals little about what Brazel told him during that first interview. He says he doesn't want to put words in Brazel's mouth. But he makes it clear that the story Brazel told him on Sunday afternoon was significantly different from the one told just a few days later when Brazel was being escorted by military officers to the offices of the *Roswell Daily Record* and then to KGFL.[2]

But the military didn't have custody of Brazel the whole time. After he had shown the debris to Marcel, he disappeared. According to Jud Roberts, Walt Whitmore, Sr., kept Brazel at his house overnight.[3] Walt Whitmore, Jr., confirmed it, saying that he had to sleep on the couch because Brazel was in his room. The next morning he found Brazel in the kitchen making himself some coffee.[4] They talked briefly, and then Whitmore, Sr., decided that he should surrender Brazel to the military.

By this time the military was, of course, suggesting that the craft found at Roswell was nothing more than a balloon. They were working hard to sell that story to the press and the public. More important, they were controlling all the witnesses and the information. Because they held all the civilian witnesses, or had silenced them, little contradictory information was available.

Walter Haut's press release suggested that a flying disk had been captured. It wasn't long, however, before there was a follow-up story on the news wire:

> Sheriff's officers in Roswell said that Brizell [sic] told them he saw it lying on the ranch, and that he picked it up and intended to keep it. They said that he did not give a complete description of the object, other than to say it appeared somewhat like tinfoil and was large— about the size of the safe in the sheriff's office.
>
> Sheriff's officers said that Brizell told them he planned to keep the object, but then heard reports of flying discs and decided to drive to Roswell and report his finding to the sheriff's office.

That was followed by the cryptic message:

```
95
FRR
    WAS TT [sic] SAME RANCH MENTIONED LAST WEEK IN FLYING
DISC HULLABALOO?
    DX CX336P 7/85
```

According to Joyce, the release "made the phones go crazy." Joyce remembered that he received an irate call from a man who identified himself only as Colonel Johnson. In a screaming voice the colonel demanded to know who the hell had told him to issue the press release. Joyce explained that he was a civilian and that there was nothing that Johnson or, for that matter, anyone else at the Pentagon could do to him. Johnson responded, "I'll show you what I can do to you."[6]

The colonel's anger was probably fueled by an Associated Press "add" transmitted at 5:09 P.M. (eastern standard daylight time) that indicated a radio reporter had broken the story. Art McQuiddy remembered that by the time Haut reached his office at the *Morning Dispatch*, the story was already on the AP radio wire.[7]

After all that had transpired, Joyce decided that he'd better find the press release and Teletype messages as they came in so that he could prove to his boss that he hadn't invented the story. He searched the station, collected all the Teletype reports, and hid them. Unfortunately someone later searched the station and found some of the hidden material, stealing it. Jud Dixon, at the United Press Association (a forerunner to the United Press International), reported the same thing had happened at his office in Santa Fe, New Mexico.[8]

Although Joyce didn't know it at that time, the cover story was beginning to kick in. The Teletype continued to print out requests for more information. Joyce was able to save some of them:

FRR

   DID ARMY CALL IT A "FLYING DISC" OR WHAT?

     DXR.

NAJ DXR

   FYI, ROSWELL REPORTS TT [*sic*] MAJOR JESSE A. MARCEL, IN-
TELLIGENCE OFFICER FOR 509TH BOMBER GROUP AT ROSWELL
ARMY AIR BASE [*sic*], IS IN FORT WORTH TEX., AT 8TH ARMY
HEADQUARTERS [*sic*], "IF HE HANT [*sic*] ALREADY STARTED BACK
FOR ROWELL [*sic*]." SUGG U GET DA IN ON IT FASTEST. TT MITE
BE WHERE DISC WAS FLOWN.

     FRR V7/8

FRR

   DA ALREADY ALERTED. HOW RE ARMY TERMINOLOGY—
"FLYING DISC" OR WHAT PLS?

     DXR

DXR

   OUR S5&4 CALLED IT "FLYING DISC." WE UNABLE GET
QUOTES FROM -4.6 OURSELVES -S 635. WE AFTER IT FASTEST.
S5&4 SAID "FLYING DISC."

     FRR V7/8

```
JD/FRR
    LETS HAVE TEST ARMY ANNOUNCEMENT FASTEST. JUST PUT ON
AS TEST AND LET ROLL IN QUOTES.
    DX NJ317P7/8
```

```
NJ DXR
    ARMY GAVE VERBAL ANNCMENT. NO TEXT.
    FRR V7/89
```

After that exchange, and the note that the army gave a verbal announcement, which referred to a press conference being held at the Fort Worth Army Air Field on July 8, the message traffic slowed. It was here that Brigadier General Roger M. Ramey showed a weather balloon, allowed reporters to photograph it, and told them that the excitement had been generated because the officers at the 509th had failed to recognize a fairly standard weather balloon with a radar-reflecting dish on it.

The Teletype printed the following change to the story:

```
FRR 8
    EEDITORS [sic]: PLEASE SUB FOR 5TH PGH AND REMAINDER OF
FRRE8

    -0-

    HOWEVER, OFFICERS AT THE ROSWELL ARMY AIR BASE HERE
NOTIFIED IMMEDIATELY BY THE SHERIFF'S OFFICE. MAJOR JESSE A.
MARCEL—INTELLIGENCE OFFICER OT [sic] THE ROSWELL BASE—
AND AN ENLISTED MAN THEN CHECKED WITH THE SHERIFF.
    SHERIFF WILCOX QUOTED BRIZELL [sic] AS SAYING THAT "IT
MORE OR LESS SEEMED LIKE TINFOIL." WILCOX SAID THAT BRIZELL
RELATED THAT THE DISC WAS BROKEN SOMEWHAT—APPARENTLY
FROM THE FALL. THE SHERIFF SAID THAT BRIZELL DESCRIBED THE
OBJECT ABOUT AS LARGE AS A SAFE IN THE SHERIFF'S OFFICE.
```

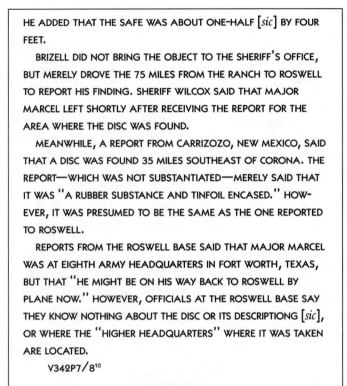

HE ADDED THAT THE SAFE WAS ABOUT ONE-HALF [*sic*] BY FOUR FEET.

BRIZELL DID NOT BRING THE OBJECT TO THE SHERIFF'S OFFICE, BUT MERELY DROVE THE 75 MILES FROM THE RANCH TO ROSWELL TO REPORT HIS FINDING. SHERIFF WILCOX SAID THAT MAJOR MARCEL LEFT SHORTLY AFTER RECEIVING THE REPORT FOR THE AREA WHERE THE DISC WAS FOUND.

MEANWHILE, A REPORT FROM CARRIZOZO, NEW MEXICO, SAID THAT A DISC WAS FOUND 35 MILES SOUTHEAST OF CORONA. THE REPORT—WHICH WAS NOT SUBSTANTIATED—MERELY SAID THAT IT WAS "A RUBBER SUBSTANCE AND TINFOIL ENCASED." HOWEVER, IT WAS PRESUMED TO BE THE SAME AS THE ONE REPORTED TO ROSWELL.

REPORTS FROM THE ROSWELL BASE SAID THAT MAJOR MARCEL WAS AT EIGHTH ARMY HEADQUARTERS IN FORT WORTH, TEXAS, BUT THAT "HE MIGHT BE ON HIS WAY BACK TO ROSWELL BY PLANE NOW." HOWEVER, OFFICIALS AT THE ROSWELL BASE SAY THEY KNOW NOTHING ABOUT THE DISC OR ITS DESCRIPTIONG [*sic*], OR WHERE THE "HIGHER HEADQUARTERS" WHERE IT WAS TAKEN ARE LOCATED.

V342P7/8[10]

On July 9 the story was dead, the army claiming they had identified the debris as part of a weather balloon and a radar target. The staged press conference in Fort Worth, including pictures of Marcel with the balloon wreckage, had convinced everyone that nothing unusual had been found in Roswell. The story, for most of the world, was finished.

But for Joyce it was not finished. While working late on the evening of July 8, after Mac Brazel had talked to reporters at the *Roswell Daily Record*,[11] he was taken to the offices of KGFL.[12]

"I remember him coming in and changing his story," Joyce said later. Brazel crouched down, about three feet from where Joyce sat at the control board, and looked at the floor as he spoke. To Joyce it looked as if Brazel were saying things he didn't believe.

"He's an old cowboy, and I told him, what you're saying is not what you were saying the other night. And then he turned around and admitted that he was . . .

that he had been told to come in or else. . . . We had some other discussions that would curl your hair."

Joyce went on, saying, "He and I were really spooked that night he came into the station. And I told him, I said, 'Look . . .' He told me what they were going to do to us, and I said, 'They're not going to do anything to us.' I yelled at him. I was really getting mad. He was really scared.

"He came in and asked me, 'You're not going to tell them anything, are you?' And I was mad by then and I say, 'I'm not going to tell them anything.' He and I were both in a fog by then. Him more than me because I think he had other influences other than the people he was dealing with."

Brazel told Joyce that he couldn't do anything else. He had to tell the new story. If he didn't, "it would go hard on him." The story of the balloon "about as large as a safe in the sheriff's office" was not the truth. And Brazel knew that Joyce knew it, too.

Joyce knew the weather balloon was a quickly manufactured cover story. When his second interview with Brazel ended, Joyce said, "The story is different, especially about the little green men." Brazel hesitated for a moment and then said, "Only they weren't green." Brazel then opened the door and walked to the military escort waiting for him outside.[13]

PART III

AFTERMATH

9

The Wright Field Connection

NUMEROUS REPORTS SUGGESTED that the material recovered by the officers and men of the Roswell Army Air Field went to Wright Field in Dayton, Ohio. Pappy Henderson took a planeload of debris there.[1] Thomas DuBose said that the debris that he'd ordered off Roswell on July 5 went to Wright Field, with a stop in Washington, D.C.[2] An FBI document dated July 8 mentioned that the "disc and balloon [were] being transported to Wright Field by special plane for examination."[3]

Almost everyone who knew anything about the bodies suggested that Wright Field was the ultimate destination for them. The nurse at the Roswell hospital said they were going to Wright Field.[4] John Tiffany said his father was dispatched from Wright Field to pick up the bodies at Fort Worth.[5] And there were those, like Norma Gardner, who suggested that the bodies were in Ohio years after the event took place.[6] Evidence had been presented and a few witnesses had been found, but the proof was still far from conclusive. Then Brigadier General Arthur E. Exon came forward.

Exon is a pilot with 135 combat missions and over three hundred hours of combat flight time during World War II. His aircraft was severely damaged by an exploding ammunition dump and he was forced to bail out over enemy territory. Captured, he spent just over a year in German prisoner of war camps. He was liberated in April 1945.

After the war, he completed an industrial administration course at the Air Force Institute of Technology and was then assigned to the Air Materiel Command (AMC) headquarters at Wright-Patterson Air Force Base. (It should be noted that Lieutenant General Nathan F. Twining was the commander of the Air Materiel Command, which controlled various intelligence functions.)

Over the next several years he held a variety of positions, finally arriving at the Pentagon as a full colonel in 1955. In 1960 he became the chief of ballistic missiles and was responsible for establishing the Jupiter Ballistic Missile system for NATO in Italy and Turkey. In July 1963 he left Europe for an assignment at Olmsted Air Force Base in Pennsylvania. In August 1964 he was assigned as commander, Wright-Patterson Air Force Base. On August 20, 1965, he was promoted to brigadier general.[7]

General Exon has had a most impressive military career. Officers are not promoted to flag rank (general officer) without having proven themselves as competent. Those who make it while on active duty, who are not rewarded with the promotion on retirement, are in a small minority. Only the top officers achieve the privilege of wearing stars.

According to Exon, "We heard the material was coming to Wright Field." Testing was done in the various labs. "Everything from chemical analysis, stress tests, compression tests, flexing. It was brought into our material evaluation labs. I don't know how it arrived, but the boys who tested it said it was very unusual."

Exon also described the material. "[Some of it] could be easily ripped or changed. . . . There were other parts of it that were very thin but awfully strong and couldn't be dented with heavy hammers. . . . It was flexible to a degree."

According to him, "Some of it was flimsy and was tougher than hell, and the other was almost like foil but strong. It had them pretty puzzled."

The lab chiefs at Wright Field set up a "special project" for the testing of the material. "They knew they had something new in their hands. The metal and material was unknown to anyone I talked to. Whatever they found, I never heard what the results were. A couple of guys thought it might be Russian, but the overall consensus was that the pieces were from space."

Exon's involvement wasn't strictly at Wright Field. He flew over the crash site, according to him, much later. But he was able to still see where the craft had come down, and he was able to confirm some of the reports that had been made in the years since.

"[It was] probably part of the same accident, but [there were] two distinct sites. One, assuming that the thing, as I understand it, as I remember flying the area later, that the damage to the vehicle seemed to be coming from the southeast to the northwest, but it could have been going in the opposite direction, but it doesn't seem likely. So the farther northwest pieces found on the ranch, those pieces were mostly metal."[8]

Exon also confirmed the gouge that Bill Brazel, among others, had reported. Exon said, "I remember auto tracks leading to the pivotal sites and obvious gouges in the terrain."[9]

When asked about the bodies, he said, "There was another location where . . . apparently the main body of the spacecraft was . . . where they did say there were bodies. . . . They were all found, apparently, outside the craft itself but were in fairly good condition. In other words, they weren't broken up a lot." This, of course, corroborates part of the testimony given by those who were on the impact site and later by Adair.

When asked if the bodies went to Wright Field, Exon said, "That's my information. But one of them went to the mortuary outfit. . . . I think at that time it was in Denver. But the strongest information was that they were brought to Wright-Pat."[10]

There has been some discussion recently about the veracity of the Exon statements. It has been suggested that Exon was a student at Wright Field during July 1947, or that he was off the base during the critical days early in the month.

But both criticisms are irrelevant. Although assigned as a student at the Air Force Institute of Technology in July 1947, he had been assigned to the headquarter staff, Air Materiel Command, until August 1946, and after graduation he was the chief of the Maintenance Data Section at Wright Field.[11] It is probably necessary to point out that the Air Force Institute of Technology was housed at Wright Field.

Although it is possible that Exon was off station during the critical July Fourth weekend, attending, as some claim, a conference, that doesn't matter. He was assigned to the base and returned after the conference had ended. He was, according to the documentation, in a position to hear of the crash and learn that material was arriving for analysis. It had not been suggested that he met the airplanes, nor was it suggested that he performed any of the analytical work.

So the documentation available, along with Exon's own words, place him in the right place at the right time. He is clear that he was repeating what he had been told by friends and colleagues at Wright Field, and his only first-hand experience was flying over the debris field and impact site sometime later.[12]

Exon was not alone in his belief that the bodies had been brought to Wright Field. John G. Tiffany reported that his father was stationed at Wright Field and that his unit, as part of their assignment, supported the 509th Bomb Group in Roswell. According to Tiffany, his father had been sent to a destination in Texas. There they picked up metallic debris and a large cylinder that reminded him of a giant thermos bottle.

Tiffany said the metal was very lightweight and very tough. It had a smooth, glasslike surface, and everything the flight crew did to mark it, bend it, or break it failed.

But what bothered the flight crew was the unusual cylinder and its unknown contents. Tiffany wasn't sure if his father had actually seen anything like bodies, but he said that two were intact. After the flight, the crew felt that they couldn't get clean. They could not "get over handling something that foreign."

Once they arrived at Wright Field, everything was off-loaded, including the giant jug. Everything was put on trucks, and once the trucks were gone, the flight crew was debriefed by a high-ranking official who told them the flight had never happened.[13]

Another witness, Sarah Holcomb,[14] who was at Wright-Patterson, reported that she held a sensitive secretarial position. She was able to supply various documents that confirmed her presence on the base and her security clearances. She also reported that she knew that bodies had arrived at Wright-Patterson.

According to her, a sergeant she knew, who had the proper clearances to get into her office, told her that he'd just come in on a special flight. He told her and the others in the office that they had brought in bodies from a flying saucer crash. He was telling them that flying saucers were real. There was no question about it. And he mentioned the bodies of the flight crew.

Not long after the sergeant left, the base commander appeared with a statement for them all to sign. He advised them, including Holcomb, that there was no truth to the rumor that the sergeant had been spreading, but they were never to talk about it, or even mention it, under a penalty of twenty years in jail and a twenty-thousand-dollar fine.

Holcomb wanted to know if she was still obligated under the oath she had signed, fearing at this late date that the military and the government would prosecute her for talking. She was very cautious, but decided that the information about the bodies should be released.

Helen Wachter talked about them after they had arrived. Wachter told of visiting a friend who had just given birth. While Wachter was in the small apartment, the husband of the new mother arrived in a state of excitement. He dragged his wife into the single bedroom and told her, in a voice that could easily be overheard through the thin apartment wall, that "alien bodies" had been brought into the base. Wachter thought at first he was referring to people from another country, but it soon became clear that he was referring to creatures from another planet.[15]

Exon also knew something of the cover-up, especially the one originated at Roswell. Because he knew Blanchard, he said, "Blanchard's leave was a screen. It was his duty to go to the site and make a determination."

Concerning the cover-up, Exon pointed out that there were no secret balloon or weather devices that could account for the debris. The lab men and officers at Wright Field, because it was their job, would have known if the debris fit into those categories. The balloon explanation was ready-made. "Blanchard could have cared less about a weather balloon," said Exon.

"I know that at the time the sightings happened, it went to General Ramey . . . and he, along with the people out at Roswell, decided to change the story while they got their act together and got the information into the Pentagon and into the president."

According to Exon, the instant they understood the nature of the find, Ramey would have alerted the chief of staff, Dwight Eisenhower. Once they had the information in Washington, control of the operation would have come from the Pentagon. The men at Roswell would have been tasked with the clean-up because they were there, on the site, but the responsibility for the clean-up would have moved up the chain of command and into the Pentagon and the White House.

According to Exon, the outgrowth of this was a top secret committee to study the phenomenon and the debris found at Roswell. An oversight committee was formed; its responsibility would be to protect the data, to control access to it, and to design studies to exploit it: a small group with control, a secondary group made up of aides, assistants, and staff from the first group, and then a third level where actual testing was done.[16]

Not all the analysis was done by men assigned to Wright Field. Some of the analysis was made by scientists outside the base. Steve Lytle reported that his father, during his long career, had worked with Robert Oppenheimer on a number of occasions and projects. Lytle's father was a mathematician and, according to Lytle, had been given one of the I beams recovered at the Roswell site, with an eye to deciphering the symbols.

Of course, the problem wasn't quite that simple. The symbols didn't represent a code that could be broken and deciphered, but was, in fact, a foreign language. Lytle could make some statistical analysis, but he would not be able to read it unless there was a great deal of additional information provided. He needed a key to crack the code.[17]

The important point, however, is that Lytle demonstrates the type of research being done. Although not a member of the military establishment or the scientific community at Wright Field, he had been involved in top secret research projects. Because of that, he was given a representative sample of the symbols and asked to make a few determinations.

Exon was sure that the material, at least some of it, would still be housed at Wright-Patterson. There would be reports, probably filed in the Foreign Technology Building, that would describe everything learned in the last forty-plus years.

There would be photographs, from the debris field and the crash site, of the bodies and of the autopsies, filed away. Everything needed to prove that Roswell represented the crash of an extraterrestrial spacecraft would be found, if those reports were ever to be released.

Like others who had been on the crash site in July 1947, and who had been in Roswell at the time of the recovery or who had been in Fort Worth when Marcel brought the material in, Exon was convinced that this was the wreck of a spacecraft. It was not something manufactured on earth. "Roswell was the recovery of a craft from space."[18]

10

The Autopsy Reports

Q UITE CLEARLY, IF bodies were recovered, there would be autopsies performed. Once the bodies were inspected on the impact site and placed in the lead-lined body bags, they were taken into the base at Roswell. Once there, according to sources, two or three of the bodies were taken to the base hospital, where some preliminary work was accomplished.

Glenn Dennis knew one of the people involved in that preliminary autopsy.[1] She was a nurse whom Dennis had dated, and, according to him, she told him that she had been on normal duties at the hospital on that day. She had been entering an examination room that was across the hall from where she was working to get some supplies. When she opened the door, she spotted two doctors, men she'd never seen at the base hospital. One of the doctors, possibly a colonel named Stanford flown in from El Paso, told her, "You stay here. We've got to have you."

As she walked in, she noticed a horrible odor. The doctors were examining three bodies . . . "foreign bodies" was the term she used. Two were badly mutilated but one looked as if it might have survived the impact and was mostly in one piece. It had apparently died of exposure some time after the crash. She said that the doctors believed the other two might have been mutilated by predators and that they looked as if they had been exposed to the elements on the high desert.

It was hard for them to stay in the room because of the odor. The doctors worked on the bodies, with her assistance, but she had to leave, feeling sick. The doctors reacted the same way and finally had to give up, sealing the bodies in mortuary bags to be taken, she believed, to the hospital's morgue.

The nurse was clear on one other point. She didn't recognize either of the doctors in the room. They were not assigned to the base at Roswell but had been flown in from the outside. She didn't see them again after that brief encounter in the hospital room.[2]

The only other doctor to be identified as participating in the brief autopsies at Roswell was Dr. Jesse B. Johnson, Jr.[3] In July 1947 he was assigned to Squadron M, 509th Bomb Group, and was the base pathologist.[4] Unfortunately Dr. Johnson died before he could be interviewed by any researchers, and if he was involved, he apparently told no one about it.[5]

The bodies, according to others, were sent from the base later that same night. The autopsies were conducted elsewhere, and one man said that later, during a meeting in the mid-1960s, he had seen slides about the autopsies performed. These were the full-blown autopsies, and not the quick, preliminary work that had been done at the base. He refused to provide much in the way of detail about the internal structures of the bodies.[6]

Len Stringfield, who originated the term *crash retrieval*, and whose research led him in several interesting directions, met with a doctor he described as "my prime medical contact." From that man he learned about some aspects of the alien body's internal structure.

Later he was able to talk with another doctor who had also participated in an autopsy of an alien body. The new source, according to Stringfield, provided a great deal of additional data. "From him, in time, I was able to envision the body entire, and the more I learned of its internal chemistry and some of its organs, or, by human equation, the lack of them."

Stringfield, from his sources, said that he was able to draw a number of conclusions. According to Stringfield, the beings are humanoid, three and a half to four and a half feet tall. They weigh about forty pounds.

The head is larger than a human head and there are two large round eyes, though one source did suggest the eyes were "Oriental or Mongoloid, deep-set and wide apart." The nose is vague, with only a slight protuberance. The mouth is a small slit and opens only into a slight cavity. The mouth apparently does not "function as a means of communications or as an orifice for food ingestion," and there are no teeth. There are no earlobes or "protrusive flesh extending beyond apertures on each side of the head."

There was no hair on the head, though, according to Stringfield, one of his sources said that it was covered with a slight fuzz. In fact, there isn't much hair on the bodies.

The neck is thin, as is the torso. The arms are long and thin, and the hands reach close to the knee. The hands, according to Stringfield's sources, have four fingers and no thumb, which agrees with what Dennis's nurse told him. Stringfield writes that "a slight webbing effect between fingers was noted by three authoritative observers." One of those who was on the impact site, however, says that there is a thumb on the hand.

Stringfield writes, "Skin description is NOT green. Some claim beige, tan, brown, or tannish or pinkish gray and one said it looked almost 'bluish gray' under deep freeze lights. . . . The texture is described as scaly or reptilian, and as stretch-able, elastic or mobile over smooth muscle or skeletal tissue. No striated muscle. No perspiration or body odor."

There was additional information supplied by Stringfield's sources. He noted that "under magnification, I was told, the tissue structure appears mesh-like, or, like a grid's network of horizontal and perpendicular lines. Clarifying an earlier reference which describes the skin of the entity as 'reptilian,' this new information suggests the texture of the granular-skinned lizards, such as the iguana and chameleon."[7]

Melvin E. Brown, a sergeant with the 509th, told family members that he had seen the bodies of alien creatures when he was given the task of guarding them. According to him, they were smaller than humans and had a skin that was yellowish-orange and like that of a lizard, meaning it was leathery and beaded, but not scaly.[8] Given the circumstances around his opportunity to observe the bodies, the discrepancy in color could have been the result of the lighting conditions. It is interesting that Brown spoke of lizardlike skin in the same way that Stringfield's sources did.

Stringfield was able to learn something of the internal structure. There are no apparent reproductive organs and no genitalia. The brain capacity is unknown. There is a colorless fluid prevalent in the body, which, according to Stringfield, is "without red cells. No lymphocytes. Not a carrier of oxygen. No food or water intake is known. No digestive system or GI tract. No intestinal or alimentary canal or rectal area described."

On July 2, 1979, Stringfield received a typewritten statement from a doctor who performed an autopsy in the early 1950s.

> Size—The specimen was 4 foot three and three-eights inches in length. It has been so long and my files do not contain the weight. I recall the length well, because we had a disagreement and everyone took their turn at measuring.

> Head—The head was pear-shaped in appearance and oversized by human standards for the body. The eyes were Mongoloid in appearance. The ends of the eyes furthest from the nasal cavity slanted upward at about a ten degree angle. The eyes were recessed into the head. There seemed to be no visible eyelids, only what seemed like a fold. The nose consisted of a small fold-like protrusion about the nasal orifices. The mouth seemed to be a wrinkle-like fold. There were no

human type lips as such—just a slit that opened into an oral cavity about two inches deep. A membrane along the rear of the cavity separated it from what would be the digestive tract. The tongue seemed to be atrophied into almost a membrane. No teeth were observed. X-rays revealed a maxilla and mandible as well as cranial bone structure. The outer "ear lobes" didn't exist. The auditory orifices present were similar to our middle and inner ear canals. The head contained no hair follicles. The skin seemed grayish in color and seemed mobile when moved.

The above observations are from general anatomical observations. I didn't autopsy or study the head portion in any great detail since this was not my area of specialty.

NOTE—Your drawing of the head should have the cheek bones removed or a smoother contour. The eyes in the nasal cavity area are not right. The recess and fold is continuous across the forehead. The neck seems too long and the shoulders do not slope as prominently. This may give you this effect. The arms are oversized in length by human standards. There was no thumb. The index finger in your drawing is longer than the middle finger. I don't believe this is correct, but my memory is hazy at this point. The chest area contained what seemed like two atrophied mammary gland nipples. The sexual organs were atrophied. Some other investigators have observed female specimens. I have not had this opportunity. The legs were short and thin. The feet didn't show any toes. The skin covered the foot in such a way that it gave the appearance of wearing a sock. However, X-ray examination showed normal bone structure underneath.

Stringfield, commenting on the above, wrote, "The statement received from the doctor, which I had requested . . . is indeed a breakthrough. . . . I hasten to say that I find no hints or obvious loose ends that would indicate a hoax. Moreover, some of the information he had related in the past year, not included in his statement, was corroborated by another source, also a doctor."[9]

There were some discrepancies between the various reports, and Stringfield was concerned about that. He was told that "there are more than one type."[10]

That doesn't matter, because there is good testimony that bodies were recovered at Roswell, and there is testimony from doctors about their involvement in autopsies. Most of the data is second hand, coming from the work of Len Stringfield. There is no doubt that Stringfield is reporting accurately what he has been told.

Further confirmation of autopsies is available from another source. Dr. La June Foster, a renowned expert and authority on the spinal cord, and who had a practice in San Diego in 1947, was called in to examine the spinal structures. She did not travel to Wright Field, but went to Washington, D.C., where she spent about a month. During Foster's absence, Dr. Laura Henderson worked in the San Diego clinic.

Because Dr. Foster had worked undercover for the FBI during World War II, and because she already had a security clearance, she was flown to Washington, D.C., to examine the spinal structures of the bodies retrieved near Roswell. She reported that it was possible that one was found alive but critically injured. According to her, it was rushed to Washington but soon died of its injuries.

Foster saw one or two of the bodies. Her task was to check the bones, the spinal cords, and vertebrae, making comparisons with the human anatomy.

Like the others, Foster described the beings as short, with large heads. She said that they had strange eyes.

According to family members, she was very upset upon her return from Washington. As she had been debriefed, she had been told that if she talked, she would lose her practice and be killed. "Someone in the government is trying to keep me quiet," she said.[11]

There have been other reports from medical people, but they refuse to allow their names to be attached to these reports. Information about the autopsies is sketchy at best. Those selected to participate were chosen because they could be trusted to remain silent.

Somewhere the reports and photographs made during the autopsies are filed away. Somewhere the data that could answer our questions is hidden. Once those files are opened for general review, we will have the answers. Until then, we are forced to rely on the incomplete information provided by second-hand sources, with little commentary by those who participated in the autopsies.

11

The Threats

A MONG THE MOST disturbing aspects of this story are reports that participants in the event, including individuals whose involvement was only
peripheral, were threatened by members of the United States military and
representatives of the U.S. government. Those telling such stories include women
and children.

George Wilcox, as the Chaves County sheriff, was one of the first civilians
involved in the case. He spoke with Brazel, saw some of the debris, and may have
been at the second site, where the bodies were found.[1] Although he worked with
the military and fielded phone calls from the press, he later claimed that he had no
involvment with the case. Some of the original investigators believed that he had
done no more than alert the 509th Bomb Group to the fact that Brazel was in town
with the strange metallic debris.

But later investigations revealed that Wilcox had a major role. He had been
warned not to talk about it. The military wanted him to remain silent.

Wilcox's granddaughter, Barbara Dugger, made the extent of the threats clear.
Her grandmother told her that the military police came to the jailhouse "and told
George and I [that if we] ever told anything about the incident, talked about it in
any way, not only would we be killed, but they would get the rest of the family."

Dugger asked her grandmother, "Did you hear them say that, Big Mom?" The
answer was that she did. Inez Wilcox had been standing next to her husband when
the threat was made.

Dugger made it absolutely clear that her grandmother believed the threat.
According to Dugger, Inez "sat up and listened. . . . She was a very loyal citizen.
[These] men were not kidding. They never contacted them again and never
threatened them again."[2]

Wilcox himself delivered a threat to Roswell mortician Glenn Dennis, who had
been in the base hospital when the bodies arrived. Earlier a red-haired captain had
warned Dennis that if he wasn't careful, he would be picking his bones out of the
sand. The black sergeant with the captain added that Dennis "would make good

72

dog food." They made it clear that they didn't want to hear later that Dennis had been in town shooting off his mouth.

The following day, Wilcox drove out to the Dennises' house and told the elder Dennis that his son was in trouble out at the base. The warning was that he better be careful. Wilcox told Dennis's father, "Glenn is in some kind of trouble at the base. I don't know what it is, but I've had a black sergeant inform me to tell you to tell your son to keep his mouth shut, because he didn't see anything out at the base." The implication was that there were people watching.

Dennis, a civilian, wasn't particularly intimidated by the threats, but another encounter was distinctly unsettling. The day after he had spoken with his nurse friend at the base, he phoned to ask if she had recovered from the illness that had interrupted their lunch. According to Dennis, "They told me she wasn't working . . . she wasn't available that day. The next day I made two or three calls, and it was also that she was unavailable. On the third day I called again. They said she'd been transferred out. They didn't know where, but she was no longer at the air base."

Then, according to Dennis, "About ten days to two weeks later, I got a letter from her . . . just a note . . . [that said] 'I can't write right now, but here's an APO [Army Post Office] number you can send mail to.' I wrote a letter back . . . probably two weeks. . . . The letter . . . was returned to me, and the envelope said, 'Return to sender,' and it had big red print that said, 'Deceased.' "

When Dennis tried to find out what happened, all he could uncover was a rumor that she had been killed on maneuvers with five other nurses. Their plane had crashed, according to the rumor, killing all on board.[3]

No evidence of the accident has ever been found. Searches of various sources such as *The New York Times Index*, the National Transportation and Safety Board, and the army have failed to confirm that such a crash took place.

Military officers continued to make the rounds in the Roswell area. Frankie Rowe reported that "the military came to our house and they basically threatened us if we said anything about it. They were going to take Mother away and they were going to take Daddy away, so we basically forgot everything we ever saw. . . . We could never talk about this. As far as we were concerned, the whole incident never happened."

It was only a few days, no more than two or three, after Rowe saw the piece of debris in the Roswell fire station that a group of mili- tary men arrived at her house. They wanted to speak to the child who had been at the fire station. When the man in charge learned who it was, he sent the younger children outside to wait with a couple of the other military men.

There were four of them, all armed with rifles, except for the leader, who was probably an officer. "One stood beside the car outside with his rifle at an angle across his body," she said. "One stood beside the guy who talked to us, in the dining room . . . and one went outside with the other three kids."

The man in charge left no doubt that he was giving orders. He forced Rowe and her mother to sit at the table and wouldn't let them stand. According to her, "He stood. We sat."

The other kids were outside with armed men. Rowe and her mother remained inside with the leader of the group and another man who was armed with a rifle. "The other guy was standing beside him with his rifle at half-mast . . . holding it pointed up right in front of their bodies."

He apparently already knew what had happened at the fire station, that a state police officer had shown some of the debris to the fire fighters and to a young girl. Once he was sure that he had the right people, he "didn't mince any words," according to Rowe. He told her that she was not to talk about this again. If she did, "they could take us out in that desert, and no one would ever find us again."[4]

Helen Cahill, Rowe's sister, remembered her father's intense anger about the menacing talk. Soldiers had also threatened all the fire fighters who had been involved. City police officers who had been involved were threatened as well. She confirmed that something had happened and that her father would not tell her a thing about it. Her mother, however, said that the family would be in trouble if Dan Dwyer ever mentioned what he had seen.[5]

Confirmation of the threats to civilians also comes from one of Wilcox's deputies who is still alive. When first contacted, he blurted, "I don't want to get shot."[6] Now he simply denies that he was involved or that he knows anything about the events of July 1947.

The threats against Ruben Anaya, his brother Pete, and his friends were indirect. When Ruben Anaya asked Joe Montoya about the events, he was told to forget it. "It's too dangerous," Montoya allegedly said. "The FBI will do away with you."[7]

A few of the civilian witnesses were only told that they were not to discuss the case with outsiders. Mac Brazel never mentioned a specific threat, but he did give his word that he would say nothing. Whenever Bill Brazel asked his father about the events of July 1947, Mac Brazel invariably said he had taken an oath that he wouldn't talk about it. He'd promised the government that he wouldn't tell.[8]

Even the military men and women involved in the retrieval weren't immune from the threats or security oaths. All, as they completed their assignments, were reminded of the various oaths they had taken.[9] In most cases, it was a gentle reminder.

Pappy Henderson told his wife, Sappho, about the case only after seeing a 1982 newspaper article. He told her that he "had been dying to tell her for years," but had been sworn to secrecy. Now that an article had been printed, he believed, incorrectly, that he was free to tell her.[10]

Edwin Easley had been on the debris field and had the responsibility for cordoning the impact site, but he was reluctant to talk. Although he freely admitted that he had been the provost marshal for the 509th Bomb Group in July 1947, he didn't want to admit that he had been involved in the events of that month. He tried to avoid the questions, saying that he wasn't free to talk. "I've been sworn to secrecy." He revealed information slowly, cautiously, over a period of months.[11]

Frank Kaufmann said that the men were taken into the briefing room in small groups so that no one man would have the names of many of the others who were involved. They were told that the retrieval was classified at the highest levels and that no one was to talk about it under any circumstances. The men were then released out one door while those waiting for the next briefing entered through another. That way no one would be inclined to ask too many questions, because he would never know who had been involved and who had not.[12]

The military went to extraordinary lengths to keep the information under wraps. In 1945, during the waning days of World War II, FBI agents and military officials requested that American citizens keep their knowledge of the Japanese balloon bombs to themselves. Although the Japanese were desperate to learn whether the bombs were reaching the American continent, the American government did not threaten citizens to ensure their silence or their cooperation. It is an interesting contrast.

At Roswell the government went after everyone who knew anything with threats of prison or death. Agents threatened entire families, expressing a willingness to murder children.

If such a report had come from a single individual, a case could be made that the person had overreacted or had misunderstood a request. But these reports came from several individuals who, though unaware of comparable testimony from others, told strikingly similar stories.

What made the events at Roswell so different that the government felt that it was necessary to threaten its own citizens? What made this secret so important that they could not rely on the veracity and the loyalty of those citizens? What made the events so different that officials believed it was necessary to remind the men and women in the military of their oaths and their obligation to keep secrets?

If there were no other information about the Roswell case, this would be sufficient to generate questions. It is a circumstance that is unique in American history. It is the only time that men, women, and children had been threatened with physical violence by representatives of the American government. It is the only time that law enforcement officials have been told that family members would be in jeopardy if they spoke of the events.

The testimony to this aspect of the case is overwhelming. No one could see the emotion of Frankie Rowe as the memories flooded back without being impressed by the depth of that emotion. These were spontaneous memories, induced not under questioning by researchers but by the New England accent of a radio talk show host.[13]

So the question remains. If the events at Roswell were explainable as a balloon, as the official government policy still suggests, why is the information still so carefully guarded? We know it is, because one of the men who was on a July 9 flight to Fort Worth reported a disturbing phone call recently. Having moved, and having changed his telephone number, he was surprised when he was confronted by an unidentified voice who knew his military nickname, his unit, and then suggested that all the MPs who had been involved had committed suicide.[14]

The MPs had not committed suicide, but the implication was clear. Those who knew about the events and who talked about them out of turn died quickly. It frightened the man enough that he decided to say no more.

These threats have been in place for more than forty years, and they are still effective. There are those who refuse to talk, and there are those who were once willing to talk but who have changed their minds. If Roswell was nothing more than a secret balloon project, why does anyone care about it now? What is the real secret of Roswell?

12

Anatomy of an Investigation

I NVESTIGATION OF THE crash at Roswell is more than just talking to witnesses. It is a search for corroborating documentation and an interpretation of the facts and testimony. It is trying to fit recollections in with the documentation and create a whole that encompasses all the facts and all the testimony.

One of the best illustrations of this is the discovery, just over a year ago, that the two men who had been dispatched by the New York office of the Associated Press from Albuquerque to Roswell were both alive and well. This small segment of the Roswell case had not been explored by any of the previous researchers. It was virgin territory and allowed us to examine it as a separate issue.

Once Walter Haut issued the press release, the world demanded more information. All authorities in the Roswell area reported they received dozens of telephone calls. George Wilcox had phone calls from London, Rome, and Hong Kong. The phone lines to the base were jammed, and Blanchard, angered because he couldn't get an outside line, demanded that Haut do something about it. As newspaper deadlines approached, the situation got worse as the reporters needed something to satisfy hungry editors.

Jason Kellahin was an AP reporter in the summer of 1947 based in Albuquerque, New Mexico. He received a call from the New York office of the Associated Press[1] telling him that he needed to get down to Roswell as quickly as possible. According to Kellahin, "We were informed of the discovery down there. . . . The bureau chief sent me and a teletype operator from the Albuquerque office." Kellahin remembered that it was Robin Adair who accompanied him.

Kellahin, interviewed in his home more than forty years later, said, "It must have been in the morning, because we went down there in the daytime. It would take a couple of hours to get down there."

77

Kellahin continued, saying, "We went down to Vaughn. Just south of Vaughn is where they found the material."

The ranch, according to him, wasn't very far from the main highway (Highway 285) from Vaughn to Roswell. They turned from that highway, just south of Vaughn, onto the Corona road. They were driving to the west and saw "a lot of cars and went over. We assumed that [this] was the place. There were officers from the air base. They were there before we got there."

Kellahin described military cars, civilian cars, and even police vehicles parked along the side of the road. In one of the fields adjacent to the road, at the far end of it, were a number of military officers, not more than five or six of them. Kellahin left his vehicle and entered the field, where he saw the scattered debris.

"This man from Albuquerque with me, he had a camera. He took some pictures of the stuff lying on the ground and of the rancher who was there. . . . Brazel was there and he [the photographer] took his picture."

Kellahin asked Brazel a few questions, interviewing him there, in the field."I talked to him. He told me his name [Brazel], and we had been told it was on his ranch."

Kellahin didn't remember much about what Brazel had said. "About the only thing he said, he walked out there and found this stuff and he told a neighbor about it, and the neighbor said you ought to tell the sheriff. . . . It was the next day [he] went down to Roswell."

Standing there in the field, near the debris, Kellahin had the chance to examine it closely. "It wasn't much of anything. Just some silver-colored fabric and very light wood . . . a light wood like you'd make a kite with. . . . I didn't pick it up. In fact, they [the military] asked us not to pick up anything. . . . You couldn't pick it up and have identified it. You have to have known [what it was]. But it was a balloon. It looked more like a kite than anything else."

The debris covered a small area, not more than half an acre. The military men were standing close by as Kellahin interviewed Brazel, but they didn't try to interfere. "They weren't paying much attention. They didn't interfere with me. I went wherever I wanted to go. They didn't keep me off the place at all. Me or the photographer." Kellahin tried to talk to the military people, but they didn't give him any information. "They were being very, very cautious because they didn't know."[2]

He didn't have much time for the interview because the military officers came over and told him they were finished and were going to take Brazel into Roswell. With Brazel gone and the clean-up of the debris finished, there wasn't much reason for the AP reporters to remain. Kellahin and Adair continued their trip to Roswell, arriving before dark.

Adair, however, when interviewed a couple of days after Kellahin, said that he was in El Paso, Texas, when he received the call from New York.[3] He had been there to repair some equipment, and it was in El Paso that the portable equipment for wire transmission was located. The Associated Press headquarters didn't care how he did it, they just wanted him to get up to Roswell as quickly as he could, even if he had to lease an airplane.

Adair landed at the Roswell municipal airport, but not before they had flown over the Brazel ranch in Lincoln County a half dozen times. "We didn't do a bit of good by it. We couldn't get any [pictures]. . . . Even then the place was surrounded by policemen, FBI people. They wouldn't let us in within three-quarters of a mile of the place. We were afraid to go too low. Afraid they would shoot at us.

"We did take a plane up there, but we couldn't land anywhere around it. We got as close as we could and we wanted to get lower, but the indication [from the ground] was that we really didn't want to." Later he said, "They [the military officers on the field] just waved. . . . You couldn't tell if they were waving us off or just politely telling us to get the hell away from there."

From the air, Adair did get a good look at what was later determined to be the debris field. "We could make out a lot of stuff . . . looked like burnt places. . . . You could tell that something had been there." The field was large, and Adair said, "I remember four indications. . . . It was rather hard to line them up from the plane. . . . I wanted to find out if they ran east to west or north to south. I never did get it square in my mind."

Even though he was in an airplane, Adair could see the gouge and tracks on the ground. He said, "You couldn't see them too good from the air. . . . Apparently the way it cut into [the ground], whatever hit the ground wasn't wood or something soft. It looked like it was metal."

Adair didn't think that it had skipped as it hit the ground. It was his impression that it had come down flat. "Right straight down and right straight back up when it left. It took off the same damned way. It didn't skid off or slide off. It went straight up just like it came straight down."

Returning to Roswell, he noticed that none of the other places they flew over had guards. They knew not to try to land in those other locations, because the terrain was rugged. Besides they were only interested in the location where there had been military guards.

Adair said that he saw two sites. "One of them wasn't very distinctive. The other was plainer."

Adair, after they landed in Roswell, linked up with Kellahin a few minutes later. That evening they went to the offices of the *Daily Record*. Adair set up the equipment to transmit from the newspaper office. According to Adair, "That sometimes runs into quite a little chore. Anyhow, got it done and got the picture moved."[4]

Kellahin confirmed some of this, saying that "we went down to the *Roswell Daily Record* and I wrote a story and we sent it out on the AP wire. . . . Adair developed his pictures and set up the wire photo equipment and sent it out."[5]

Transmitting the pictures was considered so important, or maybe such a novelty, that the *Record* ran a story on the front page of the July 9 newspaper, along with a photo of both Kellahin and Adair. They explained that the photo taken of Brazel [while he was in the newspaper office] was the first to be sent from Roswell. The story explained that the circuit had been opened through Mountain States Telephone and Telegraph directly to Denver. Adair, according to the article, said, "seven minutes were required to send the Brazel picture."[6]

The story ended saying, "Adair and Kellahin were ordered to Roswell for the special assignment by the headquarters bureau of AP in New York."[7]

Kellahin, when he left the ranch, had expected to see Brazel in Roswell the next day, but said, "I don't recall that I did. I think the military was talking to him and wouldn't let him talk to anyone else, to my recollection. . . . I saw him there, but . . . there were some military people with him."

Following the story as far as he could, Kellahin talked to Sheriff Wilcox. "When we got down there to the newspaper, he was there. I saw him there or at his office. . . . By that time the military had gotten into it. He was being very cautious."

"It was a weather balloon," said Kellahin. "In my opinion that's what it was. That's what we saw. We didn't see anything else to indicate it was anything else."[8]

Once they finished in the office, Kellahin returned to Albuquerque, and Adair was ordered to return to El Paso to finish his job there. In fact, according to him, the ride back was rough. They ran into a dust storm and tried to climb over it. At one point they hit an updraft and the pilot smacked his head against the side of the aircraft. Adair thought they were going to have to land the plane without the help of the pilot.

In El Paso he finished his assignment and then returned to the bureau office in Albuquerque.[9] El Paso, along with most of New Mexico, was directed from the office in Albuquerque.[10]

This, then, is the reconstruction based on the testimony of the two men and the documentation available in the form of newspaper articles printed in 1947. There are some contradictions, but those can be explained by the long time that passed between the events and the interviews.

Besides, the Roswell story was dead by the morning of July 9. The military had provided an explanation for what was found, and there seemed to be no reason to dispute it. By the time Kellahin returned to Albuquerque, there was a new story for him that had nothing to do with flying saucers. Another assignment that was just as important as his last.

Both Kellahin and Adair were trying to answer the questions as honestly as they could, attempting to recall the situation as it was in July 1947. However, as can be seen, they are at odds with each other. There clearly is no way for Adair to be both in El Paso and in Albuquerque.

All the facts have been gathered. The newspaper articles written in the time frame have been located. Although many of them had no byline, they did carry an AP slug and did identify the location as Roswell. Since Kellahin was the only AP reporter there, assigned by the bureau chief in Albuquerque at the request of the AP headquarters in New York, it is clear that he wrote the articles.

The first problem encountered is Kellahin's memory of getting the call early in the morning. That simply doesn't track with the evidence. First, Haut's press release was not issued until about noon on July 8.[11] That means there would be no reason for the AP to assign a reporter on the morning of July 8. There was no story until that afternoon. And by the morning of July 9, the story was dead. No reason to send anyone to Roswell because photos had already been taken of the debris in Fort Worth and the information already released. Besides, the story in the July 9 issue of *The Roswell Daily Record* makes it clear that they, Kellahin and Adair, had already arrived in Roswell, coming down on July 8.[12]

Second is the story that Kellahin saw the weather balloon on the Brazel ranch. His description of the location, south of Vaughn but just off the main highway to Roswell, is inaccurate.[13] The debris field, as identified by Bill Brazel and Bud Payne, is not close to the Vaughn–Roswell highway. In fact, the field where the debris was discovered is not visible from the road around it. It is a cross-country drive.

More important, by the time Kellahin could have gotten to that field, the balloon should have been removed. In fact, according to Marcel and the newspaper articles, the balloon was already in Fort Worth if we believe what has been reported. After all, a balloon wouldn't have taken long to collect, and Marcel had done that the day before.

It appears that Kellahin, having looked at the articles he wrote for the Associated Press, and having read *The Roswell Incident* (a copy of which was seen in his house), created a scenario that matched what he believed would have happened. He mentioned nothing of the call from the New York bureau, and calculated the situation based, not on his memory of what happened, but on what he believed would have happened.

Adair, on the other hand, tells of being ordered out of El Paso and told to rent an airplane if he needed one. Here is a set of circumstances that are out of the ordinary. It wasn't every day that he was ordered away from one assignment and told to rent an airplane to get to the next.

He mentioned the call from New York, confirmed by the news article in the *Daily Record*. This detail, which checked out, had not been mentioned by Kellahin. That call, from New York, is the kind of special detail that would stick in the mind simply because it was out of the ordinary.

An attempted review of the AP records for additional confirmation of Adair's story failed. Though searches were initiated at several levels, including offices in Albuquerque and Dallas, as well as one in New York, no records could be located that would support Adair's story. Receipts and records that might verify some of the facts are currently unavailable.[14] No significance was attached to this simply because those records would be nearly fifty years old.

Adair's statements about two sites is confirmed by other witnesses, including Brigadier General Arthur Exon, who also flew over the area. Although Exon's flight was later, his descriptions of the terrain and the gouge are consistent with those made by Adair.

Looking at it from that perspective, it seems that the testimony given by Adair is most consistent with the independent evidence that can be found. Adair's story of flying over the two sites is valuable because it corroborates other testimony and suggests, because there was a gouge and two sites, that the balloon explanation is inaccurate.

Kellahin's testimony of seeing a balloon out in the field is intriguing, not because he is an eyewitness to the balloon on the crash site, but because of what it suggests. If there was a balloon, it would mean that the army had to bring one in. In other words, they were salting the area, and that, in and of itself, would be important. It would suggest that the army had something to hide if it was involved in planting evidence.

Given the sequencing of events, based on the newspaper accounts and other testimony, the earliest that Kellahin could have been in the field was late on July 8. However, by that time, Marcel and the special flight from Roswell were already in Fort Worth. If the balloon explanation is accurate, then the evidence had long since been collected and there would be nothing for Kellahin to see.

Kellahin also said there had been photographs taken while on that field. These photos, according to Kellahin, had been transmitted from Roswell. The photo of Brazel transmitted, however, was one that had been taken, not in the field, but in the newspaper offices.[15] If there were pictures taken in the field, they have never been printed. Had they existed, even if of poor quality, they would have been printed. After all, what could be better than pictures of Mac Brazel with the debris in the field?

By contrast, the seven pictures taken in Ramey's office were printed throughout the country. All seven have been located. Even the fairly rare picture of Irving Newton was printed in Texas newspapers[16] and was used by the editors of *Look* when they printed their *Flying Saucers* special in 1966. But those that Kellahin claimed had been taken of Brazel on his ranch with the debris have never been found. That suggests that Kellahin's memory is flawed.

The evidence and testimony suggest that the call from New York went to Kellahin in Albuquerque and Adair in El Paso. Both were ordered to Roswell by the quickest way possible, including the leasing of an aircraft.

Kellahin did not stop at the ranch on his way down. He is mistaken about that. The lack of the photographs, and evidence about the location of Brazel on the afternoon of July 8, suggest it. The location that Kellahin gives is in error. The ranch was not close to Vaughn, and the debris field is not close to any road.

Adair flew over the area, searching for the crash site. His descriptions, though vague, match those provided by other first-hand witnesses. He then landed at the Roswell municipal airport, where he met Kellahin probably before dark, around seven or eight that night.

By the time they arrived and were ready, some of the pressure was off. Ramey, in Fort Worth, explained that the material found in Roswell was nothing extraordinary. No longer was New York demanding pictures. In fact, several pictures had already been taken in Fort Worth.

The interview with Brazel occurred on the evening of July 8, according to the newspaper article in the July 9 edition of *The Roswell Daily Record*. Brazel was brought in by the owner of KGFL, Walt Whitmore, Sr. Brazel was then interviewed by Kellahin, as well as a reporter for the *Daily Record*. The pictures transmitted, those of Brazel and George Wilcox, are ones that had been taken in the office for that purpose. Kellahin wrote his story, which appeared in the newspapers the next day.

With the story dead, both men were ordered to return to what they had been doing. They left Roswell. Kellahin believed that nothing extraordinary had been found, and there was no reason for the events to stick in his mind.

Adair, having seen some of the military activity on the field, knew that some-thing extraordinary had happened, but didn't know exactly what. He believed that it had nothing to do with a balloon. He suspected it might have to do with the atomic bombs, but that was only because of the presence of the 509th Bomb Group.

The point, however, is that we can take the testimonies of the two men and the documentation, and reconstruct, with a fair amount of accuracy, exactly what happened on July 8 and 9, 1947. We can do it because we are dealing with recent history. We have the men who were involved, and just as important, we have a written record from the time frame. Without those two items, we would be left to speculate.

13

The Twining Letter, Project Moon Dust, and a History of Deception

T HERE ARE THOSE who believe that a letter written by Lieutenant General Nathan F. Twining on September 23, 1947, proves that there was no crash at Roswell. Skeptics, citing the letter, claim that it shows the flaw in the thinking of the UFO community. They take it further, claiming there were no secret studies, and that the air force quit active investigation of flying saucers in 1969. None of this is true.

In the aftermath of the crash at Roswell, a number of policies were established. It would be forty years before they were understood. It would be forty years before the existence of them, as well as the documentation supporting them, would be found. But it was the discovery at Roswell that set the tone for UFO research. Had the crash not taken place so soon after the first flying saucer reports were made, and had it not happened in such a remote section of the country, the history of the phenomenon might have been radically different.

The policy of secrecy became clear when Twining wrote his response to inquiries directed to the Air Materiel Command. This letter, classified as secret in 1947, has become all things to all sides of the UFO question. To understand it, and the ramifications of it, it is necessary to look beyond it, to the reasons it was created, what it was meant to accomplish, and the mood of those in command positions during the summer of 1947.

The letter itself was drafted in response to an inquiry from Brigadier General George F. Schulgen, who was the assistant chief of staff for air intelligence.[1]

Schulgen, among others in the military and those in civilian intelligence agencies including the FBI, had noticed an apparent lack of concern by the "topside" about the flying saucer reports. In an undated page from FBI files that apparently accompanied an army air force estimate of the situation dated July 30, 1947, an officer wrote, "Lack of topside inquiries, when compared to the prompt and demanding inquiries that have originated topside upon former events, give more than ordinary weight to the possibility that this is a domestic project, about which the President, etc. know."[2]

The problem here was that the conclusion wasn't valid. The FBI had consulted with Colonel L. R. Forney of the Intelligence Division of the War Department (later the Defense Intelligence Agency). Forney told Special Agent S. W. Reynolds that the disks were not army or navy vehicles. In fact, several agencies in the U.S. government, including the Atomic Energy Commission, were denying that the disks belonged to them or that there were any secret experiments that would account for the sightings.[3]

The silence from the top said just the opposite. It appeared that the secrecy was so tight that even the highest levels of intelligence inside the army air force were kept in the dark. Reynolds, who was also in contact with Lieutenant Colonel G. D. Garrett, who served under Schulgen and who should have been in a position to know the answers, concluded that the disks were probably "a very highly classified experiment of the army or navy."[4]

There was a historical precedent for the belief. According to Garrett, when the ghost rockets were flying over Sweden in 1946, the "high brass" of the War Department "exerted tremendous pressure on the air forces intelligence to conduct research and collect information in an effort to identify these sightings." In sharp contrast, there were now sightings over the United States, and the "high brass" appeared to be "totally unconcerned."[5] This led to the conclusion that the high brass already knew the answers to the questions about the identity of the objects. They just weren't interested in sharing the answers with those in the trenches.

FBI agent Reynolds wasn't completely satisfied with the answer and called his liaison at the War Department, Colonel L. R. Forney. Forney had inquired about classified army projects and learned that the army had no idea what the disks were. Further checking by Garrett, even pressing Schulgen for an answer, demonstrated that Schulgen couldn't offer an explanation. It was agreed that the inquiry should be taken to a higher level. General Curtis LeMay, head of research and development, reported that "a complete survey of research activities discloses that the Army Air

Forces has no project with the characteristics similar to those which have been associated with the Flying Discs."[6]

It seemed that the question had been answered. Still, there were those concerned about the situation, so it was decided to make a direct request for information from the commanding officer of the Air Materiel Command headquartered at Wright Field, Ohio. Accompanying the request to General Twining was the first of the intelligence community's estimates concerning the flying saucers. Although the study contained specifics of sixteen cases, the body of the report mentions eighteen. These were the best sightings since the May 17 report from Oklahoma City, and included the Kenneth Arnold sighting, ending with a case from Elmendorf Field, Alaska. Five of the cases involved military pilots, including the Maxwell Field sighting by four pilots on June 28. Six of them were made by civilian pilots, including the July 4 sighting near Emmett, Idaho, made by a United Airlines flight crew.[7]

The estimate contained conclusions based on the information used to prepare it. It seemed that the officers did not think the flying disks were much of a mystery. They believed they were mechanical aerial objects. They just didn't know whose, but based on the lack of concern from the top, they believed that they had to be a classified U.S. project.[8] It was the only conclusion that made sense to them.

This, then, was the situation in late summer of 1947. And this was the information that Twining's staff used to prepare the report to be sent down to Schulgen. They used nothing other than the information supplied to them, adding nothing to the discussion at all.

The response from Twining must have surprised everyone. They had believed that the AMC would know all about the flying disks, yet Twining was telling them, essentially, that the phenomenon was real and should be investigated but that they, the flying disks, weren't ours.[9]

In the secret letter, General Twining, upon the recommendations of his staff, said that an investigation of the "flying discs" should be continued. The subject of the letter was "AMC Opinion Concerning 'Flying discs.' It was directed back to the Commanding General, Army Air Forces, in Washington, D.C., and was marked for the attention of Brigadier General George Schulgen.

The letter said:

> 1. As requested by AC/AS-2 there is presented below the considered opinion of this Command concerning the so-called "Flying Discs". This opinion is based on interrogation report data furnished by AC/AS-2 and preliminary studies by personnel of T-2 and Aircraft

Laboratory, Engineering Division T-3. This opinion was arrived at in a conference between personnel from the Air Institute of Technology, Intelligence T-2, Office, Chief of Engineering Division, and the Aircraft, Power Plant and Propeller Laboratories of Engineering Division T-3.

2. It is the opinion that:

a. The phenomenon reported is something real and not visionary or fictitious.

b. There are objects probably approximating the shape of a disc, of such appreciable size as to appear to be as large as man-made aircraft.

c. There is a possibility that some of the incidents may be caused by natural phenomena, such as meteors.

d. The reported operating characteristics such as extreme rates of climb, maneuverability (particularly in roll), and action which must be considered *evasive* when sighted or contacted by friendly aircraft and radar, lend belief to the possibility that some of the objects are controlled either manually, automatically or remotely.

e. The apparent common description of the objects is as follows:

(1) Metallic or light reflecting surface.

Page two began with the heading: Basic Ltr fr CG, AMC WF to CO, AAF, Wash. D.C. subj "AMC Opinion Concerning 'Flying Discs:' "

(2) Absence of trail, except in a few instances when the object apparently was operating under high performance conditions.

(3) Circular or elliptical in shape, flat on bottom and domed on top.

(4) Several reports of well kept formation flights varying from three to nine objects.

(5) Normally no associated sound, except in three instances a substantial rumbling roar was noted.

(6) Level flight speeds normally about 300 knots are estimated.

f. It is possible within the present U.S. knowledge—provided extensive detailed development is undertaken—to construct a piloted aircraft which has the general description of the object in subparagraph (e) above which would be capable of an approximate range of 7000 miles at subsonic speeds.

g. Any developments in this country along the lines indicated would be extremely expensive, time consuming and at the considerable expense of current projects and therefore, if directed, should be set up independently of existing projects.

h. Due consideration must be given the following:

(1) The possibility that these objects are of domestic origin—the product of some high security project not known to AC/AS-2 or this command.

(2) The lack of physical evidence in the shape of crash recovered exhibits which would undeniably prove the existence of these objects.

(3) The possibility that some foreign nation has a form of propulsion possibly nuclear, which is outside of our domestic knowledge.

3. It is recommended that:

a. Headquarters, Army Air Forces issue a directive assigning a priority, security classification and Code Name for a detailed study of this matter to include the preparation of complete sets of all available and pertinent data which will then be made available to the Army, Navy, Atomic Energy Commission, JRDB, the Air Force Scientific Advisory Board Group, NACA, and the RAND and NEPA projects for comments and recommendations, with a preliminary report to be forwarded within 15 days of receipt of the data and a detailed report thereafter every 30 days as the investigation develops. A complete interchange of data should be effected.

4. Awaiting a specific directive AMC will continue the investigation within its current resources in order to more closely define the nature of the phenomenon. Detailed Essential Elements of Information will be formulated immediately for transmittal thru channels.

N. F. Twining
Lieutenant General, U.S.A.
Commanding[10]

The problem for researchers today is that one paragraph about the "lack of physical evidence in the shape of crash recovered exhibits." Clearly Twining and the highest-ranking members of his staff would have been notified if a flying disk had crashed. The laboratories and facilities to examine and exploit such a find were at the Wright Field–Patterson Field complex in Dayton, Ohio. Reverse engineering of captured foreign rockets, aircraft, and weapons was accomplished at the Foreign Technology Division there.[11]

The argument can be made that no mention of the crash debris from Roswell was made because it had not been included in the reports forwarded to Twining. Since it wasn't included, Twining's staff saw no reason to inform Schulgen and others of its existence, especially since they could accomplish their task without mentioning it. While those in Washington were expecting AMC to tell them that no further investigation was necessary because the answers were held at the top, Twining was telling them that such was not the case. The investigation should be continued, and in fact, it was recommended that a priority, classified, code-named project be created for the collection of intelligence about the flying disks. It also pointed out that the AMC would continue to investigate "to more closely define the nature of the phenomenon."

There is another consideration here, and that is the level of classification of both Schulgen's original requests and AMC's eventual response. First, it must be remembered the Twining letter was classified as "secret." That meant anyone with a "secret clearance" would have access to the information. Nearly every officer in the military is routinely granted a "secret clearance." In addition, thousands of civilians working at the Pentagon and at other levels throughout the federal government also have secret clearances.

Second, if Roswell happened and debris was picked up, it would have been classified at a higher level than secret. In fact, the accepted wisdom is that the Roswell information is one of the highest and most tightly held secrets. Clearly it was classified as top secret in 1947 when the Twining letter was written, and it continues to be classified top secret today. To include the data in the report would require that the whole report be classified as top secret.

While there is no reason the report couldn't have been classified higher, the protocols for dealing with top secret material are different from those for secret. Instead of keeping it in a safe, for example, top secret requires a vault. Access to top secret is limited and requires that it be signed out. If it is to be destroyed, two officers must be present to certify the document has been properly destroyed. A single officer can destroy material classified as secret or lower.[12]

What develops is a dilemma. What is happening here? On the one hand, those at certain levels of the intelligence community could learn nothing about the flying disks; the lack of "topside" interest suggested the answers already existed, and they were going to give up. On the other, suddenly, came a directive from on high that told them it was a serious problem and that a coordinated investigation should be a priority. That meant, quite simply, the answers didn't exist at the top.

There is a second consideration here. If the flying disks were a top-secret experiment of some kind, and if it was as closely held as it appears to have been, the last thing Twining and his staff would have done is suggest a priority investigation be initiated. They would be telling lower-level officers to begin a campaign that had the mission of exposing the secret. They would put not only the resources of army intelligence into revealing the secret, but those of the FBI because of the interest shown by the Bureau.

Instead, had the flying disks been ours, Twining would have suggested that the whole project be dropped. If inquiries continued, a quiet word in the right ears would have stopped the investigation and possible compromise.

What Twining's response proves is that Twining and his staff, although aware of the Roswell crash, wanted to gather additional intelligence about the flying disks. They made the suggestion, but then added the statement about the lack of crash-recovered debris. In other words, Twining was telling those ranked below him not to bother with the stories of flying saucer crashes because the debris didn't exist. He was shutting off one area of investigation, suggesting that those reports, prominent in the press, were hoaxes or misidentifications, as had been reported. He didn't want anyone looking into those reports because they would lead back to Roswell.

Of course, none of this answers the question of the Twining claim that there is a lack of crash debris. All it does is show that there was concern at a high level and that conclusions that those at the highest levels knew all about the flying disks are wrong.

For those who think the Twining letter proves the Roswell crash didn't take place, it can be countered with the statement by J. Edgar Hoover. On July 10, 1947, FBI agent E. G. Fitch sent an "office memorandum" to D. M. Ladd about the flying disks. Schulgen had asked Special Agent Reynolds for help investigating the flying disks. Clyde Tolson, one of the top FBI men, on July 15 endorsed the memo, saying, "I think we should do this."[13]

It was then passed to Hoover, who wrote, "I would do it but before agreeing to it we must insist upon full access to disks recovered. For instance, in the La case the Army grabbed it and would not let us have it for cursory examination."[14]

The problem with this statement is the sloppy handwriting of Hoover. Many have interpreted the location as La and tried to determine what it means. On July 7, 1947, there was a hoax from Shreveport, Louisiana.[15] There is no doubt that this case was a hoax, and a not very clever one. If that is what Hoover meant in his endorsement on the letter, then the question has been answered, and we are no closer to understanding the situation in July 1947.

But the FBI was not cut out of the Shreveport case. In fact, the FBI was an important part of the investigation. The FBI reported through the commanding general at Barksdale Field, Louisiana, to the commanding general of the army air forces (General Carl Spaatz) in Washington, D.C. The report said, in part, "FBI resident agent, Shreveport, was informed and contacted FBI office, New Orleans, by phone, made initial report and later informed that office that discovery was hoax and rendered complete report of investigation. Summary of information on case will be forwarded."[16]

Because the FBI was involved heavily, because the case was an obvious hoax, and because pictures of the "flying disk" were included in the newspapers, it doesn't seem likely that this is the case Hoover mentioned, simply because the army didn't grab it and not let anyone see it.

The obvious conclusion, then, is that La refers to Los Angeles, but there are no cases from that area that fit the facts. While there were sightings in or near the Los Angeles area, and a Los Angeles–based pilot claimed to have seen an object crash into the mountains in Montana,[17] there are no reports from Los Angeles of a crashed disk. Other than the ambiguous letters on the Hoover endorsement, there is nothing to suggest that it was Los Angeles.

There are others who claim the La refers to Los Alamos. The problem is that while some of the Roswell debris was taken to Los Alamos as witnesses at Roswell have testified, it can't be called the Los Alamos case. Los Alamos is several hundred miles from the crash sites in southeastern New Mexico. The crash was near Roswell, and it has always been referred to by that location. Even in July 1947, all information was coming from Roswell, all the newspaper reports datelined the information as from Roswell, and inquiries from the press were directed to various officials in Roswell. There were, quite naturally, questions and statements from officials in Fort Worth and Washington, but those were the locations of officials and not the site of a crash.

The important thing here is that we have a trail of FBI documents that address the case in Roswell, that create a question of what was happening on July 8, and finally, a document that suggests that sometime after July 15, long after the newspapers had forgotten about Roswell, the head of the FBI was still referring to a crashed disk that the army wouldn't let him see.

Neither document, then—the Twining letter or the FBI memo—is conclusive proof. They tend to cancel each other out. But the information developed through other sources, and the documentation that exists, tend to reveal the level of secrecy inside the military establishments. Given all that, it is not unreasonable to believe that Twining, who knew all about Roswell, would not have mentioned it in his response to Brigadier General Schulgen. The mention of the lack of crash debris only points out that such debris would conclusively answer the questions, but Schulgen hadn't mentioned it in the reports forwarded to AMC for analysis. Since the letter was drawn up based on information supplied by Schulgen, it can be concluded that the suggestion about a lack of debris refers not to the reality of the situation at AMC, but to the evidence as forwarded by Schulgen.

The note by Hoover on the FBI memo suggests that something else was going on; but again, there are problems. It is ambiguous enough that researchers are forced to speculate about which crash report he meant. In July 1947 there had been several reports of debris recovered, such as the Louisiana case, one near Houston, Texas, and a reported crash with no debris near Bozeman, Montana. And, of course, the front page report out of Roswell, New Mexico.

The problem is that neither document is conclusive. Each is open to interpretation. It can't be said that Twining's letter rules out the crash at Roswell because of the circumstances surrounding its creation. There is room for Roswell to slip through the cracks. Or to be pushed through them.

Nor can it be said that the Hoover note is conclusive. It can't be said that it documents a crash at Roswell. There is room for an alternative explanation.

Once again there is proof, but the proof, in the form of the documents, leaves something to be desired. Convincing arguments can be made in both directions, but, in the end, all that can be said is that this is not the final word. Something more tangible is needed.

But the trail of documents and deceit doesn't end there. Twining's suggestion, of a classified, priority project, was accepted and implemented. This was the beginning of Project Sign, created on December 30, 1947, with a priority of 2A.

During the summer of 1948, the officers at Sign created a report, rumored to have been classified top secret, that they called *An Estimate of the Situation*. The report concluded that flying saucers were extraterrestrial in origin. The *Estimate* was forwarded to General Hoyt S. Vandenberg, at that time the chief of staff of the air force. Vandenberg rejected the report, claiming the conclusions were not warranted by the evidence presented.[18] All copies of the report were supposed to have been destroyed, but rumors persist that one or more were kept. Ruppelt, in his book, claimed to have seen one shortly after he became the head of Project Blue Book.[19]

The civilian community knew that the military was investigating UFOs, and had been told the name was Project Saucer. But that name was a cover for Project Sign. In February 1949 a second report on flying saucers was prepared. It recommended:

> Future activity on this project should be carried on at the minimum level necessary to record, summarize and evaluate the data received on future reports and to complete the specialized investigations now in progress. When and if a sufficient number of incidents are solved to indicate that these sightings do not represent a threat to the security of the nation, the assignment of special project status to the activity could be terminated. Future investigations of reports would then be handled on a routine basis like any other intelligence work.
>
> Reporting agencies should be impressed with the necessity for getting more factual evidence on sightings, such as photographs, physical evidence, radar sightings, and data on size and shape. Personnel sighting such objects should engage the assistance of others, when possible, to get more definitive data. For example, military pilots should notify neighboring bases by radio of the presence and direction of flight of an unidentified object so that other observers, in flight or on the ground, could assist in its identification.[20]

It is interesting to note that only six months or so earlier, the officers at Sign were advocating the extraterrestrial hypothesis, and then, after rejection of their report by the chief of staff, they were concluding that the project should be downgraded. Clearly they were taking their cues from General Vandenberg even if those cues were unstated.

On February 11, 1949, the project name was changed to Grudge, because, according to Ruppelt, the code name Sign had been compromised.[21] At the same time, the project lost some of its priority.

In August 1949 Grudge officers produced their own report, advising "that the investigation of reports of unidentified flying objects be reduced in scope." The closing of Project Grudge was announced on December 27, 1949.[22]

The project, however, was not abandoned. In September 1951 Major General C. B. Cabell asked Lieutenant Jerry Cummings of Grudge what was happening with the flying saucers. Told "Not much," Cabell blasted the project's disorganization and ordered an overhaul of the system.[23] Project officers must have been confused by the contradictory statements issuing from the Pentagon.

The outgrowth of this was the appointment of Edward Ruppelt to head the project with a new name, Blue Book. Ruppelt was to energize the project, which he did, appointing scientific advisors and attempting to improve the types of data collected. By March 1952, when the name was officially changed, the project was upgraded.[24]

During the summer of 1952, thousands reported flying saucers. Public interest in the phenomenon was at an all-time high. When UFOs swarmed over the capital on two successive weekends in July, the air force explanations for UFOs began to sound lame at best. The resources of Blue Book were strained to the breaking point. And although Ruppelt was trying to gather more and better information about UFOs, his system was swamped and good cases had to be ignored.

Because of the large number of sightings, Washington could no longer ignore the UFO problem. The CIA, claiming to be afraid that UFO reports could clog the intelligence-reporting channels during a time of national security, began to downplay the UFO sightings.

By December of 1952, the CIA was trying to get the UFO problem redefined as a security question. They were pressing the air force to agree to a review of the best cases from the Blue Book files. This would become the Robertson Panel, scheduled to meet in January of 1953.[25]

On January 3, 1953, the 4602d Air Intelligence Squadron (AISS) was created by Air Defense Command regulation 24-4 in what might be considered an amazing coincidence. The Robertson Panel convened about two weeks later. They reviewed the information, suggested answers for the previously listed unidentifieds, and recommended that the myth be taken from the UFO sighting reports. They suggested that the media be used to "educate" the public about flying saucers. They believed that if they could teach the public about the nature of UFOs, then the number of sighting reports would drop off.[26]

Then, just after the conclusion of the Robertson Panel, Blue Book was stripped of its investigative function.[27] Sighting reports were no longer to be sent to Blue Book and ATIC at Wright-Patterson, but to the 4602d at Fort Belvoir, Virginia. A series of new regulations and special units was created that carefully spelled out who had the responsibility for UFO investigation, and it was not Blue Book.[28]

Seven months later, on August 26, 1953, the 4602d was tasked with the official investigation of UFOs under Air Force Regulation 200-2. The regulation required that all UFO reports from inside the United States be transmitted to the 4602d before they were sent on to Project Blue Book (referred to as ATIC in the regulation).[29]

In other words, air force regulations dictated that an organization other than Blue Book and ATIC be alerted first in a UFO report. Then the 4602d would determine if it was to be forwarded to ATIC at Wright-Patterson Air Force Base. Primary responsibility for UFO-related reports was held at Fort Belvoir, Virginia.

Air Force Regulation 200-2 is an Intelligence regulation titled "Unidentified Flying Objects Reporting" (short title: "UFOB"). It deals only with UFO-related questions. In 1969, when Brigadier General C. H. Bolender wrote, "Moreover, reports of unidentified flying objects which could affect national security are made in accordance with JANAP 146 or Air Force Manual 55-11, and are not part of the Blue Book system,"[30] he knew the truth, as outlined by air force regulations. Real responsibility for UFO reports was located in Virginia and not Ohio.[31] Project Blue Book was nothing more than a public relations outfit designed to identify objects and to convince the public that something was being done.

The designation of the "special unit" at Fort Belvoir changed a number of times. The 4602d became the 1006th AISS in July 1957. In April 1960 it became the 1127th USAF Activities Group.[32] That designation became important when tracking the Project Moon Dust documents.

In November 1961 another policy was established by the air force in a document sent to various air force intelligence functions. It outlined the establishment of the "AFCIN Intelligence Team Personnel."[33] It was more proof that the air force was interested in UFOs and that it has continued its investigation of them.

There is a portion of the document deleted, but in paragraph 2, subparagraph c, it says, "In addition to staff duty assignments, intelligence team personnel have peacetime duty functions in support of such Air Force projects as Moondust, Bluefly, and UFO, and other AFCIN directed quick reaction projects which require intelligence team operational capabilities (see Definitions)."

Those definitions appear in paragraph 5. It covers not only those assigned to the teams, but also the terms used in the document itself.

> a. Linguist: Personnel who can develop intelligence information through interrogation and translation from Russia and/or Bloc country languages to English.
>
> b. Tech Man: Personnel qualified to develop intelligence information through field examination and analysis of foreign material, with emphasis on the Markings Program and technical photography.
>
> c. Ops Man: Intelligence team chief. Qualified to direct intelligence teams in gaining access to target, in exploitation of enemy

personnel and material, and in use of field communications equipment for rapid reporting of intelligence information.

d. Airborne Personnel: Military trained and rated parachutists.

e. Unidentified Flying Objects (UFO): Headquarters USAF has established a program for investigation of reliably reported unidentified flying objects within the United States. AFR 200-2 delineates 1127th collection responsibilities.

f. Blue Fly: Operation Blue Fly has been established to facilitate expeditious delivery to FTD of Moon Dust or other items of great technical intelligence interest. AFCIN SOP for Blue Fly operations, February 1960, provides for 1127th participation.

g. Moon Dust: As a specialized aspect of its overall material exploitation program, Headquarters USAF has established Project Moon Dust to locate, recover and deliver descended foreign space vehicles. ICGL #4, 25 April 1961, delineates collection responsibilities.[34]

In the discussion part of the document, the composition of the teams is defined. "Intelligence teams are comprised of three men each, to include a linguist, a tech man, and an ops man. All are airborne qualified. Cross-training is provided each team member in the skills of the other team members to assure a team functional capability despite casualties which may be incurred in employment."[35]

What this means is that the government, more specifically the air force, has a contingency plan to deal with the retrieval of material from space. It is clearly outlined that part of that responsibility surrounds UFO material, which means anything that is unidentified and could, therefore, be of extraterrestrial manufacture.

What this does is tie it all together now. The air force, right after the Robertson Panel of January 1953, created a series of special units and new regulations. These took the primary responsibility away from Project Blue Book, changing it from an active investigation into nothing more than public relations. It carefully spells out who has the responsibility for UFO investigation, and it is not Blue Book.

In a classified document originated by the Department of State and sent to "All American Diplomatic and Consular Posts" on July 26, 1973, it was ordered that "the designator 'MOODUST' [sic] is used in cases of non-US space objects or objects of unknown origin."[36]

Documents found by Clifford Stone, a researcher in Roswell, New Mexico, suggest that Moon Dust has been activated on a number of occasions. On the night of March 25–26, 1968, four objects fell in an area of Nepal. The American embassy in Kathmandu, in a secret message dated July 23, alerted the 1127th USAF Field Activities Group at Fort Belvoir that they expected full cooperation with the government of Nepal. The subject of the message was "Moon Dust."[37]

Although parts of the message were deleted, it is clear that the nature of the four objects was readily known to the personnel assigned to the embassy in Nepal, that they had seen photographs of three of the items but had not been allowed to inspect the fourth, and that "technical team should not be sent unless visual examination of fourth object is felt essential." It is also clear that three of the objects had been sent to the United States for examination and that they were expected to be returned to Nepal on July 28.[38]

Moon Dust was used on August 17, 1967, in what could easily be the retrieval of a terrestrially manufactured satellite found in the Sudan. A cube-shaped satellite weighing about three tons was found fifty miles from Kutum. The nationality of the satellite was not known because there were no inscriptions on the outer surfaces of it. According to local authorities, "in El Fasher have photographs and with difficulty cut samples."[39]

Moon Dust was mentioned in another document dated October 7, 1970, when a report from the Department of State was sent to the 1127th USAF Field Activity Group and to FTD at Wright-Patterson. It said, "Subject: (U) Moon Dust. DATT called by Minister of Interior to inspect object found. . . . Minister said object fell in area with three loud explosions and then burned for five days. . . . The object resembles a pressurized fuel tank."[40]

Those three incidents, all discovered by Stone in his search for Moon Dust documents, show that Moon Dust exists and that it was used to recover debris of unknown origin. Each of them could be explained by terrestrially manufactured craft. Of course, each could refer to something that was not made on Earth. It shows that the government had teams trained and ready to move quickly if something happened. It is those teams that would respond if something from another planet crashed.

Looking at the Kecksburg sighting of December 1965, it becomes clear that a Moon Dust team was dispatched to that area. If there were no other information available, it would be logical to suppose this simply because the various air force regulations required it. Something reentered from space; it didn't behave as a meteor would and therefore would seem to be a manufactured object. That was the proper criterion for Moon Dust to activate.

In fact, documentation from the Project Blue Book files contains a handwritten log from one of the air force command posts that supports the contention that Moon

Dust was involved. It says, "I called Maj. Quintanilla for his advice and assistance. He came to the base and called Major Liver. A further call was made to the Oakdale Radar Site in Penna. *A three man team has been dispatched to Acme, Pa to investigate and pick-up an object that started a fire* [italics added]."[41] This is the three-man team that was outlined in the air force document that was dated November 3, 1961.

Here was one "UFO" case where it was confirmed that Moon Dust was involved. There is no doubt that something was seen over parts of Canada and the eastern United States. Some people in the Kecksburg area believe they saw it crash to the ground. The air force alerted Moon Dust and sent them into the area.

In 1965 General Arthur Exon was the base commander at Wright-Patterson Air Force Base. (For more data on Exon, see Chapter 9: "The Wright Field Connection.") During several interviews with him, he explained that he would sometimes receive a call from Washington, D.C., ordering him to prepare an aircraft. According to Exon, "they'd ask for an airplane tomorrow morning, and that would give the guys a chance to get there by commercial airline. . . . Sometimes they'd be gone for three days and sometimes they'd be gone for a week. . . . I know they went out to Montana and Wyoming and the northwest states a number of times in a year and a half. . . . They went to Arizona once or twice."

Asked if they were assigned to Wright-Patterson, Exon said, "No. They would come from Washington, D.C." He also said the team might have been made up of eight, maybe fifteen people. He couldn't remember specifically. He just knew that it was a small number of trained personnel.[42]

Moon Dust was in operation while Exon was the base commander at Wright-Patterson. They were responsible for the recovery of space artifacts, and their parent unit was based in the Washington, D.C., area. It makes sense that some of the people whom Exon remembered flying into Ohio were operating under orders as part of Project Moon Dust.

Operation Blue Fly is nothing more mysterious than the control for setting up the necessary movement of personnel and equipment to the locations for a Moon Dust recovery. In the Nepal incident, it was a Moon Dust team that was referenced with the note that it wasn't necessary to send them unless they'd have access to the fourth piece of debris. If they had been dispatched, Blue Fly would have been the operation to do it.[43]

That was what we had been able to learn about Moon Dust. Response to FOIA requests and letters to various congressional representatives by military officials, however, claimed that Moon Dust never existed. Stone wrote to a U.S. senator from New Mexico, Jeff Bingaman, and Bingaman passed the request on to the air force. Stone already had the Department of State document, so he was surprised by a letter sent by the air force to Bingaman stating that Moon Dust had never existed.[44]

Lieutenant Colonel John E. Madison of the Congressional Inquiry Division, Office of Legislative Liaison, wrote, "There is no agency, nor has there ever been, at Fort Belvoir, Virginia, which would deal with UFOs or have any information about the incident in Roswell. In addition, there is no Project Moon Dust or Operation Blue Fly. Those missions have never existed."[45]

Within months after Stone and Bingaman challenged the response, Bingaman received another letter, this one from Colonel Mattingley, apparently Madison's boss. He wrote, "Upon further review of the case . . . we wish to amend the statements contained in the previous response to your inquiry." He then admitted that both Moon Dust and Blue Fly existed but that "these teams eventually disbanded because of a lack of activity; Project Moon Dust and Operation Blue Fly missions were similarly discontinued. . . . Although space objects and debris were occasionally reported and recovered by United States citizens, and subsequently turned over to Air Force personnel for analysis, such events did not require the assistance of an intelligence team."[46]

Of course, the other documents have already proven this not to be true. Moon Dust was used on a number of occasions, both inside and outside the United States. Mattingley was candid, now that his office had been caught in a series of misleading statements made to a United States senator, but he wasn't completely honest.

And his suggestion that Moon Dust and Blue Fly were discontinued is not true. Other documents obtained under the Freedom of Information Act prove this. Robert G. Todd, in a letter from the air force dated July 1, 1987, learned that the "nickname Project Moon Dust no longer exists officially." According to Colonel Phillip E. Thompson, deputy assistant chief of staff, Intelligence, "It [Project Moon Dust] has been replaced by another name that is not releaseable [*sic*]. FTD's duties are listed in a classified passage in a classified regulation that is being withheld because it is currently and properly classified."[47]

What this all means is that we can now document that there was a secret project that investigated UFOs, that it had nothing to do with Project Blue Book, and that it was designed with retrieval of material in mind. After 1953, Blue Book evolved into a public relations outfit, and by the time Blue Book was closed in 1969, its headquarters was not Intelligence, but the Office of Information.

The documents also show that the air force engaged in an attempt to mislead the public. While the left hand was in Ohio, handing out information and press releases about UFOs, the right hand was in Virginia, suppressing, according to the regulations, all information about sightings listed as unidentified.

All of this can be proven by documents that are clearly official statements. There is no question about the provenance of them. They show a pattern of deception and misinformation about a topic that the air force and the government would like us to believe doesn't exist. A pattern that began with Twining's letter in 1947 continued through the closing of Project Blue Book, and continues today. If that is the case, then why more than forty years of lies? Why not tell the truth . . . unless that truth is what we have suspected all along? UFOs are extraterrestrial spacecraft.

14

The Search for the Archaeologists

I T WAS BARNEY Barnett who introduced the concept of archaeologists into the Roswell crash case. Or rather, it was those repeating the Barnett story since Barnett died before any researchers began to investigate.[1] It was Jean Maltais who said they were affiliated with the University of Pennsylvania.[2] The stage was set for an area of investigation that would bear little fruit for more than a decade.

Bill Moore, writing in his 1985 paper about the status of his Roswell investigation, said that the link to the University of Pennsylvania had been confirmed.[3] He offered nothing in the way of evidence that it had been confirmed, just that statement.

As our investigation began in 1989, there was no reason to assume that the Barnett testimony was in error in any fashion. The conventional wisdom accepted the Barnett story at face value, and the search for the archaeologists, potential first-hand witnesses to the craft and bodies, was launched. Following the well-mapped route, we began the task of learning who was working in the state of New Mexico in July 1947, with an emphasis on those working in the area of the Plains of San Agustin.

Records were available listing who was where and what was being done. The archaeological literature provided additional clues, and while some of the records available at the Museum of New Mexico, and the Laboratories of Anthropology both in Santa Fe and the University of New Mexico in Albuquerque, might be incomplete, the articles contained acknowledgment sections listing local help and amateurs who assisted on the projects. In other words, there was a paper trail that would lead back to the archaeologists if any had been involved.

The archaeologists who were working on the Plains or near the Plains in July have been identified and eliminated. All of them have denied knowledge of anything happening there.[4] Friends of them were located and questioned, in the hope of a lead, but none developed. The only conclusion that could be drawn was that none of them had been involved.

Given the situation, it would be easy to decide that the story of archaeologists had somehow been created between what Barnett actually said and what those he spoke to heard. The Barnett end of the story was created from second-hand testimony, and it is possible that something had been misunderstood. Since no one can now interview Barnett to ask him, investigators were forced to speculate about his testimony.

It would have been easy to ignore the archaeologist connection if not for two additional facts. On February 15, 1990, just about a year after we began to actively investigate the Roswell case, a man claiming to be one of the archaeologists called.

According to him, they had been surveying the general area looking for "signs of occupation that predated the arrival of the white man."

That was interesting but entirely irrelevant. Anyone reading anything about the Roswell case would have been able to invent that detail. It was clear from the little that had been said that early-man sites were of interest to archaeologists working in New Mexico. However, when asked if he was one of the archaeologists who had been on the Plains, he said, "No. We were working north of the Capitan Mountains."

That was the new wrinkle. No one had suggested that the archaeologists had been working anywhere other than the Plains of San Agustin. He took it further, saying they had been driving cross-country, searching for evidence that the Indians had been in the area in the ancient past. They came up over a rise, and in the area below, "maybe half a mile, maybe more . . . was something that looked like a crashed airplane without wings." The caller said that it looked like an aircraft fuselage that was badly damaged, with no sign of a dome, porthole, or hatch.[5]

Interestingly, the man said that he saw another man already there. That was assumed to be Barney Barnett, but the question that must be asked now is whether it was Jim Ragsdale, the civilian who had been camping with his girlfriend. The archaeologist didn't pay much attention to the other witness, being so concerned with the crashed craft that he said he now knew wasn't an airplane. "It was more rounded." It was so badly damaged that he couldn't tell if it had been disk-shaped or not.

He only saw three bodies. They were small with big heads and big eyes. He said that the head was turned to one side, so that it was difficult to see the facial features. The beings were wearing silver-colored flight suits.

The military arrived moments later. The archaeologist thought there was an officer with them but wasn't sure. All were armed with pistols, and a couple of them had rifles. The archaeologists were ordered away from the craft and stood facing away from it. The man in charge told them that it was of vital national interest that they forget what they had seen. The man then took the names and school affiliations, telling them that grant programs and government funding could disappear if they mentioned what they had seen.[6]

They were then escorted from the area by armed guards. The archaeologist didn't mention what happened to the man who had been there first. The assumption had been that it was Barnett, who received the same treatment, but now it appears that the man left before the military arrived.

The intriguing aspects of the account were that he didn't report a disk and that they had been escorted from the site. Although nothing had been published about the military cordon, the archaeologist described it correctly, saying that there was an army car sitting at the side of the road with a couple of soldiers standing near it. They were turning back everyone who tried to use the road.

It was an interesting story and the man sounded sincere, but the same could be said for Gerald Anderson. In fact, from one point of view, the Anderson testimony was better because it wasn't anonymous and Anderson did supply some documentation. Only after it all fell apart was the Anderson story rejected for the hoax it was.[7]

The archaeologist changed, significantly, the location of the crash site. He placed it in Lincoln County, near the Brazel ranch. He changed the description of the craft and mentioned only three bodies. It was interesting corroboration of part of the Barnett story, but there were enough differences to suggest the man was relating what he'd seen as opposed to what he read. Unfortunately, with no other information, there was little that could be done to investigate.

But that wasn't the only lead to the archaeologists. After the "Unsolved Mysteries" broadcast of September 1989, Mary Ann Gardner came forward. She had been watching the program with her husband when she turned white and felt her stomach flip over. The story of the archaeologists was one that she'd heard about ten years earlier from a dying cancer patient.

The woman (Gardner couldn't remember her name) had been alone in the hospital. Feeling sorry for her because she had no visitors, Gardner spent as much time as she could listening to the woman's stories. Several times she told about the crash of the ship and the little men she had seen.

According to Gardner, "Basically . . . they had stumbled upon a spaceship of some kind and . . . there were bodies on the ground. The army showed up . . . and chased them away and . . . told them that if they ever told anything about it, that the government could always find them."

Gardner couldn't get the woman to say much other than that they had been "little people with big heads," and later she added, "large heads and large eyes."

Gardner thought that the military officers had covered the bodies the way police covered accident victims.

Under questioning, Gardner remembered that the woman had used the word "spaceship." Gardner thought that one of the men had entered the ship. He didn't explore it too far and then "the military was everywhere, the army people were everywhere."

The woman, according to Gardner, wasn't supposed to be there. They had been "looking for fossils. That's what she said. They were hunting rocks and looking for fossils. . . . She went with a friend."

Gardner said that when she first heard the story, in 1976 or 1977, she thought it was the result of a drug-induced fantasy. The woman was on painkillers because of her cancer, but she told the story half a dozen times. It wasn't until the "Unsolved Mysteries" broadcast that Gardner began to believe it.[8]

Of course, there were things to be investigated. Gardner remembered which hospital it had been and was able to provide a time frame for the event. It seemed simple enough to check the records at the hospital for the names of women who died of cancer during those years.

The hospital had been sold, but the hospital administrator said that if someone could get to Florida, the records would be available. But once that happened, there was a series of excuses as to why the records weren't available. Gardner was sure she would recognize the name if she heard it, but there was no way to learn it through the hospital.

The next best thing was to check the obituary pages of the local newspapers, but it was soon evident that the task was overwhelming. All deaths in the area, and many from the rest of the state, were listed. All hospitals were included. Without a little more information, or another way to limit the search parameters, the task was impossible.[9]

These two cases, one second hand and one from an anonymous source, suggested that the Barnett data—that a group of civilian archaeologists had stumbled onto the crash site—was accurate. It was clear through research that the archaeologists had been neither on the Plains of San Agustin nor from the University of Pennsylvania, and that was about all that was known.

There was, as outlined elsewhere, very good evidence that something unusual happened near Roswell. The Mac Brazel story had a wide range of first-hand sources, documentation, and corroboration. The Barnett story had none of these.

Tom Carey, in fact, remembered the statement made by Moore in 1985 in which Moore claimed that he had confirmed the connection to the University of Pennsylvania. He called Moore and learned that he had spoken to an archaeologist at Pennsylvania who, according to Moore, remembered the story. Moore identified him as Bernard Wailes, who was still at Penn. Wailes denied it was he, said that he hadn't arrived in this country until the 1960s and knew nothing about the UFO crash near Roswell. He didn't even remember meeting Moore.[10]

The search then had to center on the area around the Brazel ranch and the areas north of Roswell. That was where something could be documented to have happened. It was the general area identified by the anonymous archaeologist, and it was about the only clue that was left.

Those at the Laboratory of Anthropology in Santa Fe took a look at all the reports filed from the area north of the Capitan Mountains east toward Roswell. The Museum of New Mexico provided the names of those who had been working in that area from 1945 through 1955.

The two names that popped up were Donald Lehmer and Jane H. Kelly. Both were professionals who had written monographs that included information from the proper region. Lehmer, unfortunately, had been killed in an automobile crash,[11] but Kelly was alive and teaching. The scientific director of the Center for UFO Studies (CUFOS), Mark Rodeghier, spoke with her, and she said that she hadn't gotten into the region to make her study until sometime after 1948.[12] That seemed to be documented by her monograph.

Friends and advisors to Lehmer were found and interviewed. Fred Wendorff knew Lehmer well and said that Lehmer had never mentioned a thing to him. Wendorff believed that had Lehmer been involved, he would have said something. Others who knew Lehmer said that he had never mentioned it. Family members were eventually found, including a daughter, Megan, who wrote Tom Carey, "I've talked to my brothers and my father's cousin. He never mentioned anything about the Roswell incident or anything about UFOs to them."[13] That seemed to eliminate Donald Lehmer.

Since we'd already searched through the lists of professional archaeologists who had been working in New Mexico during the summer of 1947, the only thing left was to try to find the amateurs. These ranged from pot hunters to untrained people with an interest in archaeology. They rarely, if ever, produced a written record, but professionals often tapped into the amateur network as they conducted their research. Often, when they finished their reports, the names of the amateurs were appended to thank them for their assistance.

The Laboratory of Anthropology library filed not only the monographs prepared by professionals, but the surveys conducted at the request of the Bureau of Land

Management. Using those documents, it was possible to learn the names of some of the amateurs.

There were a number of amateurs who led back into Lincoln and Chaves counties. Lists of amateurs working around the Fort Stanton area, north and south of Roswell, and with the Museum and Art Center in Roswell were obtained. There are a number of important sites in the area, especially along the Hondo River valley leading to the west from Roswell. Those who had worked the sites were identified and, if still alive, contacted. It was another dead end. No one had any first-hand knowledge of the events, and no one was able to think of who it might have been.

Another amateur surfaced by the name of Cactus Jack. After the "Unsolved Mysteries" broadcast, Iris Foster called, telling of an old pot hunter she knew only as Cactus Jack. He told Foster that he had seen the "object which was round but not real big." He claimed to have seen four bodies and said they were small. Their blood, according to Cactus Jack, was like tar, thick and black, and stained the silver uniforms they wore.[14]

Foster couldn't remember Cactus Jack's real name, but her sister Peggy Sparks could. She said it was Larry Campbell, an old-timer who had drifted through parts of New Mexico, Texas, and Arizona his whole life. Campbell, she believed, had been burned a number of years earlier in a fire in Taos and lived at a nursing home in Las Vegas, New Mexico.[15]

A search initiated at the *Taos News* failed to reveal any information about a fire or Larry Campbell. Carey tried to learn if Campbell had ever been in the nursing home in Las Vegas, and the answer was no.[16] Campbell, it seemed, was another dead end.

Interestingly, another Cactus Jack was located. Unfortunately he was in prison in Anthony, New Mexico. A quick check revealed that he was not old enough to be the Cactus Jack of the Roswell crash.[17]

Long lists of archaeologists and anthropologists had been located and many of the people were interviewed. They included Joe Ben Wheat, Jesse Jennings, William Pearce, Art Jelinek, Ridgely Whitman, John Speth, Regge Wiseman, and many more. The lists ranged from people who might have been involved to people who might have known who was involved.

For two years it seemed that nothing concrete could be learned. Had it not been for Gardner and the unidentified archaeologist who called, who seemed to have some inside knowledge, it would be simple to ignore this aspect of the case. The long searches, the checks at universities all over the United States, had failed to find a clue. With few exceptions, all who were interviewed were friendly and interested. They

They wanted to help, but a point was reached when the names being given were the same ones already interviewed. There was nowhere to go.

Then Tom Carey received the break. A friend of a new member of Mutual UFO Network (MUFON) told Carey that her father, C. Bertram Schultz, had been telling the story of a crashed flying saucer for years. Although he wasn't an anthropologist, he was a vertebra paleontologist. He had spent time in Roswell and he had spoken to a group of archaeologists in Roswell who knew about the crash. He did, however, see the military cordon as he drove out of Roswell, speaking of guards on the western side of the highway. Since he didn't want to drive off to the west, he was curious but unconcerned.[18]

The big question was: could Schultz remember the names of any of those archaeologists. According to him, W. Curry Holden was the leader of the group.[19]

Holden, at one time the chairman of the Department of History and Anthropology at Texas Tech in Lubbock, Texas, was ninety-six years old when he was discovered. Holden, when interviewed in 1992, said that he had been there. He could remember nothing about the event, other than that he had been there and had seen it all. Each time the question was asked during the short meeting, he confirmed that he had seen it all.[20]

Later, both his wife and daughter said that he was easily confused. Memories from his life were jumbled and reordered, and he had never mentioned, to either one, that he had been involved in a flying saucer crash.[21] But Holden had been asked the question three separate times in three separate ways, giving him the opportunity to answer it differently, yet he always responded that he had been there.

Holden's papers, nearly a quarter of a million sheets, had been given to Texas Tech and were there for review. With luck, there would be something in the papers to answer the questions one way or the other.

The weekend when the ship crashed had been a three-day holiday. Holden's records revealed that he had written a check in Lubbock on July 3, that he had been invited to a wedding on July 8, and that he made a bank deposit on July 9. There was no way to prove that he had been in Lubbock on the critical Sunday when the archaeologists had been on the impact site.[22] With Roswell only two to three hours away, and given the history of the region, there was no reason not to believe that he had been there.

Schultz was sure that Holden had been one of the archaeologists. Schultz mentioned that he had seen the cordon himself,[23] and his daughters confirmed that he had been to Roswell many times, particularly to a region south of Roswell.[24]

There are records of Schultz's research as well. Schultz was in southern Nebraska before and after the right date, collecting samples, but again, there is no record of where he was on the critical dates. The field notes, available at the University of Nebraska, were inconclusive, and Schultz's personal diaries were not available.[25]

Interestingly, records from Texas Tech did put Schultz and Holden together at the University of New Mexico for the 46th Annual Meeting of the American Anthropological Association, December 28–31, 1947. Holden attended the meeting, and Schultz spoke about "The Lime Creek Sites: New Evidence of Early Man in Southwestern Nebraska."[26]

Here were two major finds, archaeologists who had claimed to have knowledge of the events in Roswell, one first hand and one who had both first- and second-hand information. But more important, both of them placed the site of the event in the Roswell area and not anywhere near the Plains of San Agustin.

The archaeologists had been found, but there weren't the revelations that had been expected. Holden, who died in April 1993, had been unable to share any additional data, and his age prevented a detailed questioning. Schultz, who could be interviewed, only related what he'd heard from Holden, and the little he'd seen himself.

Without these clues, the search would have been abandoned, but Carey couldn't let go. Without the data from the anonymous source and without the new data, the search would have to be ended. There would have been no hope.

But Carey stayed after it, reinterviewing those who had been found and rejected. He talked to Dr. George Agogino, who finally admitted that he had heard the story himself. He knew who had been there. When Carey read him the notes from the conversation with the anonymous source, Agogino said, "That's what he told me."[27]

Agogino didn't want to identify the archaeologist, because the man had made him promise not to tell. Fear of the government seemed to be the reason. He didn't want to get into trouble. But Agogino did tell,[28] providing a name as well as a corroborating source.

The search for the archaeologists has nearly ended. Their leader, Dr. W. Curry Holden, has been identified, and he confirmed his involvement. Corroborating witnesses have been found and interviewed. The story of archaeologists on the impact site, just north of Roswell, is true. The details provided by them have been sketchy, but we now have a better understanding of what happened on that New Mexican desert in July 1947. All that remains is to learn the names of the other witnesses and add them to the growing list of people who kept the greatest secret of the twentieth century.

PART IV

THE
EXPLANATIONS

15

Alternative Explanation Number One: A Japanese Balloon Bomb?

I N AN ARTICLE in the April 1990 issue of *Fate*, occult journalist John Keel claimed to have solved the Roswell mystery twenty years earlier. By his account, Mac Brazel found a rice-paper Japanese balloon bomb in his field. It had lain undetected on a remote part of the ranch until freakish winds accompaning a thunderstorm uncovered it. Official embarrassment about the Japanese project kept the officers of the 509th Bomb Group from revealing the true nature of Brazel's find. Keel suggests that army air force officers at Eighth Air Force headquarters then substituted a weather balloon for the balloon bomb to keep the myth of American invulnerability alive.

For this theory to work, there had to be a reason to keep such a secret in postwar America. In his *Japan's World War II Balloon Bomb Attacks on North America*, Robert C. Mikesh writes, "On January 4, 1945, the Office of Censorship asked newspaper editors and radio broadcasters to give no publicity whatsoever to the balloon incidents. This voluntary censorship was adhered to from coast to coast, a remarkable self-restraint in a free-press-conscious country." This suggests the theory may have some credence.

Mikesh then gives the reason for the request. The government feared that spies for the Japanese would read those newspaper stories and report to their headquarters that the balloon bombs were reaching the United States. Documents secured after the war told of Japanese plans to use biological warfare against the United States if the bombing was successful. But the Japanese abandoned the plan when they could confirm no reports that any of their balloons had reached the American mainland. They assumed, falsely, that all the balloon bombs had fallen harmlessly into the ocean.

The plan of censorship was abandoned in the summer of 1945 when a balloon bomb killed six picnickers in Oregon. According to the Reverend Archie Mitchell, he was on an outing with his wife and several children. While he was parking the car, his wife and the kids found the balloon in the woods. While tugging on it, they triggered one of the bombs. The resulting explosion killed Elsie Mitchell, Jay Gifford, Eddie Engen, Sherman Shoemaker, Joan Patzke, and Dick Patzke.

These six deaths were the only casualties recorded in the continental United States resulting from enemy action during World War II. In 1949 a Senate committee approved a House bill to pay twenty thousand dollars to the victims' relatives.

Following the deaths, the War Department began a "whispering campaign" to alert the general public about the dangers posed by the balloon bombs. It sponsored programs in schools, in public halls, and through various civilian agencies. *Smilin' Jack*, a popular comic strip, even carried a warning about the balloon bombs on August 7 and 8, 1945, about a month before the end of the war. The War Department thought that a well-planned, well-coordinated, low-profile program could warn the public without tipping off the Japanese that their balloons were reaching the United States.

When the war ended, the secrecy, already fading, was lifted. Grace Maurer, a reporter for a small weekly in Laurens, Iowa, remembered the balloon bombs. She had written an article telling of the discovery of a balloon bomb in Iowa on February 2, 1945. Other balloons fell near Holstein and Pocahontas, Iowa, and Civil Defense Director George Buckwalter carried the debris away.

Those finds were relatively unimportant except that Maurer was visited by the FBI in February 1945, who asked that she file her story. They explained the situation, and Maurer complied, waiting until August 16, 1945, to publish her article, a full account of the Japanese bombing of Iowa.

The censorship was probably precipitated by a *New York Herald-Tribune* story, "Balloon Bomb in Alaska," printed on January 2, 1945. The Office of Censorship issued their request two days later.

On August 16, 1945, *The New York Times* reported, "Bomb-Laden Balloons Fizzle." *The Washington Post* of January 16, 1946, reported that "nine thousand balloon bombs were used against the United States." *The New York Times* of February 9, 1946, reported "Raids by Japanese Balloons."

In fact, *The New York Times* ran a series of articles about the bombs in 1947, including "Piccard Flies Japanese Paper Balloon" on February 17, and "Balloons . . . But Japan Never Knew the Outcome" on May 29.

Among the magazine articles was a piece in *The Engineering Journal* of September 1945 on "Japanese Paper Balloons." George E. Weider, in an unclassified report for the U.S. Army, wrote about *Japanese Bombing Balloons* in January 1946.

These, along with other stories carried in local newspapers, told the public about the balloon bombs. The secrecy imposed was only for the time of the war and did not extend beyond the signing of the Japanese surrender in 1945. After the war was won, further secrecy served no purpose. There was no longer any reason to deny that the bombs reached the United States, and more important, no evidence that the topic was still classified.

Keel's claim that Brazel found a pile of rice paper in his pasture is incompatible with witness descriptions. He dismisses the testimony of witnesses who were there and who handled the material.

According to Jesse Marcel, the debris was spread over an area that was more than a million square feet in size. That was too much debris for balloon bombs, which were about thirty-three feet in diameter. In any case, such a balloon would have been easily identifiable to investigating authorities.

Marcel did mention the parchment of which Keel makes much, but Keel ignores what Marcel had to say about it. Marcel said he tried to burn some of the parchment, but it wouldn't burn. This is a critical piece of evidence that is virtually ignored because it is not explainable in the conventional.

Sheridan Cavitt, the counterintelligence agent stationed at Roswell in July 1947, responded bluntly when asked if the wreckage was the result of a balloon bomb. He said, "No way."

Bill Brazel, who also held debris that came from the wreckage, describes nothing suggestive of a balloon bomb. He saw wires reminiscent of fiber optics, foil that when wadded into a ball would straighten itself, and a small piece of metal so strong that it could not be cut or scratched with a knife. Nothing about it resembled the debris that would have been associated with a balloon bomb.

Keel draws attention to the flowerlike drawings observed on some of the wreckage; he claims that Japanese schoolchildren, whom he believes assembled the bombs, decorated them with such symbols. But, according to Robert Mikesh, the whole project was carried out under the strictest of security precautions. "While Japanese markings and stamps would normally be used to facilitate assembly of components, alphabetical letters and figures were used instead. No trace of the origin of the balloon was to be allowed, and inspectors were reprimanded on any infringement of this rule. Fear of disclosing the manufacturing location or launch site, which would result in reprisal attacks by B-29s, was responsible for these harsh measures."

But investigation is a search for the truth, whatever that truth might be. Even though Keel's contention that the balloons were classified in 1947 is wrong, and there were no remote sections of the ranch for the balloon to have remained hidden for two years, and he ignores the descriptions of the debris and the crash sites that don't agree with his theory, it was possible that his idea might have some merit.

Art McQuiddy, editor of the *Roswell Morning Dispatch*, when asked if he'd ever heard the rumor, story, or explanation that Brazel had found a balloon bomb, said, "Never, ever, ever. It's not even a theory. If anyone had suggested it, I would have heard it."

Judd Roberts was the minority owner of station KGFL in Roswell. When asked if the find could have been a balloon bomb, he said, "No. This is the first time I've ever heard it."

In July 1947 George Walsh worked at the other Roswell station, KSWS. According to Walsh, he'd heard rumors about the flying saucer but said of the balloon bomb, "That's one that missed me."

John McBoyle worked with Walsh during the summer of 1947. When asked if he'd heard the theory, rumor, or explanation that Brazel had found a balloon bomb, he said, "I don't remember it. I never heard it."

Al Stubbs worked for both daily newspapers in Roswell at one time or another. It was in 1949 that he left the *Morning Dispatch* to go to work for the *Daily Record*. When asked if he'd ever heard the explanation that Brazel had found a Japanese balloon, he said, "No. I never heard that."

Because Roswell in 1947 was a military town and because there was a good relationship between the base and the town, it was possible that the military had been able to hide the truth from the representatives of the local media. It wouldn't have been the first time reporters had missed a good story.

In July 1947 Phyllis McGuire's father, George Wilcox, was the sheriff. When asked if there was a possibility that what was found could have been a Japanese balloon bomb, McGuire said, "No, I never heard that. I don't think he [Keel] knows what a balloon bomb is. It's not logical."

Most of the deputies who worked for the sheriff in July 1947 have long since died. But one of them still lives, and his reaction to the theory was, "I never heard a thing like that. Nothing at all."

Of course, if Keel's theory was right, even the local sheriff might have been cut out of the loop. He, or in this case, his daughter and his deputy, might not have been told what Brazel found. Members of Colonel Blanchard's staff would have known. They were the men charged with cleaning up the debris.

In July 1947 Joe Briley was a lieutenant colonel and assigned as the operations officer at the Roswell base. When asked about the balloon bomb, he said, "I never heard it mentioned. There were no rumors about it. It certainly was not talked about at the base, and if it had ever been suggested, I would have heard it."

In July 1947 Patrick Saunders was a major and assigned as the base adjutant. His job would have required him to accomplish the paperwork surrounding the assigning of troops to clean up the debris, whatever it was. When asked about the recovery of a balloon bomb, he said, "I don't remember it. If it had been one, I would have remembered that."

Blanchard's provost marshal, Major Edwin Easley, when asked about a balloon bomb, said, "No. Never heard anything like that and I would have if it had been. It's an idiotic story." It should be noted that Easley was on the impact site, saw the craft and bodies, and said that it was his belief the craft was extraterrestrial.

There was always the possibility, however remote, that all these people had been kept in the dark. It is possible that the military officers were sworn to secrecy and were lying. But that doesn't explain why no one in Roswell heard that it might have been a balloon bomb. It is possible that the cover-up was so well constructed that even after forty years, it couldn't be broken by talking to the people who were there. Not very likely, but barely possible.

The Smithsonian's *Annals of Flight* reference lists nearly three hundred balloon-bomb-related incidents along with the places where the bombs were recovered. The locations range from Michigan in the east, to Alaska and Canada in the north, and to Mexico City in the south. There are no listed recoveries in New Mexico.

A check with the Museum of New Mexico in Santa Fe produced a statement from Charles Bennett, who said he knew of "no records or indications of any balloon bomb attacks." In fact, Bennett said that he looked for that sort of thing and that he'd never seen anything like it.

Bennett did say, however, that he might have missed something and suggested that Robert Torres, also with the museum, might be helpful. Torres said, "I've never seen anything like that. No indication that any [balloon bombs] did [reach New Mexico]." Torres said that he would check the various indices, records, and charts to see if anything had been found. If he learned that one or more had been reported in New Mexico, he'd be in touch. If not, he wouldn't bother. He didn't call.

But the Museum of New Mexico in Santa Fe, with all its state records, files, and documents, might have missed a single story of a balloon bomb in Chaves or Lincoln counties. David Orr, at the Chaves County Historical Museum, said he'd never heard of anything like it. "Not that I know of. Maybe it's too wide open here, so no one found anything. I have heard of them on the West Coast."

Keel might claim that all these people were kept from knowing the truth, though there is no evidence that such is the case. It might be said that after all these years, the people at the Museum of New Mexico and the Chaves County Historical Society just weren't aware of the balloon bombs. It could be that the people seeing a balloon bomb might not have recognized it as such.

In September 1947 Lewis S. Rickett was ordered to escort Dr. Lincoln La Paz around central New Mexico as they tried to determine the speed and trajectory of the device that crashed on the Brazel ranch.

According to Rickett, La Paz formed the opinion that whatever hit the Brazel ranch was a probe from another planet. At no time did La Paz tell Rickett that he thought the material was a balloon bomb. There would have been no reason for La Paz to tell Rickett it was extraterrestrial if it was a Japanese balloon bomb. According to Rickett, there was never any discussion of the Japanese balloon bombs.

And La Paz's opinion was important for one other reason. La Paz, during World War II, had investigated the balloon bombs. He worked with officers at Second Air Force Headquarters near Colorado Springs as the first of the balloons arrived. He investigated a number of reported finds, and was there when the first intact balloon bomb was captured in January 1945. La Paz would have easily recognized the material as a balloon bomb if it had been one.

Rickett, in fact, was fully aware of La Paz's research into the balloon bombs. When asked, based on his own knowledge and his association with La Paz, if it could have been a balloon bomb, Rickett replied, "No way. These people [Keel] don't know anything about this country [New Mexico], the mountains, or the winds."

Keel said that he'd talked to a local historian (in Roswell) who told him it was a balloon bomb. We are to accept this pronouncement, even though everyone contacted said they hadn't heard such a story. We are asked to believe this though Keel admits that he can't supply a name.

And Keel offers no documentation for his claims. He ignores the unit history prepared by the 509th Bomb Group. While flying saucers are mentioned, the recovery of Keel's balloon bomb is not. Since the documents were originally classified secret, there is no reason for the recovery of the balloon bomb not to be mentioned if that is what it was. In fact, in our search we have not found a single document to support the theory that Brazel discovered a balloon bomb.

It is interesting that in Keel's list of articles about the balloon bombs, there is nothing earlier than 1953. In addition to the newspaper and journal articles mentioned earlier (selected only because they predated the July 1947 find by Brazel), there is a *Reader's Digest* article from August 1950 and La Paz's article from *Collier's* on January 17, 1953. There are also unpublished histories of several military units from 1945, 1946, and 1947 that make reference to the balloon bombs.

Keel claims that in 1947 the army covered up the recovery of a balloon bomb because the military and the government wanted to maintain the myth of invulnerability. He offers no proof that this was the case.

We can prove, through a wide range of documentation, that the balloon bombs were not a secret in 1947. There were dozens of articles published about them. Keel himself admits that in the January 1991 issue of *Fate*, where he writes, "Actually there were hundreds of articles published between 1946 and 1970, particularly in regional journals and local newspapers." That's our point exactly. By 1947 there was no secrecy surrounding the balloon bombs.

The July 9, 1947, *Roswell Daily Record* may end this aspect of the controversy once and for all. In a story on page 6, a weatherman in the Albuquerque bureau is quoted. "He said that the radio-sondes periodically create excitement across the country and that two years ago they started a Japanese balloon scare."

Keel reports on rice paper and strings and ignores all the descriptions of the metal found at Roswell. He rejects the testimony of the witnesses, dismissing it with the ridiculous sentence, "I suppose by 1999 there will be thousands of Roswell witnesses from that long-gone era." (This of course, ignores the fact that the people being quoted can prove, with documentation, they were in Roswell or assigned to the base in 1947.)

Keel ignores what he can't explain, belittles what he can't ignore, and offers us nothing to prove what he says. He provides no documents, no names of witnesses for verification, no proof at all. His theory breaks down under objective research. If it had been a balloon bomb, why are there no witnesses to it? Can Keel offer a single name? If it was a balloon bomb, why is there no documentation for it? Can Keel offer a single newspaper article, a single report, or a single statement from the historical societies and museums in New Mexico supporting his claims? Can Keel offer any proof at all?

16

Alternative Explanation Number Two: A V-2 Rocket?

WAS MAC BRAZEL'S debris nothing more than the remains of an errant V-2 rocket? One writer, Ron Schaffner, has suggested that the debris came from the nose cone and parachute assembly from a German-developed V-2.

According to Schaffner, a V-2 with a faulty gyroscope strayed off course after a May 29, 1947, launch from the White Sands Proving Grounds. The missile crashed into a cemetery about a half mile south of Juarez, Mexico.

Records from White Sands indicate this was a modified V-2 made from captured German rocket parts. It was the second in a series of rockets fired by General Electric and Army Ordnance in connection with the Hermes II missile project. The official report says, "The rocket left the launching platform normally but no program was evident after 4 seconds. Observers at the emergency cut-off station realized the rocket was moving to the south slightly but judged the angle was so steep that the rocket would fall within the limits of the proving ground. Cut-off occurred at 46 seconds and the rocket landed near the site of Juarez in the Republic of Mexico."

The result of that error was a suspension of firings until the chief of ordnance was persuaded that future missile launches could be controlled. The next attempted launch was on July 3, but the V-2 never got off the pad. According to the *Chicago Sun*, "Faulty mechanism was blamed today [July 4, 1947] for a V-2 rocket accident in which eight persons were sprayed with acid yesterday."

Even if the July 3 launch had been successful, all witness descriptions of the debris, detailed elsewhere, and of the crash sites indicate the crash was not of a V-2, but of something else. When all the facts are brought into play, the area for speculation about the V-2, or any of the other rockets then being tested at White Sands, shrinks to nonexistent.

To start with, Marcel, among others, described a debris field more consistent with an aircraft accident than a rocket crash. A V-2 would have left a crater with little debris scattered over the fields, not the widespread debris described by the eyewitnesses.

The V-2 chutes Schaffner would place in Brazel's pasture consisted of two pieces: a chute of aluminum foil eight feet in diameter, made of ribbons covered with metallic mesh, deployed to slow descent, and a second chute about fourteen feet in diameter. Neither contained enough material to cover the pasture to the extent reported by witnesses.

The direct eyewitness testimony offers no support for Schaffner's theory. While it is certainly possible that Marcel, even as the head of the intelligence section of the 509th Bomb Group, might not have known about the experiments in New Mexico with the V-2, he certainly would have been able to identify the components as something of terrestrial manufacture.

And even if Marcel had somehow been fooled, would the other officers of the 509th, including the commander, have been unable to identify the foil, the parachute, and the capsule as being something made on earth? They didn't have to know it came from an errant V-2 to understand that its components were of conventional origin.

In any case, many of the men of the 509th had been in the army during World War II and had been stationed in England during the V-2 attacks there. They were not unfamiliar with the wreckage of the V-2. Pappy Henderson, a First Air Transport Unit pilot stationed at Roswell in July 1947, even had a piece of V-2 debris that he had picked up in England during the war. Yet his widow, Sappho Henderson, said her husband described the Roswell debris as "weird. It was like nothing he'd ever seen."

Captain Sheridan Cavitt denies that he ever participated in the recovery of material from a crashed V-2. "No. After the one that almost hit a town [Juarez], they made sure that no errant rockets got close to the ground again," he said. Cavitt never participated in the recovery of any rocket or missile while he was stationed at Roswell. According to him, the recovery of a crashed V-2 would not have been handled out of the base at Roswell but from nearby Alamogordo and the White Sands Proving Ground. Even though White Sands did not have complete radar coverage of the area, its personnel would have known the general location of the missile wreckage. They would have been out to retrieve it long before Mac Brazel walked into the Chaves County sheriff's office to report the debris field.

A generally similar theory has been proposed by Gerald Brown. When the debris field and the metal were described to him, Dr. Brown said that an A-9, a two-staged rocket, could have created the gouge reported on the crash site. He said that duralumin, an extremely tough metal used in the nose cone, could explain some of the debris found. He said that some of the wiring on the V-2 and A-9 was such that heat would cause the interior of the wiring to melt, leaving a hollow tube that could give the impression of fiber optics. The Germans, in labeling some of the interior structures of the rockets, used a combination of the Greek alphabet, scientific notations, numbers, and geometric symbols. Brown thought the bodies might be the remains of animals launched during a few of the experiments, possibly as early as 1947.

Duralumin also has very good high temperature properties. In other words, if Marcel had found a piece of duralumin, he might not have been able to burn it. However, repeated blows from a sledgehammer would cause it to shatter. Marcel reported that such blows failed to dent or even scratch the debris.

Brazel's description of the monofilament fishing line does not sound like a wire that has had the center melted from it. Brown acknowledged that the wire he described would be fairly brittle. Marcel's seemed indestructible.

And there are no records that any of the German A-9s were ever assembled or launched from White Sands. Full records of all the tests are available.

In fact, Brown's theories do not match what the independent witnesses who saw it remember of the material. Brown's duralumin and partially melted wire in a very gross sense resembled the material, but it did not match it closely.

Jesse Marcel, Jr., who described the symbols he'd seen, recognized none of them. Had they been from the Greek alphabet, scientific notations, Arabic numbers, or words in German, Marcel would have had some sense of what they were. He might not have been able to read them, but he certainly would have been able to identify them.

June Tyree, a lifelong resident of the Corona area, recalls no rumors of such an event among the ranchers. Even when a secret, experimental plane crashed in the mountains not far from Corona during World War II, the ranchers heard about it, and many of the local teenagers drove up to see it. But there was never a rumor of a rocket or missile from White Sands crashing so close to the town of Corona.

Brown's explanation for the bodies is particularly unconvincing. Witness descriptions make it clear that they were neither human nor animal. Even human bodies that had been burned in an intense fire would not match the descriptions. In any case, all who were on the debris field or on the impact site where the bodies were found were universal in their descriptions. There had been no fire.

Even Schaffner admits that earliest launches of rhesus monkeys occurred in the early 1950s. He found no evidence that monkeys had been used in 1947. In fact, information from the Space Center in Alamogordo, New Mexico, proves that the first use of primates was June 11, 1948, a year too late for the theory. Besides, that experiment involved rhesus monkeys, which are small animals, about the size of a large house cat, unlikely to be confused with the remains of a human pilot.

Wright-Patterson's Aeromedical Lab did conduct five biological flights using the V-2 and those experiments were badly botched. It should be noted that they failed in each of the five attempts to recover a living specimen. Each died as a result of a parachute failure, or when the missile failed to perform as programmed. And there was no attempt to cover up any of these mistakes.

What we have is speculation that what was found was the remnants of a V-2 and the suggestion that a ban on launches forced the officials at White Sands to try to cover their blunder. The descriptions of the debris by the men and women who handled it do not match that of an aluminum and mesh parachute. The debris field is too large for a V-2, the gouge is not consistent with a V-2, and the accounts of bodies do not fit the speculation that they were animals. The photos taken in Fort Worth, which Schaffner didn't examine, clearly show the remains of a rawin target device and a rubber balloon.

While it is true that men trying to protect their careers after an errant V-2 crash might hide the truth, it is not true that the cover-up would extend for over forty years. When those men moved on or retired, the evidence of the cover-up would have begun to surface.

But the most damaging items are the reports from *The Chicago Sun* and *The Los Angeles Times*, to name two sources. There is the story of that attempted launch spread over the papers for the world to see. If there was a cover-up, it wasn't very effective in 1947. Had the debris discovered near Roswell been the result of a V-2, documents to prove it would exist, and none do. The search for the truth of what happened in Roswell no longer must address the V-2 theory. It just doesn't account for all the facts.

17

Balloons, Bombs, and Experimental Aircraft

W
HEN HE SAW the debris allegedly recovered near Roswell, Brigadier General Roger Ramey declared that it was a weather balloon. He allowed reporters to photograph it, he let them interview his weather officer, Irving Newton, and he answered questions about it and the recovery. He did not, however, allow Major Jesse Marcel to answer any questions or speak with the reporters directly. Marcel was there as window dressing.

Ramey's statements, backed by other military personnel at the press conference and underscored by the ordered secrecy, effectively buried the events for the next three decades. Even UFO researchers and historians did not question the balloon identification. The Project Blue Book files contained no official reference to it.

Late in 1978, Jesse Marcel, long retired and living in a small Louisiana town, resurrected the story. He told reporters and researchers of his role in the event and insisted that the debris could not have been a balloon. Trained in radar operations, he was fully aware of the rawin-type balloons and would have recognized one instantly. Even had Marcel been lacking the training, someone at Roswell, such as the weather officer, would have recognized the balloon, had that been the solution.

With Marcel's testimony suggesting that the balloon answer offered in Fort Worth was nothing more than a cover for the real story, investigators began to probe deeper.

Yet others defended the balloon explanation, pointing to the July 9, 1947, *Roswell Daily Record* article titled "Gen. Ramey Empties Roswell Saucer." According to the skeptics, that story solved the mystery once and for all.

On the surface that newspaper article appears to be a devastating document. In it Mac Brazel speaks of finding the object on June 14. According to it, Brazel, his wife, a son, and his daughter carried most of the wreckage to the ranch headquarters. Brazel mentioned that the material was flimsy, that it was basically foil and balsa, and that he thought nothing of it until he heard about "flying saucers" a couple of weeks

124

later. Then, while in Roswell, allegedly to sell wool, he told the sheriff that he had found something out of the ordinary.

The article described the material at length, saying that the rubber was smoky gray and that it was scattered over an area about two hundred yards in diameter. There were no words or writing on it, although there were some letters on some of the parts. Considerable Scotch™ tape and some tape with flowers printed on it had been used in the construction. There were no strings or wires, but there were some eyelets in the paper to indicate that some sort of attachment may have been used.

In the story's conclusion Brazel said that he had discovered weather observation devices on two other occasions, but what he found this time did not resemble those. "I am sure what I found was not any weather observation balloon," he said, "but if I find anything else besides a bomb they are going to have a hard time getting me to say anything about it."

Though Brazel's final remarks explicitly reject the balloon explanation, the rest of the article—which contradicts virtually everything known about the circumstances surrounding the recovery—is consistent with such an explanation.

There is, in fact, no reason to believe any of this. Brazel had been in the field only four days prior to his reporting of the debris. That meant that there was no wreckage there on June 14 as the article had claimed. Brazel himself told military investigators from Roswell that he knew the material could not have been there more than four days.

The size of the debris field, as described by Marcel and Bill Brazel, is at odds with the July 9 article. Marcel and others who were on the debris field mentioned the densely packed material. Tommy Tyree, a ranch hand hired by Brazel after the events, said that Brazel had been annoyed because the material formed a barrier that the sheep refused to cross. Brazel had to drive them around the debris field to get them to water.

The balloon explanation also fails to address the descriptions of the debris given by more than three dozen people who handled it. Bill Brazel described material as being so tough, he couldn't cut it with a knife capable of slicing through barbwire. Frankie Rowe talked of foil that, when crumpled into a ball, would unfold itself with a fluid motion. Marcel, Sr., described metal that wouldn't dent under repeated blows by a sledgehammer. And Major Ellis Boldra talked of metal that dissipated the heat from an acetylene torch.

The symbols reported by some of the witnesses, including Jesse Marcel, Jr., were geometric shapes that didn't resemble anything used by people on earth for communication. Glenn Dennis reported that he had seen them on the "canoelike" structures he saw in the rear of the ambulance and didn't recognize them.

Some researchers have suggested the debris was a "cluster-balloon" launched from Alamogordo. In fact, both the *Roswell Daily Record* and the *Alamogordo News* carried stories about the cluster-balloons, complete with photographs of them.

Officers with Project Sign examined that explanation. A declassified memo, dated April 18, 1949, from the Air Materiel Command, Cambridge Research Station, reviewed the cluster-balloon launches. On July 3 cluster-balloon launch Number Eight was made. The balloon was not recovered, but it was spotted down in the Tularosa Valley just a few miles northwest of Alamogordo. There is no record of a Number Nine balloon launching, but Number Ten took place on July 5. Though not recovered, again because of the terrain, it was reported to be down northeast of Albuquerque.

These balloons, according to the memo, were twenty-foot plastic balloons with instruments. They were white, and shaped like ice cream cones. Nothing in the memo suggests that they would explode, scattering debris over a wide area, or that the material would defy the efforts of various individuals either to identify it or to cut it. The material used in the balloons, although not quickly recognizable as polyethylene, would have been recognizable as some sort of rubberized plastic. It would have burned under the torch and it would have ripped when attacked with a knife.

Others have suggested that the Roswell crash was the result of a Skyhook balloon. (Project Helios, a forerunner to Skyhook, had been canceled in the spring of 1947.) The Navy Historical Center at the Washington (D.C.) Navy Yard eliminated the Skyhook Project as a culprit by confirming that the first Skyhook launch took place on September 25, 1947, at Saint Cloud, Minnesota.

Records at Alamogordo show that a balloon, constructed of the same type of material as the Skyhook, polyethylene, was launched on July 3. It had been argued that if Brazel and the investigators who have reconstructed the sequence of events are just slightly wrong, this balloon, though not a Skyhook, could be responsible for the debris found southeast of Corona.

Those balloon launches were part of the secret air force Project Mogul, a follow-on for the navy's Project Torrid, discontinued in December 1946. The July 3 launch was of a ten-balloon cluster with a fifteen-pound payload. Watson Laboratories in New Jersey, the Department of Engineering at New York University, and the Battelle Corporation were all involved. There is no evidence that any of these cluster balloons fell on the ranch where Brazel discovered the debris or that the recovery of that debris is explainable as one of these cluster-type balloons.

About the same time, the secret Moby Dick Project, also operated by New York University, was in progress. Dr. Athelston Spilhaus was the man in charge. Balloon launches began in July 1947 but were discontinued when project officers learned of the navy's Skyhook. A balloon from a July launch, designed to reach high altitudes, was later found in Norway.

But again, the descriptions of the material and debris field, and the physical evidence, rule out the balloon answer. The first Skyhook carried a payload of sixty-three pounds. Had it crashed, ignoring the fact that no Skyhooks were launched from Holloman Air Force Base (Alamogordo) until April 1949, there would have been no gouge on the ground, and no widely scattered debris.

And though the July 3 launch fits, barely, into the four-day window of opportunity, there is no evidence to support it. It did not come down in central New Mexico, and even had it been found on the Brazel ranch, all concerned should have recognized it as a balloon, even if they couldn't name, precisely, the material from which it was constructed or identify the project to which it was attached.

Marcel said of the material, "It was not anything from this earth. That, I'm quite sure of. Being in intelligence, I was familiar with all materials used in aircraft and in air travel. This was nothing like this. It could not have been."

Other portions of the newspaper story fall apart under continued investigation. As noted, there are more than six witnesses to Brazel's trip to Roswell on July 9. Floyd Proctor, Lyman Strickland, Bill Jenkins, Leonard Porter, Frank Joyce, and Paul McEvoy are among those who saw Brazel in Roswell. Each mentioned that Brazel was accompanied by several military officers. For a story that was unimportant, the army went out of its way to make sure that the new "facts" were well publicized.

Though the newspaper claimed Brazel was not alone at the ranch when he found the object, his son, Bill Brazel, and his neighbors, including the Proctors, said there was no one at the ranch house other than Mac. The rest of the family was living in Tularosa, New Mexico, in July 1947.

In a number of interviews, Bill Brazel said that not only was his father alone at the ranch, but when Bill read the story about him in an Albuquerque newspaper, he decided that someone had to go to the ranch. No one was there when he arrived on July 12 or 13.

The article does provide a few clues, however, as to what the military was trying to accomplish. On July 5 Sherman Campbell found a strange object on his farm in Circleville, Ohio. Both Campbell and the local sheriff identified it immediately. On July 6 newspapers around the country printed a picture of Jean Campbell holding a kitelike structure from the balloon. The military did not involve itself in the episode, and, in fact, the Campbells kept the balloon for years afterward.

According to the *Roswell Daily Record* of July 9, Brazel, accompanied by Marcel and Cavitt, took the material to the ranch headquarters and tried, without success, to make it into a kite. There was no reason for Brazel or the military officers to try to make a kite out of it, unless they were attempting to duplicate the explanation and the pictures from the Circleville report.

No one thought to ask why both Campbell and the sheriff in Circleville could identify the balloon, but the officers at Roswell, some of them highly trained observers, were so surprised that they announced they had found a flying saucer. The story spread until a low-ranking officer at Fort Worth, Irving Newton, identified the wreckage as a balloon.

All of this serves to underscore the assessment of Colonel Thomas DuBose, who had been in Ramey's office and said of the balloon story, "Actually it was a cover story. . . . .The balloon part of it . . . the remnants [from Roswell] were taken from this location, and Al Clark took [them] to Washington, and whatever happened then, I have no knowledge. That part of it [the weather balloon] was in fact a story that we were told to give to the public and the news, and that was it."

In other words, no one involved in the case, from Mac Brazel to the top levels of the military command at Roswell, Fort Worth, and even Washington, D.C., took the weather (or any other type of) balloon explanation seriously.

But balloons aren't the only mundane objects to be suggested. Given the extraordinary efforts to retrieve every scrap of evidence, it stands to reason that it had to be something more extraordinary than a balloon, even one that was made of the new, and classified, material polyethylene.

One theory holds that the object was a practice atomic bomb. Practice bombs were massive things, weighing as much as a real bomb and often shaped just like them. The intelligence value for the Soviets from one of them would have been questionable, but the 509th was using them to practice its mission, and that fact was classified. Civilians, and those without a need to know, were not authorized to see the practice bombs, and had one been dropped by accident on the Brazel ranch, the military certainly would have taken precautions to keep the secret.

Of course, the practice ranges were far enough from the site of the Brazel ranch that such an accident wouldn't have happened. And the bombs, designed to be dropped from a great height so that the accuracy of the bombardiers could be graded, did not break up. They were made of iron and created a crater when they hit. They did not explode, did not break up, and usually did not skip across the ground to create a gouge.

Curt Platt, who served with the 509th, said that once the bombs had been dropped, they were recovered to be used again. Loading them onto the transport plane for the trip back to the base was quite a task. Just three of them could easily overload the transport.

Even if a practice bomb had broken up, it wouldn't have scattered the debris as widely as Marcel described, and again, Marcel would have recognized what it was. He knew all about the practice bombs. That would have been part of his job as the intelligence officer of the 509th.

True, a cover story to hide the existence of the practice atomic bombs and the accidental dropping of one could have been concocted if the circumstances demanded. There are two problems with that. One is that Marcel would not have said, in 1978, that it was nothing manufactured on earth had it been a practice bomb.

And two, the information would have been leaked by now. In 1957 the air force accidentally dropped a real atomic bomb near Albuquerque. Although the facts were hidden for a number of years, the story eventually was published in the Albuquerque newspapers.

Furthermore, the unit history of the 509th, a document originally classified as "secret," contains no reference to an accident involving a practice atomic bomb. In fact, there is nothing in any of the documentation to suggest that the debris could be accounted for by a such an event.

There are those who have suggested that the wreckage was the result of an experimental aircraft accident. The aircraft, according to the speculation, may have been an early jet that Marcel and the officers of the 509th might not have known about. But at the very least, the debris would have been recognizable as something that had been manufactured on earth.

Others have suggested that it might have been one of the flying-wing type aircraft being tested in that time frame. It is, at first, an intriguing idea. However, even the quickest search of the historical documentation often renders this explanation useless. Still, there are those who believe that the crash at Roswell can be explained as a flying wing, or more specifically, according to one researcher, a Northrop N-9M mock-up of the XB-35.

Northrop, who in August 1939 became the president and chief engineer of Northrop Aircraft, Inc., was fascinated by the flying-wing design. Although the purpose of his corporation was to develop and manufacture military aircraft, in less than a year, Northrop had the N-1M, a flying wing, ready for testing. It interested high-ranking officers of the army air corps, and they wanted it developed fully.

They changed the designation of the N-1M to N-9M, and of the full-scale model to XB-35. They told Northrop they believed it should be developed as a long-range bomber.

A contract was signed at the end of 1942, calling for the construction and testing of thirteen XB-35s. They also contracted for three additional N-9Ms. These were built of welded steel tubes and covered with wood. It looked like the larger XB-35s but contained two, rather than four, engines.

The first flight of the N-9M took place on December 27, 1942, and nearly every flight after that was shortened by a mechanical failure of one kind or another. On its forty-fifth flight, on May 19, 1943, the N-9M crashed, killing the pilot, Max Constant.

The last test flight of the N-9M took place in 1946. It was replaced by a full-scale XB-35, which first flew on June 25, 1946, from Muroc Army Air Field (later Edwards Air Force Base). On September 11, 1946, the XB-35, suffering gearbox and propeller control problems, was grounded. A full-scale flying program would not resume until February 1948. There was a series of test flights made on June 26, 1947, but the aircraft didn't crash and it didn't leave southern California. Both those points are important.

When, in July 1947, there were reports of a crash in southeastern New Mexico, speculation suggested that it was one of the Northrop flying wings. Obviously, based on the history, it couldn't have been a smaller N-9M wooden mock-up because those were no longer flying. According to *A Synopsis of Flying Wing Development 1908–1953* written by Richard P. Hallion, only one of the N-9Ms crashed, and that has been accounted for. If the flying wing was the culprit, it would have had to be the larger XB-35. Of course, those had been grounded months earlier.

On July 10 the *Chicago Daily News* reported they had asked army officers at Muroc Army Air Field if the flying wing could account for the flying disk reports. Lieutenant Robert Jones, the public relations officer at Muroc, said, "None of our flying wings has been in the air recently." Although he refused to provide much in the way of additional information, he did say, "We have just two."

The YB-49, the jet-powered version of the flying wing, made its first flight on October 21, 1947. While the gearbox problems plagued the propeller-driven craft, such problems didn't affect the jet version. Unfortunately that is several months too late to account for the Roswell crash debris.

There is a second theory that suggests that the real secret of Roswell was not the type of aircraft being tested, but the fact that the flying wings have small radar profiles. In 1947 it was believed that the United States held a huge lead over the Soviet Union in the capabilities and development of radar. Some have thought that the flying-wing technology, which negated that advantage, would be considered too important to allow to be compromised. If the Soviets were aware of the antiradar capability, they could begin a program to develop a flying wing of their own. That might have been considered important enough that the military would attempt to silence all the witnesses involved.

According to the new scenario, the secret of Roswell, then, wasn't the craft itself, but the design of that craft because it could defeat radar. It is an interesting idea, but it breaks down because there was simply nothing overly secret about the flying-wing design.

In fact, a document created by Captain N. LeBlanc for the AMC proves that. His analysis of the Horten brothers' designs and plans captured from the Nazis at the close of World War II was classified at the lowest level possible. Had the flying-wing design been considered all that important, LeBlanc's report would have been classified at a much higher level. The restricted classification meant that compromise of the material contained in it would do little harm to the national security of the United States.

There was so little secrecy around the flying wing that *The Atomic Blast*, the Roswell base newspaper, carried a picture of the YB-49 in the October 22, 1947, edition. Given the statements about the high level of secrecy around the events in Roswell in July, it doesn't make sense that just a few months later they would be publishing pictures of the flying wing if that is the explanation for the mysterious crash in July.

There were apparently two fatal crashes of flying wing-aircraft. The N-9M in May 1943, and one of the YB-49s in 1948, killing Captain Glen Edwards. (Muroc AFB was renamed Edwards in honor of the captain.) Later, the first of the YB-49s ordered was damaged in high-speed taxiing tests.

There are those who have decided that it wasn't a Northrop flying wing, but was a flying-wing type aircraft. As the Horten brothers had developed a number of such aircraft for Germany before and during World War II, the suggestion was made that it was a Horten brothers design, captured by the Soviets and used for reconnaissance. In other words, what crashed near Roswell was a Soviet spy plane.

Although some of the top officers at Roswell believed, on first hearing of the crash, it might have been of Soviet design, once they saw the wreckage, they discounted that idea. The Soviets have, in the past, attempted to penetrate the borders of the United States with spy aircraft, but most of those attempts occurred after 1950. No records have been located that suggest there were Soviet attempts in 1947.

But the theory of a stolen Soviet aircraft goes one step further. It is suggested the pilots of that aircraft were not human, just as the witnesses claim, but were, in fact, chimpanzees. For the theory to work, it must be accepted that the men on the ground at Roswell would be unable to recognize the bodies of chimps. And it overlooks the fact that there is no reason to have five chimps piloting stolen spy aircraft.

The best evidence currently available is that the Soviets didn't begin to use chimps in their space and aviation research until the 1960s. Without the chimps, and with the release of documents about spying by both the Americans and the Soviets, the question of a Horten brothers crash at Roswell has been eliminated. No evidence exists to support such a theory.

What this all means is that there were no flying wings that crashed in New Mexico in July 1947. In fact, there is no evidence that any flying wing was flying in New Mexico, or for that matter, that any were flying anywhere in the United States in July 1947. The documentation exists and has been examined for leads. And because the project was not secret and was known to the general public, there seems to be no reason to assume that there was any secret testing of flying wings that would account for the crash.

It can be taken a step further. There is no evidence that any experimental plane explains the crash at Roswell. No such experiments would be conducted during the July Fourth weekend. Searches of various records, newspaper files, including *The New York Times Index*, the National Transportation and Safety Board and the air force archives have failed to produce any documentation that suggests the crash near Roswell was the result of an experimental aircraft.

Moreover, *no one was searching for the plane*. No one suspected that anything was missing until Brazel walked into the sheriff's office to report the debris field. And once he reported it, the information did not create an immediate stir.

Other sources of information available now—and those include the notifications of death by the military, as well as records about the testing of various aircraft designs, including secret research—give no indications that a pilot or pilots were killed or injured in experimental aircraft accidents during the first week of July 1947 in New Mexico.

Once again, the unit histories of both the Eighth Air Force and the 509th Bomb Group come into play. Both documents were classified secret at the time they were written and filed. Both contain information that, if it had found its way into the hands of Soviet agents, would have adversely affected the safety and the security of the United States. Both documents were safeguarded until declassified and released into the various archives. Neither mentions a thing about the retrieval of a crashed experimental aircraft or a downed Soviet spy plane.

A History of Kirtland Air Force Base 1928–1982 covers not only the history of Kirtland but the colocated Sandia Base. Although it is a comprehensive history of research and development in Albuquerque, including pictures of the atomic weapons that were used to end World War II, there is no indication that an experimental aircraft from that base crashed in central New Mexico in early July 1947.

In short, no mundane explanation works. A craft classified as top secret in 1947 would no longer be classified today. Experiments with the SR-71, the stealth fighters and bombers, were all classified in their time. The crash of an SR-71 in the mid-1960s is still classified, to an extent, but information about it has leaked. And not only is information about the stealth technology known, but videotape of the F-117 was broadcast by CNN on the day it went into combat in the Gulf War.

Balloons, practice atomic bombs, experimental aircraft, and Soviet spy planes cannot have been responsible for the debris discovered by Mac Brazel. No alternative, nonextraordinary hypotheses account for the strange metals with strange properties described by the men and women who handled them. No evidence attests to the presence of a balloon, a practice bomb, or an experimental aircraft. Such explanations have one fatal fact in common: an utter absence of supporting evidence.

18

A Complete Examination of the Evidence

ALTHOUGH THE EXPLANATIONS offered for the material and the crash at Roswell have been thoroughly researched, there is always someone looking at it freshly who believes that he or she has found something that no one else has seen. The explanation that it was a weather balloon, a V-2, a balloon bomb, a cluster balloon from one of the many secret projects in southern New Mexico, an experimental aircraft, or a combination of these is offered without a comprehensive look at the evidence to refute such a claim. When *all* the evidence is examined, the possibility that Roswell can be explained in the mundane drops to zero.

The military was the first to offer an explanation. Within hours of Walter Haut's press release, the army was saying that it was nothing more than a radar reflector from a rawin target balloon. General Ramey, at Eighth Air Force headquarters in Fort Worth, was telling all who would listen that the officers at Roswell, caught up in the excitement of the flying disk craze, had misidentified the balloon.

This ignores, of course, the fact that the men at Roswell were hand-picked because of their expertise. All were highly trained individuals selected because of their professionalism. After all, this was the only nuclear strike force in the world at the time. The second string was not involved at Roswell.

For the moment, however, ignore that. Suppose that Marcel was fooled by the foil, balsa, and string of the normal rawin balloon and believed that he'd located something extremely unusual. His first action was, of course, to transfer the debris from the crash site northwest of Roswell to the base there for examination.

According to Marcel's records and the testimony of his son, Marcel had been trained in radar operations. Assuming that his training did not include any information about the balloons, it seems reasonable that Marcel would have been aware of them. According to the 509th Bomb Group unit history for 1947, Marcel's staff included a radar interpretation officer. Again, that training might not have included work with balloons, especially those designed to assist the weather officer in the gathering of weather data.

Marcel, however, as the air intelligence officer for the group, would have been privy to the data collected by the weather officer, and to the types of equipment, including balloons, used to gather it. In other words, there was nothing secret about the gathering of weather data that would have prohibited Marcel from seeing the operation or examining the equipment.

It is almost impossible to believe that Marcel, when he examined the debris the first time, would have been led to comment on the extremely unusual properties of it had it been nothing more than a rawin target balloon.

Three facts impact on this. First, the rawin target balloon, according to various meteorological sources, was first used in the late 1920s. It was originally designed with a highly reflective appendage that allowed those on the ground to visually track it as it climbed through the atmosphere. Later it was adapted for use with radar sets. Irving Newton said that he'd launched hundreds of such balloons during the invasion of Okinawa at the conclusion of World War II. The rawin target balloon was not of a new or unusual design that could have fooled all the highly trained men at the 509th Bomb Group.

Second, on or about July 1, Sherman Campbell, a farmer living near Circleville, Ohio, spotted the remains of one of the rawin target balloons on his ranch. Campbell, who was not trained in intelligence work, realized that he had found a balloon but believed it might explain some of the flying disk reports because of the shiny reflector carried aloft by the balloon.

Campbell called the local sheriff, who identified the balloon as mundane immediately. The local newspaper was also alerted, and an article about the find was carried by the press. The story, including a picture of Jean Campbell, the daughter (misidentified in the caption as Campbell's wife), appeared in newspapers around the country.

No one in Ohio thought the balloon was anything but a balloon. The military didn't investigate, didn't fly the debris to another part of the country, and didn't issue a press release about the find. Everyone involved, with no training at all, recognized the balloon for what it was. This in contrast to the mistakes made by trained personnel in New Mexico.

Overlooking all that, meaning the possibility that a mistake had been made, there is the testimony of Colonel Thomas J. DuBose. In July 1947 he was the chief of staff of the Eighth Air Force and knew exactly what was going on. He said, repeatedly, on both audio and videotape, "Actually, it was a cover story, the balloon part of it. . . . I don't know whether it was McMullen [Clements McMullen] or Kalberer [Colonel Alfred Kalberer Eighth Air Force chief of intelligence] or who, somebody cooked up the idea as a cover story . . . we'll use this weather balloon. That was the direction we were told. I mean, there wasn't any question about it. We were told this is the story that is to be given to the press, and that is it, and anything else, forget it."

According to Colonel DuBose, there was no question that the cover story had been designed to get the reporters off General Ramey's back. Give them an explanation that they'll accept, but don't tell them the truth.

With all that testimony from the participants, and from the facts, it would seem that the balloon explanation would fade from the scene. Clearly something crashed at Roswell, and just as clearly it was not a balloon. Balloons were used as a cover to eliminate speculation about the identification of the object that crashed.

Other types of balloons, experimental aircraft, rockets and missiles, and secret projects of all sorts have been suggested as alternative explanations for the crash at Roswell. Ignoring, for the moment, the fact that no one has been able to produce any documentation that conclusively proves this, an examination of all the testimony will eliminate all these explanations. To make any one of them work, it is necessary to reject the *eyewitness* testimony from multiple sources. When all the facts are examined, such alternatives slide beneath the waves.

Any of the alternatives might be acceptable if there were no witnesses to the crash. Prior to this work, the conventional wisdom had always been that no one saw the crash. The debris had been found already on the ground by Mac Brazel. Searches initiated after the fact located the remainder of the craft and the bodies.

But sources at several separate locations witnessed the crash. Ragsdale and Truelove saw it come down in flames during a lightning storm about 11:30 P.M. A balloon wouldn't have come down in flames and wouldn't have been visible at night.

William Woody described the object, as it fell out of the sky, as resembling a meteor. A bright white meteor trailing red. He watched it long enough to get a very good look at it. Since Woody was south of Roswell, and the debris field that Brazel found and the impact site where the craft was recovered are both far to the north of Roswell, the balloon explanation is again eliminated.

Corporal E. L. Pyles, southwest of Roswell, saw a falling star. He thought it was a falling star that was "wrapped in orange." Like the others, he believed it happened just before midnight. It clearly was something large enough and bright enough to be seen thirty or forty miles away.

The observations of all these witnesses also eliminate the experimental aircraft. What sort of experimental aircraft was being tested in New Mexico . . . at night . . . during a storm? Again, there are no records available anywhere that attest to any type of balloon experiment or experimental aircraft test late on the evening of July 4.

And, for that matter, why would such a test be scheduled for the late evening of July 4? Wouldn't it have been carried out earlier in the week? Or wouldn't they have waited until the following Monday when everyone was back at work?

And remember, all this was observed by another party. The Catholic nuns provided documentation about the crash occurring on the evening of July 4. This date alone suggests that it had nothing to do with any experiments, clandestine or other, because everyone had the day off.

The other aspect that must be considered is the testimony of MacKenzie. The object, whatever it was, had been over southern New Mexico, off and on, for nearly four days. If it had been anything belonging to the United States—if it had been a research balloon, experimental aircraft, or a rocket from White Sands—the men at Roswell or their superiors, such as General Scanlon, General Ramey, General McMullen, or General Kenny, had the authority to discover it. Had such been the case, the observations would have been suspended under orders, but they were not.

When the first-hand testimony described only the debris field and the wreckage recovered there, speculation about its nature could be made. That is, until all the eyewitness testimony was reviewed carefully.

Marcel said about the debris, "I'd never seen anything like that. I didn't know what we were picking up." He said that some of the debris was as thin as newsprint and featherlight, but so strong they couldn't dent it or burn it. He described foil-like material, I beams, and "other stuff there that looked very much like parchment that didn't burn."

Marcel was so impressed by what he had seen that he stopped at his house on the way back to the base. He wanted his wife and son to see the debris. When Jesse Marcel, Jr., saw the strange material, he asked his father what it was. Marcel, Sr., replied, "It's a flying saucer."

Marcel, Jr., said that he saw some foil material that was thicker than lead foil and that was much stronger. He mentioned the I beams, which seemed to be made out of layered foil, were embossed with writing. Marcel, Jr., described the writing as "purple. Strange. Never saw anything like it."

Within a couple of days, Marcel, Sr., returned to the house and told his family that they were not to mention what they had seen. It was now highly classified, and they weren't to tell anyone about it.

Mac Brazel, who found the debris field, was not interviewed in person by UFO investigators, but his son, Bill Brazel, was. In the months after the crash, Bill Brazel, while riding that portion of the range, searched for pieces of the debris. He says he found "oh, not over a dozen, and I'd say eight. There were three [different types of] items involved. Something on the order of balsa wood and something on the order of heavy-gauge monofilament fishing line and a little piece of . . . It wasn't really aluminum foil and it wasn't lead foil."

Brazel said the woodlike piece would flex a little. "I couldn't break it and I couldn't whittle it with my pocketknife. . . . The only reason I noticed the tinfoil was that I picked this stuff up and put it in my chaps pocket. . . . When I took it out and put it in the box, it started unfolding itself and flattened out. . . . I would fold it or crease it and lay it down and watch it. It was kind of weird."

Showing a piece of the material to his father, Brazel said his father told him, "That looks like some of that contraption I found."

Bill Brazel showed that small piece of foil to others. Sallye Tadolini was the daughter of Marian Strickland, one of Brazel's neighbors in 1947. Brazel showed her the foil, and she has the impression that it was dull in color, maybe gray, and that it was a small piece. Brazel, according to her, balled it up in his hand and then opened his hand, letting it return to its original shape. She thought it was stiff, like aluminum foil, but that it did not seem metallic.

Others around the Brazel ranch, such as Loretta Proctor, saw a small "sliver" of the debris. It was a pencil-sized piece that couldn't be cut with a knife or burned with a match. Proctor said that it looked like plastic but that she "didn't know what the stuff was."

Tommy Tyree, who was hired as a ranch hand after the events of July 1947, said that he was riding with Mac Brazel late in the summer when they spotted a piece of debris floating on top of the water in a sinkhole. Brazel told him it was a piece of the debris from the crash. Something light enough to float on top of the water.

Military men picked up the debris for shipment from Roswell to various labs around the country. Robert Smith, an NCO with the First Air Transport Unit stationed at Roswell, told how he, along with a number of other men, loaded three or four aircraft with crates. All of them were large, and many of them felt as if they were empty. Smith wasn't sure what was in them, but did say the loading took place under armed guard away from the main part of the ramp area at the airfield.

Smith did learn what was in the crates. According to Smith, "We were talking about what was in the crates and so forth and he [another of the sergeants] said, 'Oh, do you remember the story about the UFO?' . . . We thought he was joking, but he let us feel a piece and stuck it back in his pocket."

Like all the others, Smith said, "It was just a little piece of metal or foil or whatever it was. . . . It was foil-like, but it was a little stiffer than foil. . . . Being a sheet metal man, that intrigued me, being that you could crumple it up and it would flatten back out again without any wrinkles showing up in it."

Pappy Henderson, one of the pilots who flew debris out of Roswell, told a couple of friends about the debris. More important, he apparently was in possession of a piece for a number of years. He showed it to a close friend, John Kromschroeder, who had an interest in metallurgy. Kromschroeder said that he had never seen anything like it.

The metal, according to Kromschroeder, was gray and resembled aluminum but was harder and stiffer. He couldn't bend it but had to be careful because the edges were sharp. He said that it didn't seem to have a crystalline structure, and based that on the fracturing of it. It hadn't been torn.

Kromschroeder said that Henderson told him that the metal was part of the lighter material lining the interior of the craft. He said that when properly energized, it produced perfect illumination. It cast a soft light with no shadows.

That piece of debris apparently came from Major Ellis Boldra. Boldra subjected the sample to a number of tests. It was thin, incredibly strong, and dissipated heat in some manner. Boldra used an acetylene torch on the material, which didn't melt and barely got warm. It didn't glow when heated, and once the flame was removed, it could be handled in seconds.

Boldra tried to cut it with a variety of tools and failed. No one remembers if he tried to drill through it. One of Boldra's friends said that it wasn't any type of metal that he could identify.

Boldra and Kromschroeder weren't the only ones to describe the debris as incredibly strong. Lewis Rickett, the NCOIC of the counterintelligence office at Roswell, had an opportunity to see some of the debris still on the impact site. By the time Rickett arrived on July 8, the vast majority of the debris had been collected, but there were still some pieces scattered around.

As Rickett walked the field with Captain Sheridan Cavitt, he wanted to know if it was "hot." He was told that there was no evidence of radioactivity.

Rickett found one piece that was about two feet square and crouched to pick it up. It was slightly curved, but the only way he could tell that was to place it on something that was flat. He then locked it against his knee and used his arm to try to bend it. According to Rickett, it was very thin and very lightweight.

Cavitt said to Major Edwin Easley, the 509th provost marshal, "Smart guy. He's trying to do what we couldn't."

Rickett said the metal wasn't plastic and that it didn't feel like plastic, but he had never seen a piece of metal that thin that couldn't be bent.

There are others who saw the debris. Glenn Dennis saw some of it in the back of the ambulances parked outside the base hospital. He described the debris as looking like "the front part of a canoe . . . about three feet long. . . . There were some inscriptions . . . going along the contour or the wreckage."

Kevin Randle handled a small piece of material that he was told was picked up on the crash site. It looked like gray pumice, had no weight to it, some stratification, and seemed to be very tough. It didn't act like any pumice he'd ever seen.

There were three types of debris that were consistently described by the witnesses. First, by far the most common, was the foil that was thicker than normal aluminum foil, more like a lead foil. But unlike either of those, this foil, when folded or wadded into a ball, would unfold itself with no sign of a crease. Among the witnesses to the foil are Bill Brazel, Frankie Rowe, Robert Smith, Sallye Tadolini, and Jim Ragsdale.

Second, Bill Brazel talked of the lightweight material that reminded him of balsa wood but that was so strong that it couldn't be cut. Loretta Proctor handled something with similar properties. Rickett, Marcel, Easley, Boldra, Kromschroeder, and W. E. Lounsbury talked of lightweight material "as thin as newsprint" that couldn't be bent or marked.

Finally there were the wirelike pieces that Bill Brazel described as flexible. He said that he could shine a light in one end and it would come out the other no matter how he twisted the wire around. This sounds suspiciously like fiber optics.

These are the eyewitnesses who saw or handled the debris found on either the debris field or the impact site—dozens of people who saw the material and who describe it in the same terms over and over. These remains are not the stuff of balloons, experimental aircraft, or rockets. If, for example, the lead-gauge foil could be made into something stronger, and it was Jesse Marcel's opinion that it was used to make the I beams, then it could be used in the manufacture of automobiles. The next fender bender could be resolved by the drivers backing up and letting the metal return to its former shape.

The point is that no such material exists today. There are, after a fashion, molecules with a memory, but nothing that can be twisted out of shape and then return to its original shape when the pressure is released.

The question becomes, who was making material with such strange properties in 1947? Why isn't there a hint of that material anywhere today?

Of course, this argument overlooks another massive block of eyewitness testimony: the descriptions of the craft and the alien bodies found on the impact site.

Ragsdale described a craft stuck in the ground at about a thirty-five- or forty-degree angle. Not a deflated balloon of any type, not the remnants of a foil-covered target device suspended under a balloon, but a craft of some kind. With that sort of eyewitness testimony, available for the first time, it seems that the balloon explanation, all of those explanations from the rawin target balloons to a Japanese balloon bomb, can finally be eliminated.

If Ragsdale had been the sole witness to the crash site, there might be room for interpretation of it. But others who were at the impact site have corroborated Ragsdale's eyewitness account.

John McBoyle, a newsman with radio station KSWS in Roswell, was in a café in Roswell and overheard a conversation among some of the archaeologists. McBoyle convinced them to show him the location of the crash. The only description of it that McBoyle ever gave, confirmed in an interview conducted just prior to his death in 1992, was that there was an object that looked like "a crushed dishpan." An object about twenty-five to thirty feet long, impacted in a slope.

MacKenzie, one of the military men on the site, took his description of it further, saying that it had a narrow, batlike wing on it and that the front was crushed. It was stuck in the ground at an angle, suggesting that the forces at impact had been tremendous.

Another military officer, reviewing the files, reported that the craft was not of American manufacture and that it had a "scalloped wing." The object was no more than thirty feet long, had a fat fuselage, and had hit the ground with an incredible force.

Major Edwin Easley, the provost marshal at Roswell who was on the impact site, and who, in fact, was responsible for maintaining the cordon, said that the object had not been manufactured on earth. When asked if pursuing the extraterrestrial theory was right, Easley confirmed that it was the right path to follow.

Rickett, who was on the impact site after the main body of the craft had been removed, said the same thing. The material he saw was from something that hadn't been made on earth. And he was able to confirm the shape as detailed by others who had been there. It was long, thin, with a "batlike" wing on it.

The point is, the eyewitnesses, the men who were there, who were responsible for maintaining the security on the impact site, who were responsible for the retrieval of the craft and the bodies, all said the same thing. This was not a conventional aircraft manufactured on earth.

Of course, the idea that it was an experimental craft disappears with the final piece of evidence. There were five bodies on the crash site. They were not human bodies, but alien creatures.

While it might be possible to argue the points about the metallic debris, to suggest that the witnesses were exaggerating, that the metal wasn't as impressive, and therefore could be of advanced design, when the discussion returns to the bodies, the conventional explanations are eliminated. Metal is metal and wires are wires, but there is no way to explain the bodies.

When the investigation began, the rumors about bodies were little more than that. There was Barney Barnett, who might have seen something, a hint of archaeologists on the site, but no solid first-hand testimony. That objection has been eliminated.

MacKenzie made it clear that the bodies, though being more human in appearance than some of the drawings made by those claiming abduction, still were not human. They were smaller than human and they were thinner than human. Their eyes were slightly larger than human eyes. MacKenzie got close enough to examine them carefully.

Ragsdale didn't get close enough to examine the bodies carefully, but he did see them on the impact site. He couldn't provide exact details, except to say that he thought they might be dummies. They didn't look like adult humans, and he wasn't thinking in terms of beings from outer space on the morning of July 5.

Easley was reluctant to talk of bodies, but finally, before he died, said that he had seen them. He had been close enough to them to know they weren't human. He called them "creatures."

It should be remembered that Easley, as the provost marshal, would have been responsible for cordoning aircraft crash sites. The 509th Bomb Group, because of the number of flying hours it obtained, crashed a number of aircraft. Easley was on those sites as well. He had seen human bodies after they had been exposed to the forces of an aircraft accident and after they had been burned. Had the remains been those of a human, or humans, Easley would have recognized them as such. Instead, he talked about "the creatures."

That is the problem with the theories that are all too often given. They do not take into account all the testimony from all the eyewitnesses. There is a new theory, for example, that the bodies seen on the impact site were chimpanzees. The idea is that because the men on the impact site were so caught up in the excitement of the moment, and because of the time frame in which they saw the bodies, they wouldn't have recognized them as animals. Later, as theories about the extraterrestrial nature of the crash were discussed, they had "altered" their memories so that the apes, seen under bizarre circumstances, became alien beings. After all, the men at Roswell wouldn't have expected to see chimpanzees in silver flight suits lying dead outside an unconventional aircraft, so they assumed the bodies were beings from another world.

The documentable evidence suggests that no primates were used in experimentation prior to 1948. The first monkeys, according to *Mercury Primates* by Gregory P. Kennedy, were launched on a V-2 rocket on June 11, 1948. These were not chimpanzees but small monkeys, each not much larger than an ordinary house cat.

"The opportunity," according to Kennedy's report, "to place a live passenger . . . was presented two months before the planned flight. . . . By using all the space available in the capsule, it was possible, with difficultly, to place a nine-pound rhesus monkey in it."

That is interesting for another reason. There are those who believed that it was possible that the Roswell crash was the result of a V-2 with two chimpanzees on board. But the records show that chimpanzees would have been much too large, an adult male standing about five feet tall and weighing as much as four hundred pounds.

A search of the records fails to produce any suggestion that chimps were used in aviation or rocket research, either by the United States or the Soviet Union, in the proper time frame. Those records suggest that use of chimpanzees in the American space program began in the 1950s, and by the Soviets much later. The possiblity that chimpanzees comprised the flight crew killed at Roswell has been effectively ruled out.

Of course, the testimony of those on the impact site also rules it out. The face of a chimpanzee is distinctive. The eyes are small, even smaller than a human's, the facial features are not fine, and there is thick hair on the head. The head itself is not proportionally larger than a human head on a human body. And finally, the chimpanzee has large ears, but those who saw the bodies didn't mention large ears, just two small holes on the side of the head that might have functioned as ears. In other words, the descriptions of the bodies do not fit, even in the most liberal interpretation, that of a chimpanzee.

And finally, there are the archaeologists. These were men trained in the recognition of primates. While it could be argued, though ineffectively, that the officers at Roswell wouldn't have recognized the chimps, such an argument fails to explain why the archaeologists would have been fooled. They did not provide any descriptions that suggest the bodies were chimpanzees.

What we are left with, then, is a large body of eyewitness testimony to the high strangeness of the debris. Thin metal of extraordinary strength; foil that unfolds itself, assuming its original shape; strands of "wire" that sound like fiber optics; and I beams that flex. No one has been able to discover a single example of this material from that time frame. The properties described are unique.

While it is true there are always rumors of classified materials that can match those descriptions, when the conversation turns to the bodies, the debate ends. There is no way to explain them. Without eyewitness testimony, it could be suggested that the bodies were the figments of imagination. But the testimony of MacKenzie, Ragsdale, Easley, Holden, and others eliminates that. One of them might be lying, but not all of them about the same thing. And the opportunities for missed identification fall off as well. Too much of the testimony corroborates their stories.

But the real proof is the reaction of the men assigned to bury the story. It is clear that they were trying to hide something that was extremely sensitive. They went out of their way to make sure that the civilian witnesses did not talk to anyone.

Grace Maurer of Laurens, Iowa, found what she thought was the story of the century when she was informed that a Japanese balloon bomb had landed in Iowa. She wrote her story but didn't publish it until World War II had ended. She sat on the article, not because the government had threatened her, but because the FBI had visited and asked her not to publish. Maurer complied because she was convinced that it was her patriotic duty not to publish. No threats, no intimidation, no suggestion of prisons, but a request to remain silent made by government officials.

Two years later, when something crashed at Roswell, the civilian witnesses were not asked to remain quiet, they were ordered to do so. Children seven and twelve years old were confronted by armed soldiers who made threats. Frankie Rowe was told she would be taken into the desert, and no one would see her again.

Glenn Dennis, at twenty-two, was older, but the treats were no less vivid. He was told first by an officer that they would be picking his bones out of the sand, and then by an NCO that he would make good dog food. To ensure his silence, the military visited his family, as did the local sheriff.

The sheriff himself, according to his granddaughter, was threatened. If he told anyone what he had seen, he would be killed, as would his wife and his children. Not a veiled threat, but an overt threat designed to make sure that nothing leaked into the rest of the civilian community.

The threats continue today. One of the men who had been on a July 9 flight from Roswell to Fort Worth said that he received, in late 1989, a telephone call from an unidentified source. He was surprised that the caller knew his military nickname, knew that he had recently moved, and was able to obtain his unlisted phone number. The caller concluded by telling him that all the MPs involved in the Roswell case had committed suicide. The allegation was untrue, but the implication was clear. Those who knew too much and talked too much ended up dead.

If the Roswell crash was the result of a secret American project, why were these people intimidated the way they were? No other project, with the possible exception of the Manhattan Project, received that sort of treatment. Reviewing the records of the time, there is nothing that was happening then that was so highly classified it couldn't be discovered today. In fact, in the weeks that followed the Roswell crash, the government revealed a number of balloon projects that had been classified until then. The implication was that the flying disks and the crash at Roswell were explainable by those balloons.

But there is no justification for the threats made to civilians. Again, we have good first-hand testimony of those threats. Not from a single source, but from multiple sources. There is no doubt that the threats were made.

Those sorts of threats do not fit. If Grace Maurer had published her story of the balloon bomb in central Iowa, and the Japanese learned that bombing attacks were meeting with some success, then the war effort could have been hampered. Additional lives could have been lost. But even with that, a real danger, the FBI requested her assistance. At Roswell, the government demanded it.

If all the testimony about the strange qualities of the debris is ignored, if all the eyewitness testimony to the bodies is ignored, and even if all the failed attempts to explain Roswell in the mundane are ignored, there still remains that one glowing question: What was so important about the crash that the government had to threaten its own citizens to make sure they never mentioned it? What could be so important that the threats and intimidation continue today? And if Roswell wasn't extraterrestrial, then just what was it?

PART V

THE PLAINS OF SAN AGUSTIN

19

The Plains of San Agustin, Barney Barnett, and Gerald Anderson

I N CONVERSATIONS WITH friends and family, Grady L. "Barney" Barnett described how he had stumbled across a crashed saucer and the bodies of its alien crew. Barnett told each of them that he was west of Socorro, New Mexico, on the Plains of San Agustin, and that the event happened in the summer of 1947.

Barnett's close friend L. W. "Vern" Maltais said that Barnett told him the craft was metallic, dull gray, and "pretty good-sized." Barnett thought it had "burst" open. It was jammed up against a ridgeline and there was almost no wreckage scattered around it.

The creatures were all small, with pear-shaped heads, skinny arms and legs, and no hair. They all wore metallic-like, form-fitting gray suits without buttons or zippers.

While he was on the site, four or five others—Barnett thought they were archaeologists—came forward but never approached the craft or bodies as he had. Moments later the military arrived, swore them all to secrecy, and escorted them from the site.

It was a fairly basic, straightforward account of what Barnett had seen and done. It provided a location and time frame that fit, generally, into the pattern that has emerged from the investigation of the crash near Roswell. The only real problem was that Barnett quite clearly said he was west of Socorro, either northwest of Magdalena or between Magdalena and Datil.

This led a few investigators to speculate. There was no question that Mac Brazel, a rancher living southeast of Corona, New Mexico, and about 125 miles from Magdalena, had discovered a field filled with metallic debris. There was no doubt that investigators from the 509th Bomb Group, including Major Jesse Marcel, recovered the debris and said that it was nothing manufactured on earth. The question is, did a single craft start to come apart over that field near Corona, scattering debris, while the remainder of the craft stayed airborne long enough to reach the Plains of San Agustin, or were there two craft involved in some sort of midair collision?

Though all who heard the story from Barnett testified to his honesty and sincerity, extensive investigation failed to find independent corroboration. Others who heard Barnett talk of the crashed saucer, including niece Alice Knight, former boss J. F. "Fleck" Danley, and neighbor Harold Baca, could add few details, such as the claim the archaeologists were from the University of Pennsylvania.

What at first looked like confirmation of part of the Barnett story came from Robert Drake, who had been an anthropology student in 1947. Drake claimed to have heard the story of a crashed saucer while working with Wesley Hurt and Dan McKnight during a general survey of archaeological sites on the Plains during that general time frame.

Drake claimed that he had been at Bat Cave, on the southern edge of the Plains, and had seen heavy equipment tracks there. In the course of that trip, in October 1947, he, Hurt, and McKnight had stopped briefly at a ranch on their way back to Albuquerque. During their stay, Drake wandered off and discovered an old cowboy who claimed that sometime during the summer a strange ship had crashed on the Plains. There was talk of mystery bodies. Drake didn't know if the cowboy had seen anything himself or if he was relating the tale as told by an unidentified third party.

Drake also mentioned Roscoe Wilmeth, a document clerk who worked at the Los Alamos National Laboratory. Wilmeth, according to Drake, had seen secret files concerning a flying saucer crash, the bodies of its crew, and the recovery of them both. Wilmeth wanted to go to the "body site," which Drake interpreted to mean he wanted to go to the Plains of San Agustin.

Drake's story, however, became progressively more elaborate. In 1991 he recalled a conversation with students who were at Chaco Canyon on a summer field experience operated by the University of New Mexico. Drake claimed that a number of them returned from a weekend trip talking excitedly of a crashed spaceship.

Interesting as this testimony may be, all of it is, at best, second-hand. None of these people claimed to have seen anything themselves. Drake talked with others who allegedly saw something, or read something, but he knew nothing from direct observations, except the heavy equipment tracks near Bat Cave. Wilmeth never had the chance to tell his story, and the students at Chaco Canyon failed to corroborate it.

If such an event took place, first-hand witnesses existed out there somewhere. With second-hand sources, with the data filtered through others, there are too many opportunities for mistakes. After all, the location of the crash on the Plains was originally determined, not by Barnett, but by Barnett's boss, who believed that Barnett had said the Plains.

All that changed in early 1990 when a man from Springfield, Missouri, Gerald Anderson, watched the "Unsolved Mysteries" report on the events near Roswell in 1947 and then called the toll-free number. Anderson told the phone bank operator that he had been on the scene of the crash and that he had seen it all. Within days he was telling his story to all who would listen.

On February 4, 1990, Kevin Randle interviewed Anderson for just over fifty minutes. Although Anderson had been only five years old in July 1947, he provided a richly detailed account, including a description of the aliens, their craft, the location, and the military intervention. He professed surprise that anyone knew about the crash, saying that he assumed the military had successfully silenced all the witnesses. The interview ended with an invitation by Anderson for Randle to visit him if it could be arranged.

In a December 1990 interview with the Springfield *News-Leader,* Anderson added additional detail, claiming to have a family diary written at the time of the events. He told the reporter he had received it at his father's funeral several years earlier.

According to the diary, the Anderson family had arrived in New Mexico on July 4, 1947, and lived temporarily with Ted Anderson, an uncle. The next day, July 5, the Andersons drove from Albuquerque to the edge of the Plains of San Agustin to search for moss agate.

Although the diary says the event took place near Magdalena, New Mexico, Anderson later claimed it was just a mile or so from Horse Springs on the western edge of the Plains. Horse Springs is about sixty miles from Magdalena.

It was during the trip they discovered the ship and bodies. They approached the ship cautiously, believing that it might be some kind of bomb. As they neared it they spotted three entities lying in the shade cast by the domed disk. Two were motionless and a third was having trouble breathing. A fourth was sitting on the ground, unhurt. It had apparently been trying to assist its fellows.

A few minutes later, six people arrived. These, according to Anderson, were five college students and their professor, Dr. Buskirk. They had been working at some "cliff dwellings a few miles away," Anderson said. They had seen a meteor fall the night before and were out searching for it.

Anderson, feeling nauseated, sought shelter under the craft and realized that it was not just cool, but cold under it. It felt like air coming from a freezer.

It was about this time that Barnett arrived. Barnett came from the southwest, over the top of the ridge. Anderson thought that he looked like Harry Truman.

Following Barnett, so closely that Anderson wondered if Barnett hadn't led them in, was the military. Now it appeared like an invasion. The army, using jeeps, trucks, and a staff car, rolled onto the crash site. They had even blocked off a portion of the road so that airplanes could use it as an airfield. Anderson would describe it as a battalion-sized operation.

On March 24, 1991, Anderson appeared on "21st Century Radio's Hieronimus and Company," hosted by Bob Oechsler. Anderson reinforced the July 5 date and again described the aliens and the arrival of the military. But there were some changes from what he had told investigators in his first interviews in February 1990.

Now, describing the alien eyes, for example, he said, "They were enormous. . . . They were very black and very large. Almost oval-shaped." Originally he had said the eyes were a light, milky blue. According to Anderson, the eyes were "oval-shaped and very, very big. . . . They were a bluish color. Not blue like blue in human eyes . . . sort of a milky blue."

He also was now claiming that it was as much as forty-five minutes before anyone else arrived on the scene. These people were Dr. Buskirk and the archaeologists, who—again according to Anderson—were from the University of Pennsylvania.

He said there were four aliens. "There were two that were obviously dead. One that was somewhere in between, obviously critically injured, and one that had no apparent injuries at all."

All these public statements provided more than enough detail for researchers to begin a legitimate investigation of the Anderson claims. If they could be substantiated, they would go a long way to corroborating the San Agustin scenario.

Tom Carey, a researcher living in Pennsylvania and a man trained in anthropology, began a concentrated effort to locate archaeologists in general and Anderson's Dr. Buskirk in particular for just that purpose. Carey assumed that any archaeologist who had led an expedition would have written something about it at some time. He was right.

Dr. Winfred Buskirk was working on his Ph.D. dissertation in the summer of 1947. Later it was published as *The Western Apache,* and that led Carey to him.

Anderson had produced an "identikit" sketch of Buskirk and had given a description of him, including the facts that Buskirk was a tall, ruddy, balding man who spoke four languages. Comparing the author's photograph on the dust jacket with the identikit sketch Anderson had provided, Carey concluded that the man Anderson identified as the leader of the archaeological expedition was Winfred Buskirk.

One other bit of information supported this conclusion. Dan McKnight and his wife, while visiting a friend at a bookstore in Las Cruces, New Mexico, happened to see a copy of the identikit sketch. She said to her husband, "Oh, look, it's Win Buskirk."

Had Anderson's archaeologist been found? No, according to Buskirk himself, who denied being in New Mexico in July 1947. "I was in Arizona all of July 1947. I was certainly too busy on the reservation [Fort Apache Indian Reservation] to be engaged in any archaeological sideshows."

Anderson began backing off, now suggesting that the man he spoke of was not Winfred Buskirk, and, in fact, claiming the archaeologist he had seen was named Adrian Buskirk. The evidence, however, indicated otherwise. Everything Anderson claimed about Winfred Buskirk was true. Buskirk spoke four languages, he was a ruddy-complexioned man, and he was tall and bald.

The question became, if Anderson hadn't seen Buskirk on the crash site, where had he seen him? Obviously Anderson knew Buskirk from somewhere. Others suggested this proved that Anderson was telling the truth. However, in 1957 Anderson was a student at Albuquerque High School. Buskirk, a history teacher, also taught a class in anthropology at Albuquerque High. Anderson took the class.

Buskirk reviewed the records and wrote, in response to questions about his 1957 class, "Anderson was in my Anthropology Class the 1st semester, then, according to his transcript, took a French Class the second semester."

When Anderson denied this, claiming at first that he couldn't remember which high school he had attended, he was challenged to produce an official transcript. He refused. Instead he produced a copied document, which appeared to have been altered. He would not allow independent researchers to check his records to resolve the contradiction.

Additional problems with the Anderson story surfaced. Anderson produced a portion of the diary supposedly written by his uncle Ted. The "diary" was full of ludicrous errors. For example, the balloon explanation—offered by the military on July 8 to explain the Roswell crash—is represented as having appeared in the Albuquerque newspapers on the 5th, three days too early. In fact, the Albuquerque newspapers mentioned nothing about balloons on July 5.

A forensic scientist who examined the diary, Richard L. Brunelle, conducted tests that determined the paper was of a type available in 1947. The ink, however, was not available until sometime after 1974. That was in direct conflict with the story as related by Anderson.

Clearly this was not a document written by Anderson's uncle Ted. Ted Anderson could not be reached for comment. He had died several years prior to 1974.

Continued investigation broke down other parts of the Anderson story. Anderson described a patch the leader of the military team allegedly wore, claiming that it indicated the soldiers were from the White Sands Proving Grounds. At that time there was no distinctive patch for the personnel assigned to the White Sands complex.

Anderson then contradicted himself again, telling other researchers that his uncle Ted had recognized the leader as an officer assigned to the Sandia base. The patch described does not match that worn by the personnel assigned to Sandia in that time frame.

Anderson's tale continued to unravel. Anderson said that he had spoken to Randle for only twenty-six minutes. To prove it, he produced a copy of his phone records showing the length of the call. Randle, however, had a tape that lasted more than fifty minutes.

Further investigation revealed that the bill submitted by Anderson did not match the records of Southwestern Bell. In fact, documents secured with the assistance of Southwestern Bell proved that the call had lasted more than fifty minutes. John Carpenter, originally a proponent of the Anderson tale, confirmed the information. He wrote, "I finally was able to learn that Gerald had indeed had a friendly 54-minute phone call just as Randle had claimed."

Carpenter, however, went further. "We now knew four things about Gerald Anderson: (1) He was capable of constructing a very clever fake phone bill. (2) He had admitted lying to us about the first phone bill. (3) He had just been caught lying to all of the gathered researchers about this 28-minute phone bill (which means he had just constructed another phony!), and (4) Gerald was now avoiding us."

What it meant, simply, was that Anderson was caught constructing one piece of documentation. With the forensic results suggesting the diary hadn't been written in 1947, and with Dr. Buskirk writing that Anderson had been in his anthropology class, the Anderson story had disintegrated completely. He was contradicted by the physical evidence and the testimony of a number of others, and he had admitted that he had constructed some of the documentation.

With the collapse of the Anderson story, testimony to an event on the Plains reverted to its original second-hand status. Most of that testimony was from a single source, Barney Barnett. Then the Barnett story took a major hit.

Sometime early in 1947 someone gave Ruth Barnett a daily reminder book, which she turned into a diary. All that year she recorded everything in her and her husband's lives. Later, when the diary surfaced in 1990, investigators were able to trace Barnett's movements for the year. Nothing in the diary gave any hint of a crashed-saucer encounter. In fact, on the day the bodies were recovered outside Roswell, July 5, Barnett was at home in Socorro.

Other areas of corroboration were found wanting. Tom Carey located half a dozen students from the 1947 field experience at Chaco Canyon, and each told him there had been no talk of a crashed saucer, despite Drake's testimony to the contrary. None of them had heard the story.

Drake also said that on the ride back to Albuquerque, after the unidentified cowboy had told him about the crashed saucer, he, Hurt, McKnight, and Albert Dittert had discussed the event. Carey spoke to all three, who told him they remembered nothing about the crashed saucer. Hurt said he hadn't heard of it until people began calling him about fifteen years earlier. There had been no discussion of a crashed saucer on the ride back to Albuquerque.

There is one other important fact. Both Barnett and Anderson claimed that there had been archaeologists involved in the report. A complete survey of all the archaeologists or anthropologists who had been working on the Plains had been completed, and none of them knew a thing about a UFO crash. On the other hand, archaeologists who had been working just north of Roswell were located, and they confirmed they had been involved. W. Curry Holden was unequivocal about it. He had been there.

What this meant was that the story of archaeologists was true. The location was wrong. With no corroboration for a crash on the Plains, and now with the archaeologists who had been found claiming the crash was close to Roswell, the final nail had been hammered into the Plains coffin.

At this point there seems to be no evidence to an event on the Plains. The second-hand testimony used to support the theory had collapsed completely. The Barnett story, at one time the foundation of such a claim, was gone. The whole Plains scenario fails to fit the framework of the Roswell event. Without better information, without first-hand corroboration, Barnett's story, and in fact, the Plains scenario, must be discarded.

PART VI

THE TIME LINE

20

The Sequence of Events

THE STORY OF what happened at Roswell is filled with people, locations, and events. For those who haven't spent years studying the case, the sequence of the events can be confusing, especially when many of the first books and articles written about Roswell failed to include much important data. Finally, in the last two years, new witnesses and new documentation have surfaced that put a new spin on the events. Rather than beginning with Mac Brazel and near Corona, New Mexico, the events start two days earlier, when the crash occurs. Changing the sequence of events does not radically alter Brazel's role. It compresses the time frame, but it also provides clues into the thinking of the military mind in 1947.

The following sequence describes the events around the Roswell crash as reconstructed from interviews, documents, newspapers, and physical evidence. Because the events took place more than forty-five years ago, it has been a difficult task. The result is based on the investigation. Some events may be slightly out of sequence, but this is the most probable time line.

Tuesday, July 1, 1947

Radars in the Roswell, White Sands, and Alamogordo area track an object that seems to defy convention. Its speeds and maneuvers suggest that it is not a craft manufactured on Earth. Checks of the radar equipment reveal no malfunction that would account for the display.

Wednesday, July 2, 1947

At 9:50 P.M. Mr. and Mrs. Dan Wilmot see an oval object, "like two inverted saucers faced mouth to mouth," passing over their house in Roswell, New Mexico. The object, moving at a high rate of speed, is heading northwest.

Thursday, July 3, 1947

At the White Sands Proving Ground, an attempted launch of a V-2 rocket fails, never getting off the pad. Several people are injured in a spray of acid.

Steve MacKenzie is ordered to White Sands, where he spends nearly twenty-four hours watching the displays as the object flashes through the New Mexican skies.

Friday, July 4, 1947

The first of the special flights from Washington arrives. On the plane is Warrant Officer Robert Thomas. Thomas and his companions are in uniform upon arrival, but quickly change to civilian clothes. Thomas wants an on-site briefing as soon as it could be arranged. These men remain at Roswell throughout the retrieval.

William Woody and his father watch a flaming object, white with a red trail, fall toward the ground north of Roswell.

During a thunderstorm near Corona, New Mexico, W. W. "Mac" Brazel hears a tremendous thunderclap that sounds like an explosion but is somehow different from the rest of the thunder. Others in the area report the same phenomenon.

At 11:27 P.M. the radar sites continue to watch the object. It seems to pulsate a number of times, then explodes into a starburst. The belief is that the object has now crashed.

Jim Ragsdale and Trudy Truelove see a bright flash of light and hear a roaring sound that passes overhead. Ragsdale knows that something has struck the ground close to their campsite.

Saturday, July 5, 1947

Jason Ridgway,* a sheepherder in central New Mexico, finds the remains of a crashed saucer. He spends little time on the site and refuses to tell anyone about it until many years later. Ridgway is a friend of Mac Brazel.

* The name has been changed at the request of the witness.

* * *

Archaeologists, including W. Curry Holden, working the sites around Roswell stumble across the impact site where the object has crashed. One of them heads to the closest phone to tell Sheriff George Wilcox of the discovery of the remains of a crashed aircraft of some kind.

Wilcox calls the local fire department to alert them about the crash. One truck, with Dan Dwyer on it, responds to the call. The site is about thirty-five miles north of Roswell.

The Roswell Fire Department, escorted by members of the Roswell Police Department, makes a run along Pine Lodge Road northwest of Roswell. These are among the first civilians to stumble across the impact site.

At 5:30 A.M. the military, knowing the approximate location of the saucer crash, move in with a carefully selected team for the recovery of the craft. The soldiers find civilians on the site already. They escort them off while others secure the area. Five bodies are found on the site. The site is cleaned and secured in six hours.

Following the rain the night before, Brazel inspects the pastures surrounding the ranch house. Riding with him is the young son of the Proctors, William D. Proctor. During the inspection, Brazel discovers a large debris field. Scattered on the slopes and into the sinkhole and depressions are metal, plasticlike beams, pieces of lightweight material, foil, and string. The debris is thick enough that the sheep refuse to cross the field and are driven around it to water more than a mile away.

Thomas and his crew move out to the impact site. The bodies, originally covered by sheets, are now in lead-lined body bags. Only those with the highest clearance are allowed close to the center of the impact. Guards are posted, facing out, to keep the curious away.

John McBoyle, a reporter for radio station KSWS in Roswell, tries to reach the crash site. He phones to report an object looking like a crushed dishpan. He tells Lydia Sleppy, who works at the parent station in Albuquerque, to hang on. She overhears an argument and then McBoyle tells her to forget it, he has made a mistake. McBoyle is about forty miles north of Roswell.

Sleppy tries to put a message out on the Teletype. According to Sleppy, the message is intercepted by the FBI in Dallas and she is ordered not to complete the transmission.

* * *

Melvin E. Brown, who is on guard duty at the impact site, is warned to climb into the back of the truck. Although he has been ordered not to look under the tarp, the moment that everyone's back is turned, he does. He finds the bodies of the alien flight crew. They are small, with large heads and skin that is yellow or orange.

Glenn Dennis, the mortician working at the Ballard Funeral Home in Roswell, receives a call from the base mortuary officer, who asks him about small caskets.

In Roswell for a conference, C. Bertram Schultz, a vertebra paleontologist, drives north from the city on Highway 285. To the west he sees a number of guards along the highway. Schultz isn't interested in driving to the west, so he doesn't stop, nor is he bothered by the guards.

The Roswell base mortuary officer calls again. He asks Glen Dennis questions about what various chemicals would do to blood and tissue. He also wants to know the procedures for preparing a body that has lain out in the elements. Dennis suspects a fatal crash involving a VIP.

Glenn Dennis receives a call from downtown Roswell, where an airman had been injured. The funeral home where Dennis works also operates the ambulance service. Dennis drives the injured airman to the base, is waved through the gate, and stops at the rear of the hospital. Parked behind it, at the loading dock and in front of the emergency room, are three ambulances. In the rear Dennis sees small, canoelike devices and strange debris of some sort.

The bodies arrive at the base and are taken to the hospital for examination. Dr. Jesse Johnson pronounces them dead. Two doctors who are not assigned to the base but who have arrived on one of the special flights begin the preliminary autopsy.

Brazel, taking a few scraps of the material, heads to the home of his closest neighbors, Floyd and Loretta Proctor. He shows them "a little sliver" of material that he can neither burn nor cut. The Proctors suggest he take it into town to show the sheriff.

Inside the base hospital at Roswell, Dennis is confronted by two officers. A red-haired captain tells Dennis that he has seen nothing and heard nothing; if he opens his mouth, they will be picking his bones out of the sand.

* * *

Military bases along the West Coast have fighters on standby in case the flying disks are seen. A few bases in Oregon and Washington have planes equipped with gun cameras on airborne alert.

Sherman Campbell of Circleville, Ohio, reports to the sheriff that he has what he thinks is an explanation for some of the flying disk sightings. He has found a weather balloon on his farm. It is metallic, with a kitelike appendage on it. The device is displayed at the local newspaper office and then returned to Campbell. Jean Campbell (Romero), Campbell's daughter, reports that it is kept in a barn for years afterward.

Later that evening, Brazel removes the large, circular piece of the debris from the range. Brazel either loads it into the back of his truck or drags it along behind. He stores it in a livestock shed about three miles north of the crash site.

The bodies are sealed into a long crate, which is taken to a hangar. It is left there overnight with spotlights playing on it while MPs stand guard around it. They never approach it.

Melvin Brown, along with other soldiers, is ordered to stand guard outside the hangar. Brown's commanding officer approaches and says, "Come on, Brownie, let's have a look inside." But there is nothing to see because everything has been packed and crated, ready for shipment.

Sunday, July 6, 1947

Brazel gets up early, completes his chores, and then drives into Roswell, about seventy-five miles away. He stops at the office of Sheriff George A. Wilcox. Contrary to published reports, Wilcox is excited about the find and suggests the military at the Roswell Army Air Field be notified.

At 11:30 A.M. Dennis finally locates his friend, the nurse, who agrees to meet him for lunch. He drives out to the base to meet her at the officers' club.

While waiting for the military officers to arrive, Wilcox dispatches two of his deputies to the ranch. They have only the directions given by Brazel, but both men are familiar with the territory, and Wilcox believes they will be able to find the debris field.

*   *   *

William Woody and his father try to drive out toward the area where they'd seen the object coming down, but the roads are blocked. The side roads off Highway 285, from Vaughn and to the west, are guarded by military police who allow no one to pass.

Frank Joyce, a reporter and announcer for radio station KGFL, calls the sheriff and asks if anything interesting is happening at the office. Wilcox refers him to Brazel.

Colonel William Blanchard, commanding officer of the 509th Bomb Group, orders Jesse A. Marcel, the air intelligence officer, to investigate. Marcel immediately drives to the sheriff's office. Marcel interviews Brazel, examines the pieces of the material that Brazel brought in, and decides he had better visit the ranch to examine the field for himself.

Marcel, taking some of the debris with him, returns to the base and reports to Blanchard what he has seen. Blanchard, convinced that he is in possession of something highly unusual, perhaps Soviet, alerts the next higher headquarters. No one mentions any type of balloon.

Marcel returns to the sheriff's office with the senior counterintelligence agent assigned to the base, Captain Sheridan Cavitt. They escort Brazel back to his ranch and examine the debris field.

Acting on orders from Major General Clements McMullen, deputy commander of the Strategic Air Command, Blanchard obtains, from the sheriff's office, more of the debris. It is sealed in a courier pouch and loaded on an airplane to be flown on to the Fort Worth Army Air Field, where it is given to Colonel Thomas J. DuBose for transport on to Washington, D.C.

After Marcel and Cavitt leave with Brazel, the two deputies return to say they did not find the debris field but observed a burned area in one of the pastures. There the sand has been turned to glass and blackened. It looks as if something circular has touched down.

At the Fort Worth Army Air Field, DuBose and Colonel Alan D. Clark, the base commander, meet the aircraft from Roswell. Clark receives the plastic bag with the debris and walks to the "command" B-26 to fly it to Washington, D.C., and General McMullen.

* * *

Because of the distance to the ranch over roads that are less than adequate, Brazel, Marcel, and Cavitt do not arrive until after dark. They stay at the "Hines" house (an old ranch house close to the debris field), eat cold beans, and wait for daylight. Marcel runs a Geiger counter over the large piece of wreckage Brazel has stored in the cattle shed. He detects no sign of radiation.

Monday, July 7, 1947

At 2:00 A.M. a special flight leaves for Andrews AAF in Washington, D.C. Some of the debris and the bodies are on that flight.

Brazel takes the two military officers out to the crash site. It is three-quarters of a mile long and two to three hundred feet wide. A gouge starting at the northern end of it extends for four or five hundred feet toward the other end. It looks as if something has touched down and skipped along. The largest piece of debris is recovered at the southern edge of the gouge.

The debris is as thin as newsprint, but incredibly strong. There is foil that, when crumpled, unfolds itself without a sign of a wrinkle, I beams that flex slightly and have some symbols on them, and material resembling Bakelite.

Marcel and Cavitt walk the perimeter of the field and then range out looking for more details or another crash site, but find nothing else. Finally they return and spend the remainder of the day collecting debris. They load the rear of Marcel's car and then the jeep carryall driven by Cavitt. About dusk they begin the trip back to Roswell.

Lieutenant General Nathan F. Twining, the commander of the Air Materiel Command, the parent organization at Wright Field, Ohio, and the next higher headquarters for both the Alamogordo Army Air Field and the Kirtland Army Air Field, changes his plans and flies into Alamogordo.

General Carl Spaatz, commander of the army air forces, on "vacation" in the Pacific Northwest, tells reporters that he knows nothing about the flying disks or the plans of various local units to search for them.

Intrigued by the story Joyce has told him about the telephone interview he'd conducted with Brazel, Walt Whitmore, Sr., wants to learn more. Whitmore, who knows many of the ranchers and is familiar with the area, drives out to find Brazel.

Brazel, now in the company of Walt Whitmore, Sr., has been asked to stay the night in Roswell.

Tuesday, July 8, 1947

At 2:00 A.M. Marcel stops at his house on the way to the base. He awakens his wife, Viaud Marcel, and son, Jesse, Jr., to show them the material. Over the next hour they examine the debris on the kitchen floor. Marcel, Sr., says it was a flying saucer. Marcel is not breaking regulations since nothing has yet been classified. With the help of his son, Marcel loads it into the car to be taken to the base.

At 6:00 A.M. Marcel and Cavitt visit with Blanchard in his quarters and tell him what they have seen.

Blanchard calls the provost marshal and orders him to post guards on the roads around the debris field, denying access to anyone without official business. Easley is directed to locate Brazel and have him escort the MPs to the crash site.

Blanchard calls Eighth Air Force headquarters and advises them of the new find. By this time no one believes the material is from a Soviet device.

Eighth Air Force relays the message up the chain of command to SAC headquarters.

The regular morning staff meeting is moved up to 7:30 A.M. Blanchard discusses the new find and its possible disposition. Attending the meeting are Marcel and Cavitt; Lieutenant Colonel James I. Hopkins, the operations officer; Major Patrick Saunders, the base adjutant; Major Isidore Brown, the personnel officer; and Lieutenant Colonel Ulysses S. Nero, the supply officer. There is reason to believe that Lieutenant Colonel Charles W. Horton, Lieutenant Colonel Fernand L. Andry, Lieutenant Walter Haut, and Master Sergeant. Lewis Rickett may have also been there.

Whitmore, his wire-recorded interview with Brazel completed, takes Brazel out to the military base.

At 9:00 A.M. Cavitt and Rickett, having returned from assignment in Carlsbad, drive a staff car to the impact site, followed by MPs. They are stopped by the guards who are still posted. When they arrive, they see that a small containment of debris remains which Rickett is allowed to examine.

Whitmore of KGFL receives a phone call from Washington. He is told not to air the interview with Mac Brazel. If he does, the station will lose its broadcast license.

*   *   *

Blanchard and members of the staff confer by phone with higher headquarters. Brigadier General Roger Ramey orders Marcel to Fort Worth.

Military officers begin to interrogate Mac Brazel. He is taken to the guest house.

At 11:00 A.M. Walter Haut finishes the press release he'd been ordered to write and is preparing to take it into town. He takes it first to one of the radio stations. By noon he has given a copy of the release to both radio stations and to both daily newspapers.

Sheriff Wilcox, wondering what happened out at the crash site, sends two more deputies out. This time they run into the cordon thrown up by the military and are turned back. The army is letting no unauthorized personnel onto the crash site.

At 2:26 P.M. the story is out on the AP wire. The story announces: "The army air forces here today announced a flying disc had been found."

The phones at the base start ringing. Irritated at his inability to get a line out, Blanchard orders Haut to do something about all the incoming calls. Haut says there is nothing he could do about incoming calls.

Robert Shirkey, standing in the operations building, watches as MPs begin carrying wreckage through to load onto a C-54 from the First Air Transport Unit. To see better, he has to step around Colonel Blanchard.

At 2:30 P.M. Blanchard decides it is time to go on leave. Too many phone callers into the base are asking to speak with him. He, along with a few members of his staff, drive out to the debris field. Those left at the base are told to inform the reporters that the colonel is now on leave.

At 2:55 P.M. the AP reports in a "95," just under a bulletin in importance, that a flying disk had been found.

At 3:00 P.M. Marcel is told that he is going to Fort Worth with the wreckage. Only a few packages are loaded onto the plane. One, a triangular package about two feet long, is wrapped in brown paper. The other three are about the size of shoe boxes. They are so light that it feels as if there is nothing in them. The special flight, a B-29, takes off for the Fort Worth Army Air Field.

*　*　*

Calls come into Roswell from all over the world as the press release hits the various news wires.

Reporter J. Bond Johnson of the *Fort Worth Star-Telegram* is instructed to drive to the base. His editor tells him a flying saucer is coming from Roswell.

Marcel is in Ramey's office with some of the debris. The general wants to see where the debris was found. Marcel accompanies him to the map room. Once Ramey is satisfied, they walk back to the general's office, but the debris is gone. In its place is a ripped-apart weather balloon with debris scattered on the floor.

At 3:53 P.M. Roger Ramey announces that the flying disk has been sent on to Wright Field near Dayton, Ohio.

More men arrive at the debris field and are assigned to assist in cleaning it. Soldiers with wheelbarrows move across the field, tossing in the debris. When the wheelbarrows are filled, the soldiers take the debris to collection points. The debris is then loaded into covered trucks to be driven into Roswell.

At 5:30 P.M. a solution for the mystery is offered by Major E. M. Kirton who tells the *Dallas Morning News* that a balloon is responsible for all the excitement.

Warrant Officer Irving Newton is ordered from the weather office at the Fort Worth Army Air Field to Ramey's office. Newton, in front of a small number of reporters and officers of the Eighth Air Force, identifies the wreckage on the office floor as a balloon. He is photographed and then sent back to his regular duties.

At 6:17 P.M. the FBI sends a Teletype message to FBI Director J. Edgar Hoover telling him that a balloon is responsible for the reports. It is on its way to Dayton for examination by army air force experts.

At 7:30 P.M. the AP breaks into its last message with a bulletin telling the world that the Roswell flying disk is nothing more than a balloon.

Ramey, with the identity of the wreckage established, announces to the world that the officers at Roswell had been fooled by a weather balloon. Ramey also appears on Fort Worth–Dallas radio station WBAP.

* * *

An unscheduled flight from Bolling Field (Washington, D.C.) arrives. Lewis Rickett meets it at Roswell and gives the crew a sealed box with wreckage in it. He is required to get a signature before he can surrender it.

At 10:00 P.M. ABC News "Headline Edition" tells the audience that Roger Ramey has identified the Roswell wreckage as a weather balloon.

At 11:59 P.M. one of the photographs taken by J. Bond Johnson is transmitted to New York on the news wire.

Wednesday, July 9, 1947

Morning newspapers trumpet the story that the "flying saucer" found near Roswell is a weather device. Some quote Ramey while others quote "informed" sources, including senators in Washington.

Clean-up on the various sites resumes at sunup. The military is trying to get everything picked up before any more civilians stumble across the field.

At 8:00 A.M. members of the First Air Transport Unit begin loading crates into C-54s. They load three or four aircraft with an intermediate destination of Kirtland. From there they are to be taken on to Los Alamos. Armed guards watch the loading of the aircraft.

Jud Roberts along with Walt Whitmore, Sr., attempt to drive out to the debris field but run into the military cordon and are turned back.

According to Roswell Army Air Field head secretary Elizabeth Kyle, the telephones at the base are still tied up by the incoming calls.

More of the wreckage is brought into the base and is now being taken to be boxed into crates of various sizes and shapes.

Bud Payne, a rancher in the Corona area, is chasing a stray cow. As he crosses onto the Foster ranch, a jeep carrying soldiers roars over a ridgeline and bears down on him. He is carried from the Foster ranch.

* * *

At 12:00 P.M. the crate that has been sitting in the empty hangar guarded by the MPs is moved out to bomb pit number one. Nothing other than weapons has ever been stored in the bomb pit.

In Roswell Floyd Proctor and Lyman Strickland see Mac Brazel under escort by three military officers. He ignores both of them, something that he wouldn't have done under normal circumstances.

At lunch the nurse tells Dennis she is sick and wants to return to the barracks. In the course of the meal, she has provided Dennis with an account of what has happened and given him a drawing of the alien bodies.

Under military escort Brazel is taken into town and into the offices of the *Roswell Daily Record*. There he gives reporters, including R. A. Adair and Jason Kellahin from Albuquerque, a new story. Now he claims to have found the debris on June 14. He also says he has found weather observation devices on two other occasions, and what he found is no weather balloon.

Ramey's weather officer, Irving Newton, says the weather balloon is a special kind. "We use them because they go much higher than the eye can see."

An officer from the base sweeps through Roswell picking up copies of Haut's press release, including those at the two radio stations. (Art McQuiddy said that a military officer had retrieved the copies of the press release written by Haut.)

Late in the afternoon, a flight crew at the skeet range is told they have a special flight coming up. The squadron operations officer, Edgar Skelly, tells the aircraft commander to keep everyone together.

The aircraft loaded by Robert Smith and other members of the First Air Transport Unit takes off for Albuquerque. The crates will eventually reach Los Alamos. All the crates are marked with stencils saying TOP SECRET.

Members of the flight crew pulled from the skeet range quickly preflight their aircraft. Once that is accomplished, they taxi out to the bomb pit. The only places on the base where the bomb pit can be observed are the tower and portions of the flight line.

A sealed, unmarked wooden crate is brought out and loaded into the bomb bay of the B-29, tail number 7301. Six armed MPs guard it, never allowing it out of their sight.

At Fort Worth a number of officers meet the aircraft. One is a man the bombardier recognizes as a mortician with whom he went to school.

When the crate is unloaded and taken from the flight line, Jesse Marcel is driven out to the aircraft. He and the crew are told to return to Roswell. There was no debriefing given to them at Fort Worth. It is clear now that this flight was a diversion. The bodies had already been sent to Andrews.

At 6:00 P.M. Joseph Montoya returns to the base to catch the courier flight to Kirtland. He wants to get out of Roswell and forget what he has seen.

Mac Brazel calls on Frank Joyce, this time with a new story, significantly different from the one he told on Sunday. When Joyce points that out, Brazel responds that it "would go hard on him" if he didn't tell the new story.

At 8:00 P.M. the flight crew is back. Again, they were not debriefed, but are told that they have flown the general's furniture to Fort Worth. They are cautioned not to tell anyone, including their families, what they have done. As far as everyone is concerned, the flight has not taken place.

Upon his return, Marcel confronts Cavitt in the intelligence office. Marcel wants to see the reports filed in his absence, but Cavitt refuses. Marcel points out that he is the senior officer but is told the orders came from Washington. If he has a problem, he is to "take it up with them."

The *Las Vegas Review-Journal,* along with dozens of other newspapers, carries a United Press story. "Reports of flying saucers whizzing through the sky fell off sharply today as the army and the navy began a concentrated campaign to stop the rumors." The story also reports that AAF headquarters in Washington "delivered a blistering rebuke to officers at Roswell."

Thursday, July 10, 1947

As he reads the morning newspaper, Bill Brazel learns about his father's activities in Roswell. He realizes that no one will be at the ranch and makes plans to get down there to help.

* * *

At the debris field and impact site men are working to get everything cleaned up. They want nothing left and no signs of their presence.

Military personnel return to Sheriff Wilcox's office and ask for the box of debris he has been storing for them. Wilcox surrenders it without protest.

Mac Brazel is being held in the guest house on the base. The officers there are still trying to convince him that he is not to say anything about what he has seen. They are also trying to keep him out of the way of reporters. He is given a physical by doctors at the base hospital.

Sheriff Wilcox calls on Glenn Dennis's father, telling him that his son has gotten himself into trouble out at the base. The sheriff had been visited by a sergeant who wants to ensure Glenn's silence.

Major W. D. Prichard from Alamogordo claims that a unit from his base in Roswell launched balloons around June 14. That, according to the article reported in the *Roswell Daily Record,* is undoubtedly what Brazel had found.

Friday, July 11, 1947

The debriefings of all the participants are under way. Participants are taken into a room in small groups and told that the recovery is a highly classified event. No one is to talk about it to anyone. Everyone is to forget that it ever happened.

When he tries to contact his nurse friend, Glenn Dennis is informed that she has been transferred from the base and that no one knows where she has gone.

Members of the military warn those civilians around Roswell who know something of the events that they can never talk about what happened. In some cases, the witnesses are threatened with death should they speak to anyone.

Saturday, July 12, 1947

Bill Brazel and his wife, Shirley, arrive at the ranch, but no one is around. Brazel begins his work, first surveying the ranch to see what needs to be done. He sees no evidence of a continued military presence. The trucks, jeeps, soldiers, and cordon are gone.

This weekend no aircraft with gun cameras search for the flying disks. No aircraft on standby wait for orders to take off. In fact, all aircraft are ordered grounded to prevent further searching.

Tuesday, July 15, 1947

Mac Brazel returns from Roswell. All he will say about his experience is that his interrogators kept asking him the same questions over and over again and that Bill is better off not knowing what happened. Besides, Mac has taken an oath that he will never reveal, in detail, what he saw. By now most of the world has forgotten that a flying saucer supposedly crashed in New Mexico.

Late July 1947

A deeply upset Mac Brazel tells the Lyman Stricklands what happened in Roswell. Through he complains bitterly about his treatment there, he honors his oath of secrecy and says nothing about what he found.

Bill Brazel finds one of the pieces of foil-like material his father had described. Brazel shows this bit of debris to Sallye Strickland (later Tadolini).

August 1947

Mac Brazel and ranch hand Tommy Tyree spot a piece of wreckage floating in the water at the bottom of a sinkhole. Neither man bothers to climb down to retrieve it.

September 1947

Lewis S. Rickett is assigned to assist Dr. Lincoln La Paz from the University of New Mexico. La Paz's assignment is to determine, if possible, the speed and trajectory of the craft when it hit. According to Rickett, they discover a touchdown point five miles from the debris field where the sand has crystallized, apparently from the heat, and they find more of the foil-like material. La Paz, who apparently does not know that bodies were recovered, concludes that the object was an unoccupied probe from another planet.

* * *

Dennis learns that his nurse friend has been killed. A letter returned as undeliverable indicates the addressee is deceased. Nurses at the Roswell base tell him that she was killed in an aircraft accident while stationed in London, England.

November 1947

Arthur Exon, assigned at Wright Field, flies over the debris field and the impact site. The tracks of the trucks and jeeps are still visible, as is the gouge.

September 1948

Rickett, while in Albuquerque, meets with La Paz. La Paz remains convinced that an unoccupied probe from another planet crashed in New Mexico the year before. In his secret dealings with various government projects La Paz has found nothing to cause him to change his mind.

October 1948

Rickett meets with John Wirth, another CIC agent. Rickett asks Wirth about the status of the material recovered at Roswell and is told that they had yet to figure it out. According to Wirth, they hadn't been able to cut it.

Summer 1949

From time to time in the two years following the crash, Bill Brazel has found "scraps" of the craft. His father confirms this, saying, "That looks like some of the contraption I found." Bill Brazel, in Corona, mentions his discoveries. The next day Captain Armstrong and three others from the Roswell base arrive and ask for the material. Armstrong reminds Brazel that his dad cooperated with them. It is the younger Brazel's patriotic duty to give it up. Brazel can't think of a good reason to deny it to them and surrenders it.

Summer 1950

Boyd Wettlaufer discusses the crash of an alien spacecraft with Dr. Lincoln La Paz.

1952

Major Ellis Boldra, an engineer stationed at Roswell, discovers samples of the debris locked in a safe in the engineering office. In the course of his experiments, he tries to burn and melt it with an acetylene torch and to cut it with a large variety of tools. Although extremely thin, the metal resists his efforts. When crumpled, it quickly returns to its original shape.

1961

UPI stringer Jay West is working in Alamogordo, in the area of White Sands Missile Range, when the base public information officer confides he has found a file that mentions the Roswell crash. The file includes a map. The PIO obtains a topographical map of the crash site. He and West make several trips out to try to locate the site. The maps show the debris field and then, to the east, a second site.

1969

As Americans walk on the moon, Melvin E. Brown tells his family that he has seen the wreckage of an extraterrestrial craft and the bodies of the crew. He assisted in the recovery, taking the bodies into Roswell.

1972

Inez Wilcox tells her granddaughter Barbara Dugger of the involvement of the Chaves County sheriff in the events of 1947. She says her husband, Sheriff Wilcox, was informed that one of the beings survived the crash. Mrs. Wilcox says military personnel used death threats to keep the family from talking about the events.

1978

Pappy Henderson confides in his close friend John Kromschroeder that he flew wreckage from a crashed saucer out of Roswell and to Dayton, Ohio. He shows Kromschroeder a fragment of the debris and tells his friend that he saw alien bodies.

Jesse Marcel is interviewed by a number of researchers, including Leonard H. Stringfield and Stanton Friedman. Marcel tells them that he is sure the wreckage is nothing from earth. Later, Marcel grants interviews to various news organizations, but those reports do not gain wide dissemination.

December 1979

Reporter Bob Pratt interviews and later publishes his interview with Jesse Marcel in which Marcel "admitted that he was the intelligence officer who had recovered the parts of a flying saucer."

1980

Syndicated television program "In Search Of" airs an episode about UFO cover-ups and interviews Marcel. In the course of that interview, Marcel again insists the material he saw had no earthly origin.

January 1980

Charles Berlitz and William L. Moore publish *The Roswell Incident,* the first attempt at a comprehensive analysis of the events at Roswell. In the course of his research, Moore located and interviewed more than seventy witnesses who had some knowledge of the event.

1982

After reading a story about the events at Roswell in a tabloid newspaper, Pappy Henderson tells his wife, Sappho, that everything in the story was true. He knows from his own personal involvement. He is surprised that the story is being released and, moreover, that it is accurately reported. He says even the descriptions of the bodies are accurate.

October 1988

Jim Parker's son sees a strange pickup truck on the ranch where the debris was found in 1947. Parker and his son chase it down and discover two men sitting in a U.S. Air Force pickup with a camper on the back. Inside are maps of the local area. The men are in their late twenties or early thirties and apparently of low rank. They claim they are surveying the area to put in a radar site to monitor low-flying aircraft, but then ask if Parker knows about the Roswell crash, mentioning that the site is somewhere close. Parker doesn't know what they are talking about. The men leave the ranch then. No one from the air force has asked permission from the owners to enter the ranch and no one has checked with the Bureau of Land Management about the availability of property in the area for use.

Fall 1989

The J. Allen Hynek Center for UFO Studies makes the first scientific expedition to the crash site. This is only the preliminary investigation. Weeks later, the ranch foreman reports that someone has been driving all over the site where the expedition conducted its search.

July 1991

Avon Books releases *UFO Crash at Roswell,* a detailed account of the events in Roswell. It includes the supporting testimony of more than three hundred witnesses, almost half of them first-hand.

21

Afterword

THIS BOOK IS going to annoy a large number of people. We are taking the conventional wisdom about the Roswell UFO crash and tossing it out. We are beginning again, using the testimony and the documentation that we have been able to discover during the last four years of intensive investigation.

But what has been more distressing than the time, money, and effort investigating the case is the reaction of those who claim to be interested in the truth. Rather than wait to see the evidence and have an opportunity to evaluate it, some are already attacking it, labeling various witnesses as liars and suggesting that there is no corroboration for the testimony.

All this is probably confusing to those who have read or heard nothing about the Roswell case. What is the truth? How can different people, supposedly investigating the same event come to completely different conclusions? And how can the reader, without the time or the money to conduct a personal investigation make any kind of intelligent decision about what to believe?

Take the date of the event, for example. For years people have been claiming the crash took place on July 2, 1947. No one questioned the date. It has appeared in dozens of books and hundreds of magazine articles. T-shirts have been printed using the July 2 date. It is fixed and believed to be immutable. And, it is wrong.

Trying to trace the origin of the acceptance of the crash date is a difficult task. It appears in the literature of the case as a fact. However, it seems that it is based, not on testimony of witnesses, but on an early assumption by an investigator. It is the date that Dan Wilmot witnessed an object in the sky over Roswell heading, coincidentally, to the northwest. It was assumed, by those first investigators, that this was the object that had crashed. There is no reason to believe it, but that is what has been documented for the last fifteen years.

Better information, based on both the written record, as outlined earlier in this book, and on eyewitness testimony suggests the crash took place on July 4. Of course, that generates the question of why anyone should accept the new date over the old one.

First, there is a written record. This is, of course, the best evidence. It shows that the crash took place late on the evening of July 4.

Second, there is the testimony of a number of eyewitnesses. Independently, they all related the date as the Fourth of July weekend. In 1947 it was one of the few three-day weekends and, because of that, people were able to remember the events in relation to the beginning of the long holiday. People were in places they normally wouldn't have been because they had three days off. There were a number of witnesses who made mention of the weekend. One man even said that he was out, with a woman, away from Roswell because it was a three-day weekend and everyone else was in town.

When the information is examined, it is clear that the July 2 date is in error and that the new date is accurate. This is based on the evidence and research and not speculation. And it is rejected by those who don't want to hear the truth.

But this is a minor problem and easily resolved. A look at the documents and the testimony proves the date of the crash. Other problems are not so easily resolved. And, there are other factors at work, adding to the confusion of those who are not as deeply involved in the case as we are.

For example, we are now confronted with the work of a former CIA employee who in November, 1992, injected himself into the Roswell case. He traveled to Roswell to interview witnesses. He broke no new ground during his investigation, learned nothing that hasn't been reported by others, and has made a number of negative statements about the witnesses he did interview.

In fact, he spent time in Roswell telling people that he had solved the Roswell case. When he returned to Washington, he reported that the crash at Roswell was nothing more spectacular than a Northrop Flying Wing mock-up designated as a N–9M. The long list of reasons why that explanation doesn't work has been examined. The point is, had he spent thirty minutes in the library, he would have learned that identifying the wreckage as that of an N–9M, or any of the Northrop Flying Wings, fails to answer the questions.

But the real damage done by this man and his supporters at the Fund concerns the eyewitness testimony. Because of his intervention, we lost permission to use one man's name in the text of this work. Although we had named him in earlier drafts, we are now forced to refer to him by another name. Had these third parties not injected themselves, using information that we had gathered and provided for them, this situation wouldn't exist.

We should also point out that this one man has decided that the witness is lying. There is no good reason for this conclusion, but they are spreading it nonetheless.

And that is the real problem for the reader. Without the man's name, how can he or she determine the truth?

Again, let's look at some of the facts. First, if this witness was alone, telling a story that didn't match those told before, it would be simple to reject his testimony. It wouldn't mean that he was lying, but until there was independent corroboration, his testimony should be filed. After all, when dealing with testimony, there are many factors that come into play, only one of which is that the witness is lying. He could be telling the truth, the truth as he believes it, the truth as he thinks he saw it, or any of a number of hallucinations, illusions, and confabulations that he has incorporated into a truth he believes but that has no basis in reality.

This witness, however, told us a story that deviated from the conventional wisdom, changing the date of the crash, the location of the bodies and craft, the shape of the ship, and the circumstances surrounding its discovery. Because of that we needed to proceed with caution. He was either an inept liar, or he was telling us the truth as he believed it.

Take the location, for example. Everyone assumed that the debris field, found seventy-five miles northwest of Roswell, was the main site. This new witness talked of a location no more than forty miles almost due north of Roswell. It was not the conventional wisdom.

Then Edwin Easley, the provost marshal for the 509th Bomb Group, who has been identified by others as a participant, confirmed, in writing, the location north of Roswell. As did Bill Rickett, who talked of a short ride north of town. As did Jim Ragsdale, who provided a location just north of Roswell, but who used the Pine Lodge Road to get out there rather than Highway 285. (Our source later told us that they had learned, after the first day, that the easier way to get out to the impact site was on the old Pine Lodge Road.) And, it was confirmed by a fourth, military source, who used a series of maps to show us where the craft came down.

In other words, our witness, who had gone against the conventional wisdom, had been right. His information was corroborated by four other sources. To be fair, one of them knew him well, but they had not spoken for several years. And, one of those sources, Ragsdale, didn't know him at all.

Or take the shape of the craft. Everyone assumed it was a flying saucer, meaning it was disk-shaped, but our source told us, no. It was narrow with a batlike wing. It was only fifteen to twenty feet wide and about twenty-five to thirty feet long. That certainly didn't fit the conventional wisdom.

Again, there was independent corroboration. Bill Rickett independently confirmed the shape. As did Jim Ragsdale. And, if we examine the information from the first of the flying saucer reports, we learn that the shape is not a disk but "crescent." Kenneth Arnold reported a crescent and William Rhodes photographed a crescent over Phoenix, Arizona, on July 7, 1947.

In other words, we did not accept the information of this witness without learning the truth from many others. Unlike some of the UFO cases from the past where we needed to accept the word of a single source, we had multiple sources who were corroborating one another and who were going against the conventional wisdom. They couldn't have read the information in a book and then repeated it because the data hadn't been published. The information that had been published was inaccurate, but the witness didn't repeat it. He was giving us new data based on his first-hand experiences.

We could continue, pointing out the areas of corroboration, the areas where documentation supported the witness testimony. We could show the arguments against those who believe he is lying, but in the end, it is up to you, as the reader, to decide.

But this also points out something else. There is no reason to reject this testimony at this time. None. Yet there are those in the UFO community who are doing just that. They don't want to—and are not going to—believe it. The only reason seems to be politically motivated. It is data that was developed by us and therefore must be suspect.

This attitude goes back to the creation of our first book on the subject. Several people, in an attempt to block the publication of that book, wrote or called the publisher alleging copyright infringement, plagiarism, the theft of research materials, and other unethical practices.

Allegations concerning our research techniques were also made. It was suggested that we asked leading questions in an attempt to get a witness to say what we wanted to hear. They suggested that we were manufacturing evidence and had "screwed up" the Roswell investigation.

None of the allegations were true and threatened lawsuits never materialized. In fact, the criticisms about the investigation seemed to be motivated, not by a design to get at the truth, but by jealousy. We had a book contract and they didn't.

The point is that our credibility was challenged, not because of something we wrote or because our work was flawed, but because we succeeded in signing a book contract. The proof of this is, of course, letters that were sent to our publisher, and suggestions that our material was stolen. Fortunately, because we had named sources that no one else had, and because we had all the interviews on audio or videotape, the publisher decided that there was no merit to the claims. The attempt by colleagues in the UFO community to sabotage our book failed.

Further proof can be found in one of the reviews written. While it is acceptable to attack the information inside a book, it is something different to attack its authors, claiming, for example, that we are petty, we had bragged about other books, and that we made assumptions that weren't in evidence.

Of course, we can prove that the charges are not accurate, but what's the point? What we should be concentrating on is the information contained in the work. And, for the reader, explaining exactly how the information was obtained. That is the reason that there is a comprehensive bibliography, a list of all the agencies, organizations, and research centers we used, and a list of the important first- and second-hand witnesses we interviewed ourselves. It is why there are footnotes and cross-references for corroboration. We don't expect the reader to believe what we write without some form of independent corroboration.

And that leads to the real point. Don't accept what we say without verification. Look at what we write and decide whether, in the context of the Roswell case, it makes sense. Don't look at the material and believe it because it is what you want to believe, but believe it because there are facts and testimony to back it up.

In the weeks to follow, there will be criticism. Look at it and decide if it is criticism that is deserved, or more of the same politically motivated nonsense that has been spread before. Is, for example, one of our witnesses lying, or is there reason to believe him because of the corroboration of his testimony? Examine the criticism and remember that much of it will be politically motivated.

And remember that one of the witnesses withdrew permission to use his name after other investigators decided that he was lying. His story is corroborated, but they weren't interested in that. They are only interested in reducing the importance of our work by whatever method possible.

The reader is the final authority on whether this work will stand or fall. Did we do our homework, follow the proper leads, and find proper corroboration? Have we been fair and objective in our reporting, or have we shaded the facts to promote one point of view over another? Are the criticisms valid or are they leveled out of political motivation?

In the final analysis, we have attempted to provide you with all the data needed to make an intelligent choice. When confronted with contradictory data, ask yourself if you are being manipulated, or if the criticisms are justified. If not, reject them.

This work will rise or fall on the research we did, on the credibility of our investigation and the accuracy of our reporting. Don't let others drag you from the path that is important by clouding the issues and muddying the water. When the dust settles, you'll find that we were right . . . again.

Above: Early on the morning of July 5, 1947, one of the trucks of the Roswell fire department responded to a call. Dan Dwyer said they saw the wreckage of some type of flying craft. This photo was taken of members of the fire department several years after the events outside Roswell. *(Photo courtesy of Frankie Rowe)*

Left: Brigadier General Martin F. Scanlon was involved in the clandestine retrieval of the craft at Roswell. *(Photo courtesy of Jack Rodden)*

Above: Walter Haut wrote the press release that caused a worldwide stir until the officers at Eighth Air Force Headquarters insisted that the crash be officially attributed to the wreckage of an air balloon. *(Photo courtesy of Kevin Randle)*

Below: George "Judd" Roberts was told by officials in Washington D.C, that if they broadcast their interview with Mac Brazel, who stumbled across the debris field in his pasture, they would lose their radio license. *(Photo courtesy of Kevin Randle)*

Opposite: Brigadier General Roger Ramey and Colonel Thomas J. DuBose examine the balloon that was passed off as wreckage found near Roswell. *(Photo courtesy of the* Fort Worth Star-Telegram Photograph Collection, *Special Collections division, University of Texas at Arlington Libraries)*

Above: Brigadier General Thomas J. Dubose (right) pictured with co-author Don Schmitt, confirmed his orders came from Washington to cover up the true nature of the incident. *(Photo courtesy of Stan Friedman)*

Right: Lieutenant Colonel Joe C. Briley confirmed that Colonel Blanchard's leave was just a "blind," when in actuality he was at the impact site. *(Photo courtesy of the RAAF Yearbook)*

Right: The 509th Bomb Group Staff in July 1947. *(Photo courtesy of Walter Haut)*

Below: Sheriff Wilcox's daughter, Elizabeth, with her husband, Jay Tulk. Tulk and Wilcox discussed the crash in the sheriff's storeroom where the box of debris brought in by Mac Brazel was kept for military confiscation. *(Photo courtesy of Paul Davids)*

Left: The home of Jesse Marcel in July 1947 where Jesse spread craft debris across his kitchen floor to show his wife and son. Later, the military requested he return it all to them, which he did. *(Photo courtesy of Kevin Randle)*

Below: Jesse Marcel, Jr., who handled the debris of the spacecraft brought home by his father, prepares for the hypnotic regression session in May 1991. *(Photo courtesy of Kevin Randle)*

Bottom: Although former Captain Sheridan Cavitt denies all involvement in the case, he was the OIC of the CIC at Roswell in July 1947. *(Photo courtesy of Kevin Randle)*

Above: Don Schmitt stands on the site that one man identified as the site of a second UFO crash. Behind him is the Plains of San Agustin. No evidence to support the idea of a second crash has been found. *(Photo courtesy of Kevin Randle)*

Left: Dr. Wesley Hurt who worked the Plains of San Agustin in 1946 and 1947 but who heard nothing about a crash until UFO researchers began to call him about twenty years ago. *(Photo courtesy of Tom Carey)*

The International UFO Museum and Research Center at 400 North Main Street in Roswell, New Mexico. *(Photo courtesy of Kevin Randle)*

The Investigation Continues

F OR THOSE WHO would like additional information on the topic of UFOs in general, please write:

J. Allen Hynek Center for UFO Studies
2457 West Peterson Avenue
Chicago, IL 60659

The Roswell investigation continues. For that reason, we have created a quarterly newsletter to update those interested on the progress of the investigation. An hour-long video chronicling the Roswell story is also in production. For information, please write:

The Roswell Update or Video
P.O. Box 85
Hartford, WI 53027

Both Kevin Randle and Donald R. Schmitt are available for lectures. For information, please write:

Kevin Randle and Donald Schmitt
P.O. Box 264
Marion, IA 52302

PART VII

APPENDICES

Appendix A

The Majestic-12 Hoax

DOCUMENTATION PROVING THAT the Roswell crash was real and extraterrestrial has been difficult to find. There are hints in some of the documentation that has been examined, but those documents are subject to various interpretations. The exception is the Majestic 12, or MJ-12, briefing that was allegedly prepared for President-elect Eisenhower in November 1952. If the briefing is legitimate, then all questions about the UFO phenomenon have been answered, and the story of a crash near Roswell is proven.

The document surfaced in 1987 when William Moore and Jaime Shandera announced they had received it, in a brown paper wrapper on 35-mm film, which they had to develop. Once they printed the pictures, they discovered the briefing, which told not only of the recovery of the ship and bodies at Roswell, but of a second crash that had taken place just over three years later.

Analysis of the document, provided by Moore, Shandera, and Friedman, suggested that it was authentic. Friedman, in fact, with sixteen-thousand dollars provided by the Fund for UFO Research, produced *The Final Report on Operation Majestic 12,* in which he concluded, "In North American courts it is required that the prosecution establish the guilt of a defendant. It is not the job of the defendant to establish innocence. With regard to questioned documents, the burden of proof is on those who claim that the documents are forgeries as opposed to being on those who claim that the documents may be genuine. After several years of sometimes very intense research with regard to Operation Majestic 12, I have still been unable to find any argument of the dozens put forth that demonstrates that any of the three primary documents are fraudulent. I have been able to demonstrate that there is a very great deal of information in them not known to anybody not on the inside at the time the documents were received. Therefore, I am forced to conclude that the documents are genuine."

It would seem, based on the amount of money spent and on the time used to create the report, this would be the final word on MJ-12. It seemed that the MJ-12 document was legitimate, based on the superficial nature of the discussion, but there were problems with it.

Critics were quick to point out that the date as it appears on the document, 18 November, 1952, is a mixture of both military and civilian formats. Elsewhere in the document, the date includes a "positional" zero, 07 July, 1947. While neither "error" is dramatic in and of itself, when taken together, according to Joe Nickell and John F. Fischer, "[these errors] are quite distinctive. Neither we nor Friedman has been able to demonstrate the combination in a genuine U.S. government document of the period."

What this meant, simply, was that there was a major flaw in the MJ-12 document that seemed to be inconsistent with authenticity. But a mistake in the date, no matter how strange, certainly isn't sufficient to label a document as potentially explosive as the MJ-12 briefing as a hoax. It is the type of mistake that could be overlooked, if the rest of the document were without question.

A careful examination of the whole document, however, reveals other, similar stylistic errors. For example, both places where the name of the base at Roswell is mentioned, the name is wrong. The ranks of some of the men listed on the MJ-12 committee are wrong. And there are misspellings that suggest the document is not a high-level briefing but a clever hoax.

Data included in the text of the document are also inaccurate. For example, the MJ-12 briefing claims, "On 07 July, 1947, a secret operation was begun to assure recovery of the wreckage of this object for scientific study." The date the recovery operation began is July 5. It would seem that men on the inside would have been aware of this fact.

The briefing also claimed that "four human-like beings had apparently ejected." Testimony from those who were there and involved in the retrieval suggest that there were five bodies. It would seem that men on the inside would have been aware of this fact.

The briefing continued, saying, "All four were dead and badly decomposed due to action by predators and exposure to the elements during the approximately one week time period that elapsed before their recovery." And again, testimony from those involved suggests that at most, the bodies were exposed to the elements for twelve hours. It would seem that men on the inside would have been aware of this fact.

What all this demonstrates is that the information contained in the document, which should have been completely accurate is, in fact, wrong. There is no excuse for it, unless the document is a fraud, and those creating the briefing hadn't been fully aware of the Roswell case. The document actually reflects the state of the investigation in 1987 and not the reality of the situation.

The second MJ-12 document appeared at the same time as the first. It was a short memo attached to the briefing paper and was the executive order authorizing the creation of the MJ-12. It was the last document on the 35-mm film received by Shandera.

Nickell and Fischer, reviewing the memo, wrote, "Even at first reading, we saw what appeared to be a serious problem with the Truman memo." According to them, memos of the era did not contain a greeting or salutation such as the "Dear Secretary Forrestal," that appears on the document. Since that was something reserved for letters, Nickell and Fischer conclude, based on their search of "countless Truman letters and memoranda" and because the "odds are thousands to one against such an incompetent hybrid memo/letter's having originated from Truman's office," that the MJ-12 document is fraudulent.

Barry Greenwood, editor of *Just Cause,* published by Citizens Against UFO Secrecy, discovered another major error with the documents. He wrote, "Page 2 of the Briefing Paper refers to the formation of MJ-12 'by special classified executive order of President Truman on 24 September, 1947. . . ' We have checked the Truman Library's listing of executive orders and found that no orders were issued on 9/24. Executive order numbers 9891–9896 were issued respectively on 9/15, two on 9/20, 9/23, 9/30 and 10/2/47, none even closely resembling the MJ-12 subject. There is no gap in the number sequence for these dates so none are missing. Further, the number quoted in Attachment 'A' of the Briefing Paper, #092447 . . . is not an executive order number but the date of President Truman's memo, 9/24/47. Executive orders are not numbered by date but are numbered sequentially, and at the time the numbers were only four digits."

Friedman had a rationalization for this as well. He explained that the briefing paper was only designated an executive order five years after the memo was written. In a letter to Nickell, Friedman wrote, "[We] don't have any definition of what is meant by 'special executive order.' "

Analysis by Nickell and Fischer showed that the memo was being cited by Hillenkoetter (according to the document) as an executive order, and he should have known what it was. According to Nickell and

Fischer, "Besides, the document seems to function as an EO [executive order] when it states that 'you are hereby authorized to proceed with all due speed and caution upon your undertaking.' " They write that a "genuine EO would necessarily explain what the undertaking was . . . a genuine EO would necessarily cite the authority under which the President was acting." They conclude, "In short, the document's content, like its format, seems incompatible with authenticity."

The third MJ-12 document is the so-called Cutler-Twining letter, discovered by Moore and Shandera in a search at the National Archives for corroborating documentation. In a box of recently declassified material, they located a single sheet that rescheduled an MJ-12 SSP briefing. It had been written by Robert Cutler, special assistant to the president, and directed to General Twining.

But like its predecessors, there were problems with it. First, it was found in a place where it didn't belong. Air force intelligence officers had reviewed all the material in the box, and had the memo been there when they searched, they would have withdrawn it rather than declassify it.

Ed Reese, of the National Archives, wrote to Robert Todd, reporting, "In none of these reviews was the Cutler-Twining memorandum identified as present and requiring any special attention. But the declassification guidelines used by both the Air Force and the National Archives would not have permitted them to declassify National Security Council documents. If discovered in the files during any of these reviews such a documents [sic] would have been withdrawn and provided to a National Security Council declassification specialist for final determination. It was never so identified."

A second major problem with the document is the classification of "Top Secret—Restricted." That is a combination of two security classifications. The Eisenhower Library reported, "The classification marking this memorandum is one that we have never seen on an Eisenhower document. 'Top Secret' and 'Restricted' are two different levels of classification."

Taking it a step further, the strange marking of "Top Secret Restricted Information," according to the acting director of the Freedom of Information Office of the National Security Council, did not come into use until the Nixon administration. The Eisenhower Library, as mentioned earlier, confirmed that this classification was not in use any time during the Eisenhower administration.

The conclusion to be drawn, because there are so many things wrong with the Cutler-Twining memo, is that it, like the MJ-12 briefing document and the Truman letter, is a hoax. It was, after all, found in a place where it didn't belong with a classification that was incorrect.

The controversy surrounding both the Cutler-Twining letter and the MJ-12 briefing was such that the National Archives issued a "Memo for the Record," raising some questions about the authenticity of the Cutler-Twining letter in particular and MJ-12 in general. Jo Ann Williamson wrote, "When certifying a document under the seal of the National Archives we attest that the reproduction is a true copy of a document in our custody. We do not authenticate documents or the information contained in a document."

What Williamson was doing was undermining the reason the Cutler-Twining memo had been planted in the National Archives. One of the major problems with all MJ-12 documents was that there was no provenance for them. No one could point to an originating agency. Planting the Cutler-Twining memo at the National Archives was an attempt to provide it with a pedigree. If it were authentic, it would go a long way to validating the MJ-12 briefing.

Friedman, in his *Final Report on Operation Majestic 12,* touches on Williamson's statement but then dismisses it, accusing her of "a number of statements made in her review [that] are misleading." Ignoring the criticisms raised by others, Friedman creates his own misleading statement when he writes, "Their [Williamson's] statement was based on a limited investigation and was later changed."

In the updated version of the "Memo for the Record," Williamson corrected a mistyped date and added the words "a representative sample of documents . . . in the sample . . . and bond paper. The onionskin carbon copies have either an eagle watermark or no watermark at all," to one of the paragraphs. In other words, the changes were insignificant and did nothing to alter the fact that the archivists believed that MJ-12 was not authentic.

The important change was Williamson's last statement claiming that they were not authenticating the document with their reproductions, merely certifying that it was an exact duplicate of a document in their possession. In other words, the Cutler-Twining memo did nothing to authenticate MJ-12 but further suggested it was all a hoax.

In all of this, everyone arguing about the authenticity of the MJ-12 documents was overlooking the fourth and most damaging of those documents, known as the Aquarius Telex. This was an AFOSI report that referred to MJ-12. Again, if authentic, it would validate the existence of MJ-12. But checks with AFOSI headquarters revealed that no message in that form had been sent. The AFOSI headquarters consider it to be a hoax.

Richard Hall of the Fund for UFO Research was able to shed some light on this aspect of the controversy. He reported in a letter dated April 3, 1983, "The AFOSI document is not authentic in the sense of not being an original; Moore has retyped it and done a cut and paste job, as he acknowledged in answer to my direct questioning when he attended our meeting three weeks ago."

Hall followed this with another letter dated May 16, 1989, to clarify his meaning in the earlier letter. "The situation is described in the letter [of] Moore attending . . . [a meeting] of the Fund for UFO Research Executive Committee and acknowledging to those present (including Maccabee) that he retyped (rewrote is not quite accurate) the Aquarius document and pasted the various markings onto the retyped copy. My understanding is that he did so only because the original was not sharp enough to reproduce clearly. I don't condone his doing this without saying so, but I did not then nor do I now think he faked or fabricated anything."

Moore later denied that he had done any such thing. Responding to questions raised by T. Scott Crain, Jr., Moore wrote, "I did not retype the document, nor do I know who did. . . . I know the version I was handed was a retype, because I had seen the original earlier on. The reconstructed version which appears in *Focus* [a publication edited and published by Moore] is the combined product of both my and Rick Doty's memory."

Later, in July 1989, Moore suggested that the whole Aquarius Telex was the result of a disinformation campaign that might have been mounted to discredit the researcher who released it. But the important fact is that everyone agrees that the Aquarius Telex is a hoax.

What we have, then, is a series of documents, including the Aquarius Telex, of dubious provenance. All the documents offered for MJ-12 have passed originally through the hands of Moore and Shandera. In fact, all attempts to trace the history of the documents hit a single wall when they reach Moore and Shandera. Nothing can be traced beyond them, and that includes the Aquarius Telex, which everyone agrees is a hoax. And there are contradictory statements about Moore's retyping of the Aquarius Telex.

Moore also made two statements that impact on all this. According to Friedman, among others, Moore had suggested as early as 1982 that he wanted to create a Roswell document, thinking that it might open doors that were closed. And in the April 1991 issue of *Fate*, Moore said that the disclosures he and Shandera planned to make were with the express permission of the government agents with whom they worked. These disclosures would contain both good information and disinformation because that was how the government worked.

What Moore was saying was that he had been working with the government and that he was passing disinformation along to other researchers. The question becomes, was MJ-12 disinformation from those government sources, or was it something of Moore's own design?

Others had thought the same thing. Jacques Vallee, in *Revelations,* writes, "Skeptics like Philip Klass went so far as to suggest that Bill Moore had manufactured the documents [MJ-12] and mailed them to his friend."

There is another, subtle suggestion about MJ-12. Robert Pratt said that he was working on a novel with Moore concerning MJ-12, though, according to Pratt, it was designated "Majik." The book was about UFOs and touched only briefly on a secret report that was labeled "Majik," with several references to the MJ-12.

Pratt said that the writing of the book was done in 1982 or 1983 and that Moore had given him some documents or notes dated from 1981. When the MJ-12 documents surfaced, Pratt said that he wasn't surprised because the term sounded familiar to him. He said that he and Moore had been talking about something like that, MJ-12, for years. Because of that, Pratt believed, when he learned of the documents, that they were fraudulent.

Given the wide range of problems with the documents themselves, the revelations about Moore and his contradictory statements, and that no evidence has been found that the MJ-12 documents were created by any government agency, the only conclusion to be drawn is that they are faked. In fact, the air force, barraged with requests for information about the MJ-12 documents, issued a series of statements. The air force removed the "Top Secret—Eyes Only" classification markings on the copy they had and replaced them with a stamp that said, "[This is] not a U.S. Government document."

Major Richard M. Cole reported that the new markings were added after several government agencies could not establish the authenticity of the documents or the existence of MJ-12. Even the chief of the research division in the USAF's Historical Research Center at Maxwell Air Force Base believes the document is a forgery.

Colonel Richard L. Weaver, deputy for Security and Investigative Programs in the Office of the Secretary of the Air Force, took another step. He stamped the MJ-12 document "Not an official USAF document, not classified, suspected forgery or bogus document."

UFO magazine's Don Ecker (P.O. Box 1053, Sunland, CA 91041) contacted Moore and asked him about the new statement by the air force. According to Ecker's report, Moore said, "Since the MJ-12 documents are not Air Force, Colonel Weaver cannot label the documents as forgeries."

But forgeries they are. Without any type of provenance, without some independent corroboration, without good answers for the questions that have been asked, no other conclusion is possible. The MJ-12 committee never existed as such, and the documents relating to it are fakes.

Friedman has said, "In North American courts it is required that the prosecution establish the guilt of a defendant. It is not the job of the defendant to establish innocence. With regard to questioned documents, the burden of proof is on those who claim that the documents are forgeries as opposed to being on those who claim that the documents may be genuine." But the analogy doesn't work, because we're not dealing with a criminal case. We are attempting to determine if the documents are authentic. Without any provenance, and with the internal inconsistencies in the documents, it is up to those claiming them authentic to prove the case. Regardless of what is claimed by the proponents, they have failed to do so.

Appendix B

The Witnesses

HERE ARE THOSE who looked at the list of witnesses we supplied and decided that all of them were third- or fourth-hand. There were those who didn't understand that a great many of the people were first-hand witnesses, describing events they had seen themselves. If we were called into court and followed the strictest rules of evidence, these would be people who could testify. To clarify the situation, we have broken the list down into first-hand and second-hand witnesses, and those who provided us with additional information that proved valuable to our research.

There are two things to remember. One, the first group is made of first-hand witnesses. They participated in the activities in Roswell in 1947. Second, there are those who were first-hand witnesses but who refused to allow their names to be used. They corroborated much of what we already knew.

BRAZEL, Shirley: conducted in person, February 1989, October 1989, September 1990, September 1991

BRAZEL, William: conducted in person, February 1989, March 1989, September 1990, September 1991, July 1992; by phone, 1989–1993

BRILEY, Joe: conducted by phone, October 1989, April 1990, December 1990

CASHON, Charles A.: conducted by phone, January 1990, December 1990

CAVITT, Mary: conducted in person, January 1990, March 1993; by phone, August 1991, October 1991, May 1992, February 1993

CAVITT, Sheridan: conducted in person, January 1990, March 1993; by phone, August 1991, January 1992, May 1992, August 1992, October 1992, February 1993

CRUIKSHANK, Arthur W.: conducted by phone, July 1990

DENNIS, Glenn: conducted in person, November 1990, January 1991, March 1991, September 1991, March 1992, April 1992, September 1992, February 1993, May 1993, August 1993; by phone, 1990–1993

DE VAUGHN, Bill: conducted in person, January 1990, July 1990, February 1991

DOBSON, S. M. (Sav): conducted in person, September 1990

DUBOSE, Thomas: conducted in person, August 1990, October 1991; by phone, October 1990, March 1991, August 1991

EASLEY, Edwin: conducted by phone, October 1989, February 1990, May 1990

EXON, Arthur: conducted in person, June 1990, July 1990; by phone, 1990–1993

HAUT, Walter: conducted in person, April 1989, August 1989, January 1990, July 1990–1993

HOLDEN, W. Curry: conducted in person, November 1992

JOYCE, Frank: conducted in person, August 1989, September 1990–1993

KAUFMANN, Frank: conducted in person, January 1990, September 1990, January 1991, January 1992–1993

LOVE, Thaddeus: conducted by phone, May 1989

MARCEL, Jesse, Jr.: conducted in person, August 1989, May 1990, July 1990, June 1991, November 1993

MARCEL, Viaud: conducted in person, May 1990

MARTUCCI, Felix: conducted by phone, December 1989

MCBOYLE, John: conducted by phone, May 1990, December 1990

MCEVOY, Paul: conducted by phone, April 1989

MCGUIRE, Phyllis: conducted in person, January 1990, July 1990, November 1990

MONDRAGON, Joseph: conducted in person, June 1992, March 1993

NEWTON, Irving: conducted by phone, March 1990, January 1991

PAYNE, Bud: conducted in person, January 1990, September 1991

PORTER, Robert: conducted in person, May 1990, July 1990

PROCTOR, Loretta: conducted in person, July 1990, November 1990

PYLES, E. L.: conducted by phone, November 1993

RICKETT, Lewis: conducted in person, November 1989, January 1990, August 1990, October 1991, April 1992, October 1992; by phone, 1989–1992

ROBERTS, George: conducted in person, January 1990, September 1990, January 1992

ROWE, Frankie: conducted in person, November 1990, September 1991–1993

SAUNDERS, Patrick: conducted by phone, June 1989, December 1990

SHIRKEY, Robert: conducted in person, January 1990, July 1990, November 1990

SKELLY, Edgar: conducted by phone, November 1990

SLUSHER, Robert: conducted in person, March 1991, September 1992

SMITH, Robert E.: conducted in person, March 1991; by phone, May 1991, April 1992

TADALANI, Sallye: conducted by phone, December 1990

THOMPSON, Tommy: conducted by phone, January 1990

TULK, Elizabeth: conducted in person, January 1990, July 1990–1993

TULK, Jay: conducted in person, January 1990, November 1991

TYREE, Tommy: conducted in person, August 1990

WHITMORE, Walt, Jr.: conducted in person, June 1993, September 1993

WOODY, William: conducted in person, November 1990

ZORN, Vernon D.: conducted by phone, April 1990, March 1991

There are other people who were first-hand witnesses to some of the events on the base, and second-hand to other aspects of the case. Bill Brazel, for example, could talk of finding bits of debris and where the debris field was. That is first-hand testimony. He can also describe his father's story, about being held on the base. That is second-hand testimony. Others, such as Marian Strickland, can talk of Mac Brazel as a neighbor. Again, that is first-hand. And telling of Mac Brazel being "held in jail in Roswell," is second-hand. Brazel said he was held in Roswell, but Strickland didn't see that.

The people on the following list have first- and second-hand knowledge. It probably should be mentioned that their testimony would be allowed in a court under normal rules of evidence.

ANAYA, Pete: conducted in person, January 1992; by phone, June 1993

ANAYA, Ruben: conducted in person, September 1991, November 1991; by phone, June 1993

BEAN, Beverly: conducted in person, March 1990, January 1991

BLANCHARD, Anne: conducted by phone, August 1989

BROWN, Ada: conducted in person, January 1991

CAVITT, Joe: conducted by phone, December 1989, August 1991

DENNIS, Robert: conducted in person, September 1991, September 1993

DUGGER, Barbara: conducted in person, March 1991, April 1992

FRIEND, Robert: conducted by phone, August 1990, December 1990

HOLCOMB, Sarah: conducted by phone, June 1990, December 1990, May 1991

HENDERSON, Sappho: conducted in person, August 1989, August 1990

JOHNSON, J. Bond: conducted by phone, February 1989, May 1989, May 1990, August 1990

JOHNSON, Mrs. Jesse B., Jr.: conducted by phone, April 1989

KROMSCHROEDER, John: conducted in person, July 1990, August 1990

KYLE, Elizabeth: conducted by phone, August 1989

LINDE, Shirley: conducted by phone, January 1991

LOUNSBURY, W. E.: conducted in person, July 1990, August 1990

MALTAIS, L. W.: conducted in person, August 1989, July 1990

McQUIDDY, Art: conducted in person, January 1990, November 1990

PORTER, Leonard: conducted by phone, May 1990

STRICKLAND, Marian: conducted in person, September 1990

WEST, Jay: conducted in person, November 1989

YOUNG, Loretta: conducted by phone, August 1993

In the course of the investigation, it became clear that we were going to have to rely on family members to assist us. In many cases, because the events were more than forty-five years old, the principals had died, some in aircraft accidents, some in the wars fought, and some because age and disease had caught up with them. These second-hand witnesses could relate stories told them by those involved. Again, if we were forced into a court, the majority of these people could testify. In a few cases, we were dealing with what amounted to death-bed statements.

ANDERSON, Gerald: conducted by phone, February 1990

ANDERSON, Peggy: conducted by phone, November 1991, December 1991, March 1992

ARGENBRIGHT, E. J.: conducted by phone, August 1990, December 1990

BACA, Harold: conducted by phone, June 1991

BOEHMS, Jo: conducted by phone, August 1991

BOLDRA, Greg: conducted by phone, January 1992

BUSH, George: conducted by phone, January 1992; in person, March 1992, January 1993

CHAPMAN, Richard: conducted by phone, June 1990, September 1990

CLARK, Charlie: conducted by phone, January 1992

CLARK, Denise: conducted by phone, January 1992

DANLEY, J. F. (Fleck): conducted by phone, October 1990, June 1991

DAYS, Jan: conducted in person, September 1992

FOARD, John: conducted by phone, February 1992

FOSTER, Iris: conducted by phone, February 1990, May 1991

GARDNER, Mary Ann: conducted in person, December 1990; conducted by phone, February 1990, April 1990

GROODE, Mary Katherine: conducted in person, August 1990

HALL, L. M.: conducted in person, March 1993

HARRISON, Peter: conducted in person, November 1991

HENDERSON, Bill: conducted by phone, August 1990

HENDERSON, Ned: conducted by phone, August 1990

HILLMAN, Imholtz: conducted by phone, September 1990

HOBBS, Alma: conducted in person, September 1990

KNIGHT, Alice: conducted in person, September 1990, October 1990

LITTEL, Max: conducted by phone, August 1990

LYTLE, Steve: conducted by phone, February 1990

MANN, Allene: conducted in person, November 1990

MANN, Johnny: conducted by phone, October 1989, December 1989

McBOYLE, John, Jr.: conducted by phone, May 1991

OLNEY, Hugh: conducted by phone, January 1992

PROCTOR, Norris: conducted by phone, February 1991, December 1991

RAMEY, LaTone: conducted by phone, March 1991

REYNOLDS, Charlie: conducted by phone, January 1992

RICHARDS, Myra: conducted by phone, January 1990

RODDEN, Jack: conducted in person, September 1989, November 1990, January 1992–1993

SAGER, Edward M.: conducted by phone, August 1990

SAUNDERS, Dan: conducted in person, November 1991

SPARKS, Elaine: conducted by phone, December 1989

SPARKS, Peggy: conducted by phone, July 1991, September 1991

SPURLIN, F. E.: conducted by phone, February 1990

STRINGFIELD, Leonard: conducted in person, June 1989, February 1990, May 1990–1993

SULTEMEIER, Juanita: conducted in person, January 1990, November 1990

TIFFANY, John G.: conducted in person, September 1990

TRACEY, Tom: conducted in person, September 1992

TUCKER, Merle: conducted in person, August 1989, September 1991

TYREE, June: conducted in person, August 1989

VALENZUELA, Juanita: conducted by phone, June 1993

VEGH, Elaine: conducted by phone, February 1990, March 1990

WACHTER, Helen: conducted by phone, March 1990

WALSH, George: conducted by phone, December 1990

WELSH, Patty, conducted by phone, May 1991

WILMOT, Terry: conducted by phone, August 1989

WILLMUTH, Nettie: conducted by phone, September 1991

Throughout the investigation there were dozens of people who assisted us. Some of them were in New Mexico in 1947, and their jobs, either with the military, the government, or the private sector, put them in a position to testify about the events of July 1947.

BUSKIRK, Winfred: conducted by phone, June 1991, August 1991, November 1991
CHAVEZ, Caroline: conducted in person, June 1991
DICK, Herbert: conducted by phone, February 1989, June 1991, July 1991
DRAKE, Robert: conducted by phone, May 1991, July 1991
DUTTON, Bertha: conducted by phone, February 1990, April 1991
FARR, Dave: conducted by phone, August 1991
GIRARD, Harry: conducted by phone, October 1991
HAMILTON, Colin: conducted by phone, September 1990
HIBBEN, Frank: conducted by phone, June 1991, September 1991
HUBBLE, Frank: conducted by phone, July 1991
HUDON, Betsy: conducted by phone, February 1989, June 1989, February 1989
HURT, Wesley: conducted by phone, July 1991
JONES, Milton: conducted by phone, August 1989
JOSEPH, Paul: conducted in person, February 1991
KELLEY, J. H.: conducted by phone, December 1989, June 1991
KRAFT, Gerald: conducted by phone, August 1991
LYTLE, Chester: conducted in person, February 1989, April 1989, November 1990
MARTIN, Francis: conducted by phone, April 1989
McKNIGHT, Daniel: conducted by phone, July 1991
NORTHROP, Stuart: conducted by phone, July 1991
PARKER, Jim: conducted in person, September 1989
PLATT, Curtiss: conducted in person, April 1990, March 1991
SPICZKA, Florian: conducted by phone, December 1991
STUBBS, Al: conducted by phone, January 1989
TOOMAN, William: conducted by phone, August 1990
TOULESE, Carmey: conducted by phone, March 1990
TULK, Christine: conducted in person, July 1990, January 1992
WEBER, Robert: conducted by phone, July 1991
WILLIAMEE, Ben: conducted by phone, November 1991
WILLIAMEE, Geraldine: conducted by phone, November 1991
YOUNG, Gary: conducted by phone, August 1991

As our knowledge of the events in and around the Roswell area increased, it became clear that archaeologists, both amateur and professional, were working in the area during the time of the crash.

We contacted approximately two hundred and fifty archaeologists whom we had reason to believe might have seen or heard about the crash. While most leads proved to be dead ends, the list below, which presents roughly 25 percent of those we interviewed, records a part of our search for the archeologists.

ADEN, Robert, worked for University of New Mexico, at Chaco Canyon, 1947; contacted in Murfreesboro, TN
AGOGINO, George, of Eastern New Mexico University, contacted in Portales, NM
BANNISTER, Bryant, of the University of Arizon, contacted in Tucson, AZ
BECKETT, Patrick, of the New Mexico Pipeline Archaeology; contacted in Las Cruces, NM

BICE, Richard, a geologist, contacted in Albuquerque, NM

BLUHM, Elain, affiliated with the University of Chicago in 1947, contacted in Buffalo, NY

BLUMENTHAL, Earnest, affiliated with the University of New Mexico, contacted in Albuquerque, NM

BUSKIRK, Winifred, affiliated with the University of New Mexico in 1947, contacted in San Antonio, TX

CAMPBELL, T. N., affiliated with the University of Texas, contacted in Austin, TX

COTTER, John, with the National Park Service in 1947, contacted in Philadelphia, PA

DANSON, Edmund, a Harvard graduate student in 1947, contacted in Sedona, AZ

DICK, Herbert, a Harvard graduate student in 1947, contacted in Glenwood, NM, shortly before he died

DITTERT, Alfred, a University of New Mexico graduate student in 1947, contacted in Mesa, AZ

DRAKE, Robert, affiliated with the University of New Mexico and working on the Chaco Canyon dig in 1947, contacted in Boisevin, Manitoba, Canada

DUTTON, Bertha, affiliated with the Laboratory of Anthropology, contacted in Santa Fe, NM

EGGAN, Fred, formerly affiliated with University of Chicago, contacted in Santa Fe, NM, shortly before he died

EIDENBACH, Peter, affiliated with Salvage Archaeology, contacted in Alamogordo, NM

FERDON, Ed, affiliated with the Laboratory of Anthropology, contacted in Tucson, AZ

GRANGE, Roger, affiliated with the University of Chicago, contacted in Tampa, FL

HARVEY, Herbert, affiliated with the University of Minnesota, contacted in Minneapolis, MN

HAURY, Emil, formerly affiliated with the University of Arizona, contacted in Tucson, AZ, shortly before he died

HAYES, Alden, affiliated with the Laboratory of Anthropology, contacted in Santa Fe, NM

HAYNES, Vance, worked for the National Parks Sevice, contacted in Portal, AZ

HIBBEN, Frank, affiliated with the University of New Mexico and working on the Chaco Canyon dig in 1947, contacted in Albuquerque, NM

HOLDEN, W. Curry, formerly affiliated with Texas Tech, contacted in Lubbock, TX, shortly before he died

HURT, Wesley, a University of Michigan graduate student in 1947, contacted in Albuquerque, NM

JELINEK, Arthur, affiliated with the University of Arizona, contacted in Mesa, AZ

JENNINGS, Jesse, worked for the National Park Service in 1947, contacted in Eugene, OR

KELLY, J. Charles, a University of Texas graduate student in 1947, contacted in Alpine, TX

KELLY, Jane Holden, a Texas Tech student in 1947, contacted in Calgary, Alberta, Canada

LAMBERT, Marjorie, affiliated with the Laboratory of Anthropology, contacted in Santa Fe, NM

LANGE, Charles, affiliated with University of New Mexico and working on the Chaco Canyon dig in 1947, contacted in Santa Fe, NM

LESLIE, Robert, an amateur archaeologist, contacted in Hobbs, NM, shortly before he died

LONGACRE, William, affiliated with the University of Chicago in 1947, contacted in Tucson, AZ

McKNIGHT, Dan, working on the Plains of San Agustin 1946-1947, contacted in Glenwood, NM

MEYER-OAKS, William, affiliated with Texas Tech, contacted in Lubbock, TX

MUNDT, Michael, a Texas Tech graduate student, contacted in Lubbock, TX

NETTING, Robert, affiliated with the University of Chicago in 1947, contacted in Tucson, AZ

NORTHROP, Stuart, geologist, contacted in Albuquerque, NM

PEARCE, William, affiliated with Texas Tech, contacted in Lubbock, TX

PECKHAM, Stewart, affiliated with the National Park Service, contacted in Santa Fe, NM

PIERSON, Lloyd, affiliated with the University of New Mexico and working on the Chaco Canyon in 1947, contacted in Moab, UT

PLOG, Fred, contacted in Alamogordo, NM, shortly before he died

ROOSA, William, a University of New Mexico graduate student in 1947, contacted in Albuquerque, NM

SCHELLEY, Phillip, affiliated with Eastern New Mexico University, contacted in Portales, NM

SCHROEDER, Albert, affiliated with the National Park Service, contacted in Santa Fe, NM, shortly before he died

SCHULTZ, Bertrand, a paleontologist affiliated with the University of Nebraska, contacted in Lincoln, NB

SLOANE, Morton, affiliated with the University of New Mexico and working on the Chaco Canyon dig in 1947, contacted in Morristown, NJ

SPETH, John, affiliated with the University of Michigan, contacted in Ann Arbor, MI

STERN, Theodore, a University of Pennsylvania graduate student in 1947, contacted in Eugene, OR

TOULOUSE, Carmy, contacted in Albuquerque, NM

WAILES, Bernard, affiliated with the University of Pennsylvania, contacted in Philadelphia, PA

WEBBER, Robert, a geologist, contacted in Socorro, NM

WEISMAN, Regge, affiliated with the Laboratory of Anthropology, contacted in Santa Fe, NM

WENDORFF, Fred, affiliated with Southern Methodist University, contacted in Dallas, TX

WHEAT, Joe Ben, a University of Texas graduate student in 1947, contacted in Boulder, CO

WHITHOFT, John, affiliated with the University of Pennsylvania, contacted in West Chester, PA

WORMINGTON, Marie, affiliated with the University of Denver, contacted in Denver, CO

Appendix C

The Documentation

DURING THE LAST few years, hundreds of documents relating to UFOs have been released. They dribbled out for years, but recently thousands have been obtained. They relate a tale of deceipt and deception that began in July 1947 and has lasted until today. The few documents that follow are a representative sample of the material that investigators have uncovered with FOIA (the Freedom of Information Act) requests, library searches, and queries to official organizations. There are, literally, thousands of such documents now, but these demonstrate better than most that UFOs are real and the government knows it.

In a handwritten note on the letter dated July, 10, 1947, below, J. Edgar Hoover referred to the crashed disks recovered. No other information explaining this note has been found, and no one has been able to determine which cases Hoover meant. Many of the cases from that era have proven to be hoaxes, and, according to other documents available, the FBI was involved in exposing them. Clearly Hoover was referring to an event other than the hoaxes in this note.

Memorandum for Mr. Ladd

       Mr. ▒▒▒▒ also discussed this matter with Colonel L. R. Forney of MID. Colonel Forney indicated that it was his attitude that inasmuch as it has been established that the flying disks are not the result of any Army or Navy experiments, the matter is of interest to the FBI. He stated that he was of the opinion that the Bureau, if at all possible, should accede to General Schulgen's request.

SWR:AJB

ADDENDUM

I would recommend that we advise the Army that the Bureau does not believe it should go into these investigations, it being noted that a great bulk of those alleged discs reported found have been pranks. It is not believed that the Bureau would accomplish anything by going into these investigations.

DML

(Clyde Tolson)

I think we should do this
7-15

(J. Edgar Hoover)

I would do it but before agreeing to it we must insist upon full access to discs recovered. For instance in the Sw. case the Army grabbed it and would not let us have it for cursory examination.

- 2 -

H

For years the air force denied that there was an investigation other than the publicly acknowledged Project Blue Book. However, air force regulations clearly task another unit located at Fort Belvoir, Virginia, with the investigation of UFOs. The responsibility for the investigation rested with the 4602d AISS and not ATIC or Project Blue Book.

*AFR 200-2
1-5

AIR FORCE REGULATION }
NO. 200-2   }

DEPARTMENT OF THE AIR FORCE
WASHINGTON, 12 AUGUST 1954

INTELLIGENCE

Unidentified Flying Objects Reporting (Short Title: UFOB)

1. Purpose and Scope. This Regulation establishes procedures for reporting information and evidence pertaining to unidentified flying objects and sets forth the responsibility of Air Force activities in this regard. It applies to all Air Force activities.

2. Definitions:

a. *Unidentified Flying Objects (UFOB)*—Relates to any airborne object which by performance, aerodynamic characteristics, or unusual features does not conform to any presently known aircraft or missile type, or which cannot be positively identified as a familiar object.

b. *Familiar Objects*—Include balloons, astronomical bodies, birds, and so forth.

3. Objectives. Air Force interest in unidentified flying objects is twofold: First as a possible threat to the security of the United States and its forces, and secondly, to determine technical aspects involved.

a. *Air Defense.* To date, the flying objects reported have imposed no threat to the security of the United States and its Possessions. However, the possibility that new air vehicles, hostile aircraft or missiles may first be regarded as flying objects by the initial observer is real. This requires that sightings be reported rapidly and as completely as information permits.

b. *Technical.* Analysis thus far has failed to provide a satisfactory explanation for a number of sightings reported. The Air Force will continue to collect and analyze reports until all sightings can be satisfactorily explained, bearing in mind that:

(1) To measure scientific advances, the Air Force must be informed on experimentation and development of new air vehicles.

(2) The possibility exists that an air vehicle of revolutionary configuration may be developed.

(3) The reporting of all pertinent factors will have a direct bearing on the success of the technical analysis.

4. Responsibility:

a. *Reporting.* Commanders of Air Force activities will report all information and evidence that may come to their attention, including that received from adjacent commands and from civilians.

b. *Investigation.* Air Defense Command will conduct all field investigations within the ZI, to determine the identity of any UFOB.

c. *Analysis.* The Air Technical Intelligence Center (ATIC), Wright-Patterson Air Force Base, Ohio, will analyze and evaluate: All information and evidence reported within the ZI after the Air Defense Command has exhausted all efforts to identify the UFOB; and all information and evidence collected in overseas areas.

d. *Cooperation.* All activities will cooperate with Air Defense Command representatives to insure the economical and prompt success of an investigation, including the furnishing of air and ground transportation, when feasible.

5. Guidance. The thoroughness and quality of a report or investigation into incidents of unidentified flying objects are limited only by the resourcefulness and imagination of the person responsible for preparing the report. Guidance set forth below is based on experience and has been found helpful in evaluating incidents:

a. Theodolite measurements of changes of azimuth and elevation and angular size.

b. Interception, identification, or air search

*This Regulation supersedes AFR 200-2, 26 August 1953, including Change 200-2A, 2 November 1953.

AFR 200-2
5-7

action. These actions may be taken if appropriate and within the scope of existing air defense regulations.

c. Contact with local aircraft control and warning (AC&W) units, ground observation corps (GOC) posts and filter centers, pilots and crews of aircraft aloft at the time and place of sighting whenever feasible, and any other persons or organizations which may have factual data bearing on the UFOB or may be able to offer corroborating evidence, electronic or otherwise.

d. Consultation with military or civilian weather forecasters to obtain data on: Tracks of weather balloons released in the area, since these are often responsible for sightings; and any unusual meteorological activity which may have a bearing on the UFOB.

e. Consultation with astronomers in the area to determine whether any astronomical body or phenomenon would account for or have a bearing on observation.

f. Contact with military and civilian tower operators, air operations officer, and so forth, to determine whether the sighting could be the result of misidentification of known aircraft.

g. Contact with persons who might have knowledge of experimental aircraft of unusual configuration, rocket and guided missile firings, and so forth, in the area.

6. ZI Collection. The Air Defense Command has a direct interest in the facts pertaining to UFOB's reported within the ZI and has, in the 4602d Air Intelligence Service Squadron (AISS), the capability to investigate these reports. The 4602d AISS is composed of specialists trained for field collection and investigation of matters of air intelligence interest which occur within the ZI. This squadron is highly mobile and deployed throughout the ZI as follows: Flights are attached to air defense divisions, detachments are attached to each of the defense forces, and squadron headquarters is located at Peterson Field, Colorado, adjacent to Headquarters, Air Defense Command. Air Force activities, therefore, should establish and maintain liaison with the nearest element of this squadron. This can be accomplished by contacting the appropriate echelon of the Air Defense Command as outlined above.

a. All Air Force activities are authorized to conduct such preliminary investigation as may be required for reporting purposes; however, investigations should not be carried beyond this point unless such action is requested by the 4602d AISS.

b. On occasion—after initial reports are

submitted—additional data is required which can be developed more economically by the nearest Air Force activity, such as: narrative statements, sketches, marked maps, charts, and so forth. Under such circumstances, appropriate commanders will be contacted by the 4602d AISS.

c. Direct communication between echelons of the 4602d AISS and Air Force activities is authorized.

7. Reporting. All information relating to UFOB's will be reported promptly. The method (electrical or written) and priority of dispatch will be selected in accordance with the apparent intelligence value of the information. In most instances, reports will be made by electrical means: Information over 24 hours old will be given a "deferred" precedence. Reports over 3 days old will be made by written report prepared on AF Form 112, Air Intelligence Information Report, and AF Form 112a, Supplement to AF Form 112.

a. Addresses:
(1) Electrical Reports. All electrical reports will be multiple addressed to:
(a) Commander, Air Defense Command, Ent Air Force Base, Colorado Springs, Colorado.
(b) Nearest Air Division (Defense). (For ZI only.)
(c) Commander, Air Technical Intelligence Center, Wright-Patterson Air Force Base, Ohio.
(d) Director of Intelligence, Headquarters USAF, Washington 25, D.C.
(2) Written Reports:
(a) Within the ZI, reports will be submitted direct to the Air Defense Command. Air Defense Command will reproduce the report and distribute it to interested ZI intelligence agencies together with notation that the formal report will be forwarded to the Director of Intelligence, Headquarters USAF, Washington 25, D.C.
(b) Outside the ZI, reports will be submitted direct to Director of Intelligence, Headquarters USAF, Washington 25, D.C. as prescribed in "Intelligence Collection Instructions" (ICI), June 1954.

b. Short Title. "UFOB" will appear at the beginning of the text of all electrical messages and in the subject of written reports.

c. Negative Data. The word "negative"

AFR 200-2
7-8

in reply to any numbered item of the report format will indicate that all logical leads were developed without success. The phrase "not applicable" (N/A) will indicate that the question does not apply to the sighting being investigated.

d. Report Format. Reports will include the following numbered items:

(1) Description of the object(s):
(a) Shape.
(b) Size compared to a known object (use one of the following terms: Head of a pin, pea, dime, nickel, quarter, half dollar, silver dollar, baseball, grapefruit, or basketball) held in the hand at about arms length.
(c) Color.
(d) Number.
(e) Formation, if more than one.
(f) Any discernible features or details.
(g) Tail, trail, or exhaust, including size of same compared to size of object(s).
(h) Sound. If heard, describe sound.
(i) Other pertinent or unusual features.

(2) Description of course of object(s)?
(a) What first called the attention of observer(s) to the object(s)?
(b) Angle of elevation and azimuth of the object(s) when first observed.
(c) Angle of elevation and azimuth of object(s) upon disappearance.
(d) Description of flight path and maneuvers of object(s).
(e) Manner of disappearance of object(s).
(f) Length of time in sight.

(3) Manner of observation:
(a) Use one or any combination of the following items: Ground-visual, ground-electronic, air-electronic. (If electronic, specify type of radar.)
(b) Statement as to optical aids (telescopes, binoculars, and so forth) used and description thereof.
(c) If the sighting is made while airborne, give type aircraft, identification number, altitude, heading, speed, and home station.

(4) Time and date of sighting:
(a) Zulu time-date group of sighting.
(b) Light conditions (use one of the following terms): Night, day, dawn, dusk.

(5) Locations of observer(s). Exact latitude and longitude of each observer, or Georef position, or position with reference to a known landmark.
(6) Identifying information of all observer(s):
(a) Civilian—Name, age, mailing address, occupation.
(b) Military—Name, grade, organization, duty, and estimate of reliability.
(7) Weather and winds-aloft conditions at time and place of sightings:
(a) Observer's account of weather conditions.
(b) Report from nearest AWS or U.S. Weather Bureau Office of wind direction and velocity in degrees and knots at surface, 6,000', 10,000', 16,000', 20,000', 30,000', 50,000', and 80,000', if available.
(c) Ceiling.
(d) Visibility.
(e) Amount of cloud cover.
(f) Thunderstorms in area and quadrant in which located.
(8) Any other unusual activity or condition, meteorological, astronomical, or otherwise, which might account for the sighting.
(9) Interception or identification action taken. (Such action may be taken whenever feasible, complying with existing air defense directives.)
(10) Location of any air traffic in the area at time of sighting.
(11) Position title and comments of the preparing officer, including his preliminary analysis of the possible cause of the sighting(s).
(12) Existence of physical evidence, such as materials and photographs.

e. Security. Reports should be unclassified unless inclusion of data required by d above necessitates a higher classification.

8. Evidence. The existence of physical evidence (photographs or materiel) will be promptly reported.

a. Photographic:
(1) Visual. The negative and two prints will be forwarded, all original film, including wherever possible both prints and negatives, will be titled or otherwise properly identified as to place, time, and date of the incident

3

AFR 200-2
8-9

(see "Intelligence Collection Instructions" (ICI), June 1954).

(2) *Radar.* Two copies of each print will be forwarded. Prints of radarscope photography will be titled in accordance with AFR 95-7 and forwarded in compliance with AFR 95-6.

b. *Materiel.* Suspected or actual items of materiel which come into possession of any Air Force echelon will be safeguarded in such manner as to prevent any defacing or alteration which might reduce its value for intelligence examination and analysis.

9. Release of Facts. Headquarters USAF will release summaries of evaluated data which will inform the public on this subject. In response to local inquiries, it is permissible to inform news media representatives on UFOB's when the object is positively identified as a familiar object (see paragraph 2b), except that the following type of data warrants protection and should not be revealed: Names of principles, intercept and investigation procedures, and classified radar data. For those objects which are not explainable, only the fact that ATIC will analyse the data is worthly of release, due to the many unknowns involved.

BY ORDER OF THE SECRETARY OF THE AIR FORCE:

OFFICIAL:

K. E. THIEBAUD
Colonel, USAF
Air Adjutant General

N. F. TWINING
Chief of Staff, United States Air Force

DISTRIBUTON:
8; X:
    ONI, Department of the Navy 200
    G-2, Department of the Army 10

Although the air force denied that there had ever been a "Project Moon Dust," various documents prove not only that it existed, but that it operated both inside and outside United States borders. The documents (three samples appear below) also prove that Moon Dust dealt with UFO material. What this means, simply, is that the United States had regulations and teams trained in the recovery of "space debris."

CONFIDENTIAL BADR

Department of State EXCISE

TELEGRAM

SP 16
69458

E 2 43

6 OCT 69 22 03z

DISTRIBUTION

ACTION: Amembassy STOCKHOLM

INFO: DIA 802B
1127th USAFFLDACTYGP FT BELVOIR VA
AFSC ANDREWS AFB MD
CONAD ENT AFB COLO
FTD WPAFB OHIO

refer
for concurrence
rec. E B114

STATE

JOINT STATE/DEFENSE MESSAGE
SUBJ: MOON DUST
REFS: A. Stockholm 2805
B. Stockholm 3005
C. State 114584 14 Feb 68

B1A4

Can offer no further instructions beyond ref C and D

at this time. However, correlation if any between

finding of this object and tracking and decay data on

known space objects will be forwarded FYI soon as

received. In meantime Embassy's action outlined reftels

A and B is satisfactory.

GP-3   END

DRAFTED BY DIA/Mr. McCarey/
PM/AE:JTKendrick:bpw | DRAFTING DATE 10/6/69 | TEL. EXT. 21147 | APPROVED BY: PM/AE - Mr. W. Rochmann
CLEARANCES:
EUR/SCAN - Mr. Hughes (S-L)   SCI - Mr. Nesbitt (S-L)
NASA CODE I previously informed

CONFIDENTIAL, BADR
Classification

FORM DS-322
4-68

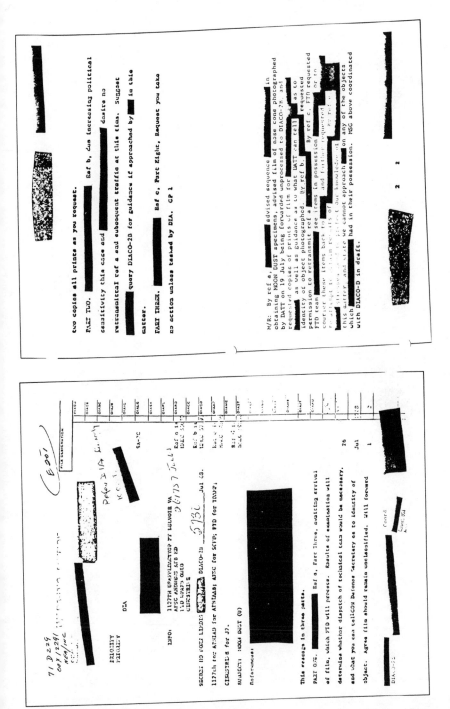

DEPARTMENT OF THE AIR FO ?
HEADQUARTERS UNITED STATES AIR FORCE
WASHINGTON 25, D.C.

RCS: AFCIN-1E-O/Colonel Bata

SUBJECT: (U) AFCIN Intelligence Team Personnel

DATE: 2 NOV 1961

TO: AFCIN-1E
AFCIN-1
IN TURN

FROM: Winston P. Jacobs
Lt Colonel, USAF

PROBLEM:

1. (U) To provide qualified personnel for AFCIN intelligence teams.

FACTORS BEARING ON THE PROBLEM:

2.

a. In addition to their staff duty assignments, intelligence team personnel have peacetime duty functions in support of such Air Force projects as Moondust, Bluefly, and UFO, and other AFCIN directed quick reaction projects which require intelligence team operational capability. (see Definitions).

b. Normal personnel attrition, through PCS, discharge, retirement, etc., has reduced the number of intelligence team qualified personnel below a minimum requirement, and programmed personnel losses within the next ten months will halve the current manning.

c. Personnel actions within the authority of AFCIN, AFCIN and AFCIN-1E can be taken to reverse the trend toward diminishment of the intelligence team capability.

3.

---

4. Criteria.

a. Intelligence team personnel can perform effectively only with an adequate background of training and experience. Inadequately qualified personnel in such assignment would be a liability rather than an asset to successful accomplishment of the mission.

5. Definitions.

a. Linguist: Personnel who can develop intelligence information through interrogation and translation from Russian and/or Bloc country languages to English.

b. Tech Man: Personnel qualified to develop intelligence information through field examination and analysis of foreign materiel, with emphasis on the Markings Program and technical photography.

c. Ops Man: Intelligence team chief. Qualified to direct intelligence teams in gaining access to target, in exploitation of enemy personnel and materiel, and in use of field communications equipment for rapid reporting of intelligence information.

d. Airborne Personnel: Military trained and rated parachutists.

e. Unidentified Flying Objects (UFO): Headquarters USAF has established a program for investigation of reliably reported unidentified flying objects within the United States. AFR 200-2 delineates 1127th collection responsibilities.

f. Blue Fly: Operation Blue Fly has been established to facilitate expeditious delivery to FTD of Moon Dust or other items of great technical intelligence interest. AFCIN SOP for Blue Fly operations, February 1960, provides for 1127th participation.

g. Moon Dust: As a specialized aspect of its over-all material exploitation program, Headquarters USAF has established Project Moon Dust to locate, recover and deliver descended foreign space vehicles. ICGL #4, 25 April 1961, delineates collection responsibilities.

DISCUSSION:

6.

a. Headquarters USAF (AFCIN) maintains intelligence teams as a function of AFCIN-1E (1127th USAF Field Activities Group). Personnel comprising such teams have normal AFCIN-1E staff duties, and their exploitation of qualifications for intelligence team employment is in addition to their normal staff duties. For example, the Chief of AFCIN-1E-OO, the Domestic Operations Section, additionally participates as approximately 16 hours of training per month for intelligence team applicant. Such training includes physical training, classroom combat intelligence training, airborne operations, field problems, etc.

People often believe that the Freedom of Information Act (FOIA) opens all doors. Such is not the case. Through a series of mistakes, the Department of State released the "Airgram" with only a few paragraphs censored. The air force, under FOIA, responded with a document that was nearly blank. The first pages are from the Department of State, and the second from the air force. Everything in the air force version was deleted from the routing slip to the name Rogers.

DEPARTMENT OF STATE

AIRGRAM

SECRET

TO : ALL AMERICAN DIPLOMATIC AND CONSULAR POSTS

DEPARTMENT OF STATE

Jul 26 9 47 AM '73

REVIEWED BY _____ DATE 9/13/82

PORTIONS DENIED AS INDICATED

FROM : Department of State   DATE:

SUBJECT : Guidance for Dealing with Space Objects Which Have Returned to Earth
REF : State 114584 (DTG 132148Z Feb 68)

E. O. 11652: XGDS-2
PFOR, PINR, TSPA, UN

This message supersedes previous instructions contained reftel which have been in effect for past five years and provides revised guidance to all US personnel serving abroad in an official capacity for dealing with space objects which have survived reentry and have impacted on the earth.

All posts should ensure that appropriate personnel, especially those who serve as duty officers, are aware of the guidance contained herein.

Background: The term "space object" is not clearly defined by international treaty. However, in general it may be construed to mean any object, including component parts, which has been placed in earth orbit or beyond. In addition to functioning satellites of various types, spent boosters, shrouds, fuel tanks, rocket nozzles, ballast, dummy payloads, etc., could also be considered space objects. For the purpose of this guidance, any hardware (whether intact major components or debris) from launches which were intended to achieve earth orbit but failed to do so should be

Attachment:

Extracts from Various Space Treaties and UN Resolutions Re Space

SECRET

FORM 10-64 DS-323

/AE:ARTurrentine/ds   Drafting Date: 7/18/73   Phone No.: 21835   Contents and Classification Approved by: PM/AE:HGHandyside
nces:SCI/SAM-Col Bassedo IO/UNP-Mr. Buback L/UNA-Mr. Neilson
/RSG-Mr. Finch D OD/ISA-Mr. Avierson DOD/USAF/INT-Mr. Foley
A/I-Mr. Mounsher CIA/FMSAC-Mr. George

A-6343

SECRET 2

considered as space objects. The procedures outlined herein would not apply to debris from surface-to-surface missile tests, even though the missiles may have passed through "outer space" during the ballistic phase of their flight.

In general, most space objects not specifically designed to withstand reentry burn up in the earth's atmosphere when they decay from orbit. However, from time to time a few space objects do survive reentry through the atmosphere and impact on the surface of the earth.

When a space object impacts on the earth and is recovered, a number of considerations and interests must be taken into account.

_____ in deciding how to proceed in [such case], a careful assessment of these sometimes competing intercsts and obligations will be made by the interested agencies in Washington and a program of action will be designed to produce the maximum benefit to the US.

In all space object cases, it is the responsibility of the Department of State to insure that US interests are served --

SECRET

A-6343

SECRET 3

The designator "MOODUST" is used in cases involving the examination of non-US space objects or objects of unknown origin.

In the examination of an object, the following information should be obtained and reported to the extent possible:

1. Pre-impact observations, direction of trajectory, number of objects observed, time of impact, characteristics of impact area, and circumstances of recovery.

2. Description of any injury or damage caused by the object. Provide precise details to extent possible, but in making inquiries avoid stimulating claims, especially trivial or nuisance claims.

SECRET

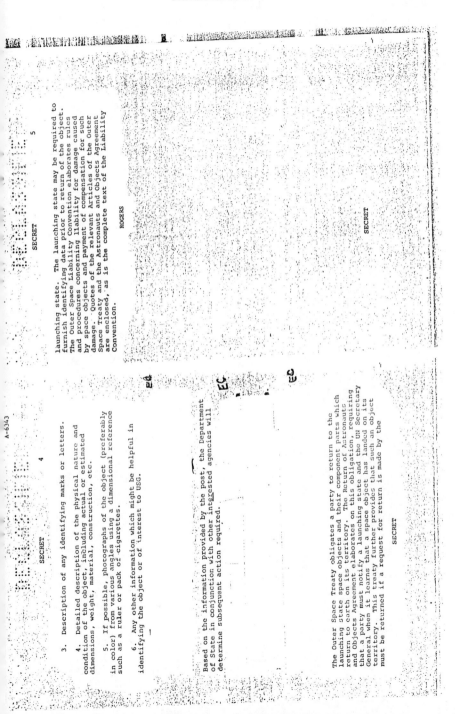

A-6343

SECRET

3. Description of any identifying marks or letters.

4. Detailed description of the physical nature and condition of the object, including actual or estimated dimensions, weight, material, construction, etc.

5. If possible, photographs of the object (preferably in color) from various angles using a dimensional reference such as a ruler or pack of cigarettes.

6. Any other information which might be helpful in identifying the object or of interest to USG.

Based on the information provided by the post, the Department of State in conjunction with other interested agencies will determine subsequent action required.

The Outer Space Treaty obligates a party to return to the launching state space objects and their component parts which return to earth on its territory. The Return of Astronauts and Objects Agreement elaborates on this obligation, requiring that a party must notify a launching state and the UN Secretary General when it learns that a space object has landed on its territory. This treaty further provides that such an object must be returned if a request for return is made by the

SECRET

SECRET

launching state. The launching state may be required to furnish identifying data prior to return of the object. The Outer Space Liability Convention elaborates rules and procedures concerning liability for damage caused by space objects and payment of compensation for such damage. Quotes of the relevant Articles of the Outer Space Treaty and the Astronauts and Objects Agreement are enclosed, as is the complete text of the Liability Convention.

ROGERS

SECRET

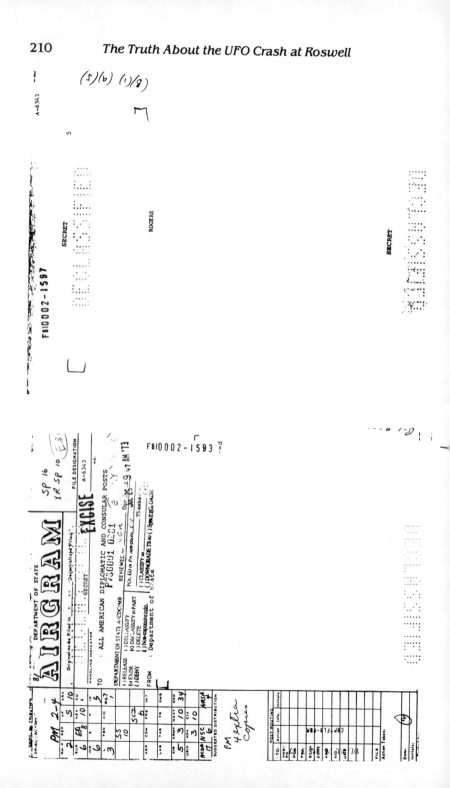

The air force, when confronted with the documentation, admitted that Project Moon Dust and Operation Blue Fly existed after insisting they didn't. Although more candid in the updated letter, shown on the next two pages, they still weren't completely honest. The letter demonstrates that the pattern of deceit continues today.

DEPARTMENT OF THE AIR FORCE
WASHINGTON DC 20330-1000

OFFICE OF THE SECRETARY

APR 1 4 1993

The Honorable Jeff Bingaman
United States Senator
114 East 4th Street, Suite 103
Roswell, New Mexico 88201

Dear Senator Bingaman:

    This is in reply to your inquiry in behalf of Mr. Clifford E. Stone on the accuracy of information we previously provided to your office. Upon further review of the case (which was aided by the several attachments to Mr. Stone's letter), we wish to amend the statements contained in the previous response to your inquiry.

    In 1953, during the Korean War, the Air Defense Command organized intelligence teams to deploy, recover, or exploit at the scene downed enemy personnel, equipment, and aircraft. The unit with responsibility for maintaining these teams was located at Fort Belvoir, Virginia. As the occasion never arose to use these air defense teams, the mission was assigned to Headquarters, United States Air Force in 1957 and expanded to include the following peace-time functions: a) Unidentified Flying Objects (UFOs), to investigate reliably reported UFOs within the United States; b) Project MOON DUST, to recover objects and debris from space vehicles that had survived re-entry from space to earth; c) Operation BLUE FLY, to expeditiously retrieve downed Soviet Bloc equipment.

    These teams were eventually disbanded because of a lack of activity; Project MOON DUST and Operation BLUE FLY missions were similarly discontinued. The Air Force has no information that any UFOs were ever confirmed downed in the United States. Although space objects and debris were occasionally reported and recovered by United States citizens, and subsequently turned over to Air Force personnel for analysis, such events did not require the assistance of an intelligence team. The unit at Fort Belvoir continued to receive reports relating to UFOs or Project MOON DUST/Operation BLUE FLY, which it would then forward to the appropriate authority.

    Beginning in the late 1940s, the Air Force investigated UFO reports under a succession of programs, the last of which was known as Project Blue Book. In 1969, the Secretary of the Air Force, Robert C. Seamans, Jr., terminated the program after determining it did not merit the continued expenditure of resources. In announcing this decision, he noted the program concluded that no evidence had been uncovered that UFOs

constituted a threat to national security, or that they
represented technological advancements beyond the scope of
contemporary scientific knowledge, or that they were, in fact,
extraterrestial vehicles. Subsequently, all Project Blue Book
records have been retired to the National Archives (Attachments 1
and 2). The Air Force refers inquiries on Project Blue Book and
current UFO sightings to the National Archives or private
organizations such as the Center For UFO Studies, 2457 West
Peterson, Chicago, Illinois, 60659.

Since the Air Force discontinued its investigative interest
in UFOs in 1969, reports of UFO sightings are now recorded and
forwarded only if there is a prior interest in the source of the
UFO sighting. For example, Enclosures 3 and 4 of Mr. Stone's
letter pertain to debriefings of two Soviet sources who were being
interviewed for possible military information of interest. Their
recounts of UFO sightings, even though they had occurred many
years earlier, were included in the report for historical interest
and were incidental to the main purpose of the report.

The Air Force does maintain an interest in space objects that
survive re-entry. When referred to the Air Force, such objects
are forwarded to the Foreign Aerospace Science and Technology
Center at Wright-Patterson AFB, Ohio, for analysis. If the object
or debris is determined to be of foreign origin, the launching
country is notified by the State Department in accordance with the
Treaty governing such matters.

We regret that the information in our previous letter was not
more accurate and sincerely apologize for any confusion it may
have caused. We trust this information is helpful.

Sincerely,

GEORGE M. MATTINGLEY, JR., Colonel, USAF
Chief, Congressional Inquiry Division
Office of Legislative Liaison

Attachments

REFERENCES

Glossary

AAF: Army Air Forces.

ADC: Air Defense Command.

AISS: Air Intelligence Service Squadron.

AMC: Air Materiel Command.

AP: Associated Press.

ATIC: Air Technical Intelligence Center at Wright-Patterson Air Force Base in Dayton, Ohio. At one time it was the controlling agency for Project Blue Book.

ATOMIC BLAST: The base newspaper of the 509th Bomb Group in Roswell in 1947.

B-25: A twin-engine army air forces bomber used widely during World War II. Many of them have been converted to use as staff and command planes for officers at various headquarters.

B-29: A four-engine bomber used by the army air forces at the end of World War II.

C-54: A four-engine cargo plane used by the army air forces in 1947.

CIC: The army's Counterintelligence Corps.

CUFOS: Center for UFO Studies.

EIGHTH AIR FORCE: Parent unit to the 509th Bomb Group. It was located at the Fort Worth Army Air Field, later Carswell Air Force Base.

FOIA: Freedom of Information Act. It was designed so that citizens would have access to government information. Often FOIA requests are denied on the grounds of national security.

FIRST AIR TRANSPORT UNIT: Located at the Roswell Army Air Field in 1947. First Air Transport aircraft flew much of the wreckage out of New Mexico.

FLYING DISK: One of the first names applied to UFOs.

FLYING SAUCER: One of the first terms applied to UFOs. In time it became a derogatory name.

FUFOR: Fund for UFO Research, P.O. Box 277, Mt. Ranier, MD 20712.

INTELLIGENCE: Any information that can impact a military mission or is necessary for the completion of it. Intelligence can include weather data, local terrain, customs, and industrial complexes. It is not limited to enemy activities or capabilities.

IUR: *International UFO Reporter,* published by the J. Allen Center for UFO Studies, 103 Oldtowne, Seguin, TX 78155.

MUFON: The Mutual UFO Network, Seguin, TX.

NCOIC: Noncommissioned officer in charge.

OIC: Officer in charge but not necessarily a commanding officer.

OPERATION BLUE FLY: The logistical support for operations supporting Project Moon Dust.

PROJECT BLUE BOOK: The official air force study of UFOs that was closed in 1969.

PROJECT MOON DUST: The official, though classified, project designed to retrieve returning space debris of foreign or unknown origin.

PROJECT SAUCER: The cover name given to the first of the air force UFO projects. It was circulated in the civilian community but was not an official project.

RAAF: Roswell Army Air Field. Later it was Walker Air Force Base.

RAWIN TARGET DEVICE: The weather balloon and reflector that some claim is responsible for the events at Roswell.

SETI: Search for Extraterrestrial Intelligence. It is the scientific communities search of life on other planets. Funding for SETI projects was recently cut from the budget.

S-2: Military designation for intelligence. The S-2 would be on a battalion or group staff, the G-2 would be on a general staff, and the AC/AS-2 refers to the head of army air forces intelligence on the staff of the chief of staff.

Notes

Chapter 1: On the Impact Site

1. Jim Ragsdale, personal interview conducted March 1993.

2. Jim Ragsdale, personal interview conducted January 1993.

3. William Woody, personal interview conducted November 1990.

4. Records held by the Franciscan Catholic nuns.

5. Tom Carey, personal interview conducted September 1993.

6. Jim Ragsdale, personal interview conducted September 1993.

7. Because of intervention by third parties, a source who had been willing to go on the record withdrew that permission. Although we were under no obligation to change the name, out of courtesy we did so. But this shows what happens when others interject themselves into a situation they do not understand. Without the intervention of these third parties, entering the investigations in November 1992, this change would not have had to be made.

8. Various personal interviews conducted January 1992, June 1992, March 1993.

9. W. Curry Holden, personal interview conducted November 1992.

10. Kevin D. Randle and Donald R. Schmitt, *UFO Crash at Roswell* (New York: Avon Books, 1991).

11. Mary Ann Gardner, personal interview conducted March 1990.

12. Tom Carey, personal interview conducted September 1993.

13. Tom Carey, personal interview conducted September 1993.

14. It is important to note that various witnesses have identified the impact site as being north of Roswell. These include first-hand witnesses of Woody, Easley, and various archaeologists, including Schultz and Holden. Second-hand sources, including Frankie Rowe and Barbara Dugger, also indicated that the impact site was close to Roswell, and to the north. None of these people knew what the others had said, but each put the site north of Roswell, in contradiction of the conventional wisdom. In fact, other sources, using maps of the area, also identified the site as north of town. If any of them had been confabulating, they would not have all selected the same site.

15. C. Bertram Schultz, personal interview conducted May 1993.

16. Donna Wilcox, personal interview conducted May 1993.

17. Jim Ragsdale, personal interview conducted March 1993.

18. Various documentation has placed Easley at Roswell in July 1947, confirming his position as the provost marshal. These include the microfilmed history of the 509th Bomb Group, the base phone book for August 1947, and the yearbook produced in 1947. In addition, Easley confirmed that in personal interviews conducted October 1989.

19. Jim Ragsdale, personal interview conducted January 1993.

20. Adair should not be confused with Robin Adair, the AP man who would enter the case on July 8 after he was alerted to the situation in Roswell by AP headquarters in New York.

21. Confirmation of Blanchard and Henderson's involvement comes from Sappho Henderson, Walter Haut, Thomas J. DuBose, and various staff members of the 509th Bomb Group.

22. Various interviews conducted in June and July 1993.

23. Louis (Bill) Rickett, personal interview conducted October 1992.

24. Jim Ragsdale, personal interview conducted March 1993.

25. Randle and Schmitt, 1991.

26. According to various sources, one of the threats made by the military officials concerned the fact that all of the archaeologists had been soldiers during the war and were using the G.I. Bill to pay for their college education. If they ever mentioned Roswell, their funds for school would be eliminated.

27. It should be noted that the men on the impact site were overwhelmed by what they were seeing. Later, many of those involved would have personal problems and drinking problems. Some of those who saw the bodies, including one of the nurses at the base hospital, would be devastated by the sight.

28. Jim Ragsdale, personal interview conducted March 1993.

29. Various personal interviews conducted September 1990.

30. Conventional wisdom has also suggested that four bodies were recovered. However, the eyewitness testimony from those on the site confirms the number five. Others, such as Melvin K. Brown and the nurse, saw fewer bodies, but that is explainable by circumstance. It means they only saw a smaller number, not that they were wrong.

31. Edwin Easley, personal interview conducted February 1990.

32. Robin Adair claimed that he flew over the site in a small plane on July 8, but this probably has nothing to do with the activity on the site prior to that.

33. Edwin Easley, personal interview conducted February 1990.

34. William Woody, personal interview conducted November 1990.

35. Several different sources confirmed the roadblocks and the fact they were stationed along the highway north from Roswell. There is no doubt that these sources were referring to a situation north of town and not to one far to the northwest as the conventional wisdom demands.

36. Various personal interviews conducted in May and June 1993.

37. The use of body bags, or mortuary bags, as they were called in 1947, has been confirmed by Glenn Dennis, the Roswell mortician, the nurse, Frankie Rowe, and Frank Kaufmann.

38. Beverly Bean, personal interview conducted by Brad Radcliffe in January 1991, with videotape furnished to Randle and Schmitt.

39. Glenn Dennis, personal interview conducted November 1990.

40. Frank Kaufmann, personal interview conducted June 1992.

41. Jack Rodden, personal interview conducted January 1993.

42. Jack Rodden, personal interview conducted November 1990.

43. Various personal interviews conducted January 1993.

44. Beverly Bean, personal interview conducted by Brad Radcliffe.

45. Confirmation of the flights available through interview with crypto operator stationed at Roswell, who reviewed the message traffic. Interview conducted in November 1991. Source requested anonymity. Flights confirmed by Kaufmann and Robert Slusher, among others.

46. Documentation supplied by Sappho Henderson.

47. Edwin Easley, personal interview conducted February 1990.

48. Various personal interviews conducted January 1993.

49. Robert Smith, personal interview conducted March 1991.

50. Ibid.

51. Edwin Easley, personal interview conducted October 1989.

52. Friends and family of Edwin Easley reporting why he refused to tell them more than that he had seen the bodies. These include Nancy Strickland.

53. Edwin Easley, personal interview conducted June 1990.

54. Edwin Easley, personal interview conducted February 1990.

Chapter 2: Glenn Dennis and Ruben Anaya

1. Glenn Dennis, personal interview conducted November 1990.

2. Ibid.

3. Ibid.

4. Frankie Rowe, personal interview conducted January 1993.

5. Ibid.

6. Helen Cahill, personal interview conducted September 1993.

7. Ibid.

8. Frankie Rowe, personal interview conducted June 1991.

9. George Bush, personal interview conducted January 1992.

10. Montoya family members have been reluctant to speak about any of these activities, claiming there was no involvement by Joe Montoya. The records show that Montoya was the lieutenant governor in 1947 but that he went on to become a powerful senator from New Mexico.

11. Ruben Anaya, personal interview conducted November 1991. It should be noted that the description of the craft and bodies are second hand.

12. Ibid.

13. Pete Anaya, personal interview conducted January 1992.

14. Ruben Anaya, personal interview conducted November 1991.

15. Pete Anaya, personal interview conducted January 1992.

16. Mary Anaya, personal interview conducted January 1992.

17. Ruben Anaya, personal interview conducted November 1992.

18. Pete Anaya, personal interview conducted January 1992.

19. Ruben Anaya, personal interview conducted November 1991.

20. Mrs. Moses Burrola, personal interview conducted January 1992.

21. Ruben Anaya, personal interview conducted November 1992.

22. Normally we are reluctant to use any information that can't be attributed to a specific source. Again, we have lost permission to use a name due to the intervention of a third party. This source, however, is confirming information that can be attributed to named sources. We have met with him a dozen times and he always provided interesting and accurate information. Since this is only corroboration for data received from named sources, we decided that we would include it.

23. Glenn Dennis, personal interview conducted November 1990.

24. Ibid.

Chapter 3: Mac Brazel and the Debris Field

1. Based on various eyewitness accounts and weather records available for July 1947.

2. Loretta Proctor, personal interview conducted July 1990.

3. Based on various eyewitness accounts, including Bill Brazel, Bud Payne, and Jesse Marcel, Sr.

4. Ibid.

5. Tommy Tyree, personal interview conducted August 1989.

6. Jesse Marcel, Sr., based on an interview conducted by Bob Pratt, December 1979.

7. Loretta Proctor, personal interview conducted April 1989.

8. Loretta Proctor, personal interview conducted July 1990.

9. Loretta Proctor, personal interview conducted April 1989.

10. Jay Tulk, personal interview conducted January 1990.

11. Frank Joyce, personal interview conducted September 1991.

12. Jesse Marcel, Sr., based on an interview conducted by Bob Pratt, December 1979.

13. Location and designation of "Hines house" based on both the Pratt interview of Marcel and interviews with Bill Brazel.

14. Len Stringfield, *The UFO Crash/Retrieval Syndrome* (Seguin, TX: MUFON, 1980), p. 17.

15. Jesse Marcel, Sr., based on an interview conducted by Bob Pratt, December 1979.

16. Ibid.

17. George "Jud" Roberts, personal interview conducted September 1990.

18. Ibid.

19. Edwin Easley, personal interview conducted February 1990.

20. Bill Brazel, personal interview conducted February 1989.

21. "Send First Roswell Wire Photos from Record Office," *Roswell Daily Record* (July 9, 1947).

22. "Harassed Rancher Who Located 'Saucer' Sorry He Told About It," *Roswell Daily Record* (July 9, 1947).

23. Bill Jenkins, personal interview conducted September 1991.

24. Frank Joyce, personal interview conducted September 1992.

25. Edwin Easley, personal interview conducted February 1990.

26. Marian Strickland, personal interview conducted September 1991.

27. Various interviews conducted September 1991, January 1992, and April 1992.

28. Various interviews conducted January 1992, March 1992, and September 1992.

29. Bill Brazel, personal interview conducted February 1989.

30. Various interviews conducted March 1989, April 1992, and June 1992.

31. Tommy Tyree, personal interview conducted August 1989.

32. Bill Brazel, personal interview conducted February 1989.

33. Tommy Tyree, personal interview conducted August 1989.

Chapter 4: Sheriff George Wilcox

1. Various interviews with members of the Clark family, January 1992.

2. Various interviews with local residents in 1990 and 1991.

3. Jay Tulk, personal interview conducted January 1990.

4. Phyllis McGuire, personal interview conducted January 1990.

5. Phyllis McGuire, personal interview conducted July 1990.

6. Jay Tulk, personal interview conducted January 1990.

7. Various interviews with various eyewitnesses, including Jud Roberts, C. Bertram Schultz, and Edwin Easley.

8. "Sheriff Wilcox Takes Leading Role in Excitement Over Report 'Saucer' Found," *Roswell Daily Record* (July 9, 1947).

9. Barbara Dugger, personal interview conducted March 1991.

10. Phyllis McGuire, personal interview conducted January 1990.

11. Barbara Dugger, personal interview conducted March 1991.

Chapter 5: Major Jesse Marcel and the Debris Field

1. Jesse Marcel, Sr., based on an interview conducted by Bob Pratt, December 1979.

2. Ibid.

3. Jesse Marcel, Jr., personal interview conducted May 1991.

4. Jesse Marcel, Sr., based on an interview conducted by Bob Pratt, December 1979.

5. Jesse Marcel, Jr., personal interview conducted May 1991.

6. Jesse Marcel, Sr., based on an interview conducted by Bob Pratt, December 1979.

7. Robert Porter, personal interview conducted July 1990.

8. Walter Haut, personal interview conducted April 1989.

9. Jesse Marcel, Sr., based on an interview conducted by Bob Pratt, December 1979.

10. Irving Newton, personal interview conducted March 1990.

11. Various interviews, including those with Irving Newton and Thomas J. DuBose.

12. Jesse Marcel, Sr., based on an interview conducted by Bob Pratt, December 1979.

13. Various interviews, including those conducted with Jesse Marcel, Jr., Thomas J. DuBose, and Edwin Easley.

14. Robert Slusher, personal interview conducted March 1991.

15. Jesse Marcel, Jr., personal interview conducted May 1991.

16. Jesse Marcel, Sr., based on an interview conducted by Bob Pratt, December 1979.

17. Lewis Rickett, personal interview conducted October 1992.

18. Various documents, including the RAAF phone book, August 1947, which includes a listing for the weather office.

19. Jesse Marcel, Sr., based on an interview conducted by Bob Pratt, December 1979.

Chapter 6: The Press Accounts

1. We conducted the first interviews with J. Bond Johnson. Since he was identified, others have spoken to him, and the story, as related by him, has changed significantly. Our reconstruction of the events is based on the uncontaminated first interview with Johnson, and the written record, including the newspaper article that Johnson claimed as his own.

2. In the original interview, Johnson had said that he'd only taken two photographs. Research, however, revealed that there had been four. On review, Johnson said that he believed that he had taken two film holders instead of the one he had told us of originally.

3. J. Bond Johnson, personal interview conducted February 1989.

4. J. Bond Johnson, personal interview conducted April 1989.

5. "Suspected 'Disk' Only Flying Weather Vane," *Dallas Morning News* (July 9, 1947).

6. Irving Newton, personal interview conducted June 1990.

7. Based on interviews with various individuals about the events in Ramey's office, including Irving Newton and Thomas DuBose.

8. Based on the review of the photographs from Ramey's office by various weather forecasters.

9. Based on the personal interview with Thomas DuBose, the Eighth Air Force telephone directory, and the Eighth Air Force unit history.

10. Thomas J. DuBose, personal interview conducted August 1991.

11. Alan Clark was the base commander in Fort Worth in July 1947. This means that he was in charge of the base facilities, the maintenance of them, and the physical base. Brigadier General Roger Ramey was Eighth Air Force commander. Clark was a member of Ramey's staff.

12. The exact date of this flight is in question. It is possible that the debris to which DuBose referred was picked up on Saturday, July 5, as the military officials explored the impact site. It is also possible, given the circumstances, that DuBose was referring to a small amount of debris collected by Brazel and surrendered to the Chaves County sheriff. Both scenarios provide for the special flight to Washington, D.C., by Clark.

13. Thomas J. DuBose, personal interview conducted August 1991.

14. Based on various interviews, including those with Johnson. It should also be noted that DuBose said that Marcel was not allowed to speak to the reporters. Marcel's interview with Bob Pratt confirms this view.

15. Audiotape of the "ABC News Headline Edition" discovered by CUFOS scientific director Mark Rodeghier.

16. Various newspapers, including the *Des Moines Register* and *Circleville Herald* (July 5, 6, and 7, 1947).

17. "Local Weatherman Believes Disks to Be Bureau Devices," *Roswell Daily Record* (July 9, 1947).

18. "Ramey Says Excitement Is Not Justified," *Roswell Daily Record* (July 9, 1947).

19. Various newspaper articles, the 509th unit history, and the morning report records for the headquarters, 509th Bomb Group.

20. "Harassed Rancher Who Located 'Saucer' Sorry He Told About It," *Roswell Daily Record* (July 9, 1947).

Chapter 7: The Story of the Century

1. The three hours is based on the time frame from the moment that Walter Haut provided the news release to the time that Ramey was providing a solution to the first of the reporters in Fort Worth, Texas.

2. Walter Haut, personal interview conducted April 1989.

3. Art McQuiddy, personal interview conducted January 1990.

4. "AP Wires Burn with 'Captured Disk' Story," *The Daily Illni* (July 9, 1947).

5. Ibid.

6. *San Francisco Chronicle* (July 8, 1947).

7. "AP Wires Burn with 'Captured Disk' Story," *The Daily Illni* (July 9, 1947).

8. Ibid.

9. J. Bond Johnson, personal interview conducted February 1989.

10. "AP Wires Burn with 'Captured Disk' Story," *The Daily Illni* (July 9, 1947).

11. J. Bond Johnson, personal interview conducted February 1989.

12. "AP Wires Burn with 'Captured Disk' Story," *The Daily Illni* (July 9, 1947).

13. Ibid.

14. J. Bond Johnson, personal interview conducted March 1989.

15. "AP Wires Burn with 'Captured Disk' Story," *The Daily Illni* (July 9, 1947).

16. Walter Haut, personal interview conducted April 1989.

17. "Sheriff Wilcox Takes Leading Role in Excitement Over Report 'Saucer' Found," *Roswell Daily Record* (July 9, 1947).

18. "Suspected 'Disk' Only Flying Weather Vane," *Dallas Morning News* (July 9, 1947).

19. "AP Wires Burn with 'Captured Disk' Story," *The Daily Illni* (July 9, 1947).

20. Copy, FBI Teletype message, July 8, 1947.

21. Thomas J. DuBose, personal interview conducted August 1991.

22. Irving Newton, personal interview conducted July 1991.

23. "AP Wires Burn with 'Captured Disk' Story," *The Daily Illni* (July 9, 1947).

24. "ABC News Headline Edition" (audiotape), July 8, 1947.

25. Ibid.

26. Caption on photograph transmitted by AP, of activities in Ramey's office, July 8, 1947, from Bettmann Photo Archives.

27. " 'Disk' Near Bomb Test Site Is Just a Weather Balloon," *The New York Times* (July 9, 1947).

28. "Army, Navy Move on 'Flying Disc' Rumors," *El Paso Herald-Post* (July 9, 1947).

Chapter 8:
KGFL, Walt Whitmore, and Frank Joyce

1. Based on Joyce's remarks that he spoke to Mac Brazel on the afternoon of July 6, 1947.

2. Frank Joyce, personal interview conducted September 1991.

3. George "Jud" Roberts, personal interview conducted September 1991.

4. Walt Whitmore, Jr., personal interview conducted September 1993.

5. Teletype message supplied by Frank Joyce.

6. Frank Joyce, personal interview conducted September 1991.

7. Art McQuiddy, personal interview conducted January 1990.

8. Frank Joyce, personal interview conducted September 1991.

9. Teletype message supplied by Frank Joyce.

10. Ibid.

11. "Harassed Rancher Who Located 'Saucer' Sorry He Told About It," *Roswell Daily Record* (July 9, 1947).

12. Frank Joyce, personal interview conducted September 1991.

13. Ibid.

Chapter 9: The Wright Field Connection

1. Sappho Henderson, personal interview conducted August 1991.

2. Thomas J. DuBose, personal interview conducted August 1991.

3. Copy, FBI Teletype message, July 8, 1947.

4. Glenn Dennis, personal interview conducted November 1990.

5. John Tiffany, personal interview conducted August 1989.

6. Kevin D. Randle and Donald R. Schmitt, *UFO Crash at Roswell* (New York: Avon Books, 1991).

7. Official biography of Arthur Exon, published by the USAF Office of Information.

8. Arthur Exon, personal interview conducted May 1990.

9. Letter from Arthur Exon to Kevin Randle, dated November, 24 1991.

10. Arthur Exon, personal interview conducted May 1990.

11. Official biography of Arthur Exon, published by the USAF Office of Information.

12. Exon was quick to point out that he didn't have much in the way of first-hand testimony. However, his presence on the base and his overflight of the crash sites place him in a unique position of knowing about the crash and seeing the evidence of it.

13. John Tiffany, personal interview conducted August 1989.

14. Because of the intervention of third parties, this witness, who originally allowed her name to be used, has revoked that permission. We have verified, through documentation, that she was present in the position that she claimed to have held at Wright Field.

15. Helen Wachter, personal interview conducted March 1990.

16. Arthur Exon, personal interview conducted June 1990.

17. Steven Lytle, personal interview conducted February 1990.

18. Arthur Exon, personal interview conducted May 1990.

Chapter 10: The Autopsy Reports

1. Glenn Dennis, personal interview conducted November 1990.

2. Ibid.

3. Johnson's position as a pathologist has been verified by a number of the former members of the 509th Bomb Group.

4. Verified by the 509th yearbook and the RAAF unit history.

5. Verified by interviews with various family members and former colleagues.

6. Verified by various interviews with former members of the 509th Bomb Group. This is another example of how the intervention of third parties has hindered investigation. One of the sources, after speaking to another so-called researcher, rescinded permission to use his name.

7. Len Stringfield, *The UFO Crash/Retrieval Syndrome* (Seguin, TX: MUFON, 1980).

8. Beverly Bean, personal interview conducted by Brad Radcliffe January 1991.

9. Len Stringfield, *The UFO Crash/Retrieval Syndrome* (Seguin, TX: MUFON, 1980).

10. Ibid.

11. Various interviews conducted by Don Schmitt.

Chapter 11: The Threats

1. Barbara Dugger, personal interview conducted March 1991.

2. Ibid.

3. Glenn Dennis, personal interview conducted November 1990.

4. Frankie Rowe, personal interview conducted January 1993.

5. Helen Cahill, personal interview conducted September 1993.

6. The source does not want to be identified because he doesn't want any trouble. He is, of course, known to us.

7. Ruben Anaya, personal interview conducted November 1991.

8. Bill Brazel, personal interview conducted February 1989.

9. Various interviews, including Edwin Easley, Frank Kaufmann, Bill Rickett, and Jesse Marcel, Sr. (as told to his son).

10. Sappho Henderson, personal interview conducted August 1991.

11. Edwin Easley, personal interview conducted February 1990.

12. Frank Kaufmann, personal interview conducted January 1990.

13. Rowe remembered none of this until she was about to be interviewed over the phone by a radio talk show host in Boston. His New England accent frightened her, and Schmitt, who was in the room, said that the blood drained from her face and she was unable to speak. Randle, on a separate phone line, had no idea what happened until the radio show ended.

14. The witness now refuses to come forward, afraid for his life. Prior to the phone call, he had been willing to share his information freely.

Chapter 12: Anatomy of an Investigation

1. Jason Kellahin, personal interview conducted January 1993.

2. Ibid.

3. Robin Adair, personal interview conducted February 1993.

4. Ibid.

5. Jason Kellahin, personal interview conducted January 1993.

6. "Send First Roswell Wire Photos from Record Office," *Roswell Daily Record* (July 9, 1947).

7. "Send First Roswell Wire Photos from Record Office," *Roswell Daily Record* (July 9, 1947).

8. Jason Kellahin, personal interview conducted January 1993.

9. Ibid.

10. Robin Adair, personal interview conducted February 1993.

11. Walter Haut, personal interview conducted April 1989.

12. "Send First Roswell Wire Photos from Record Office," *Roswell Daily Record* (July 9, 1947).

13. The location of the Brazel debris field is based on information provided by Bill Brazel and Bud Payne.

14. The result of personal searches at various AP offices conducted by Schmitt and Randle and employees of the AP.

15. Location of photos determined by a review of them.

16. " 'Disk' Fizzles . . . Army Sizzles Over Rumor," *The Midland Reporter-Telegram* (July 10, 1947).

Chapter 13: The Twining Letter, Project Moon Dust, and a History of Deception

1. Schulgen's position and rank confirmed by *Register of the Army of the United States* for 1947.

2. Michael D. Swords, "The Summer of 1947: UFOs and the U.S. Government at the Beginning," *The Roswell Report* (Chicago: CUFOS, 1991).

3. "Army Shrugs Off 'Flying Saucers,'" *The Daily Current-Argus* (July 6, 1947).

4. Swords, 1991.

5. Ibid.

6. Ibid.

7. Ibid.

8. Ibid.

9. Letter, General Twining to General Schulgen, September 24 1947.

10. Text of letter from photocopy available in Project Blue Book files.

11. Lois E. Walker and Shelby E. Wickam, *From Huffman Prairie to the Moon: The History of Wright-Patterson Air Force Base* (Wright-Patterson AFB: Office of History, 2750th Air Base Wing).

12. Personal experience of Randle as an air force intelligence officer.

13. FBI office memorandum, July 10, 1947, from E. G. Fitch to D. H. Ladd (handwritten note by Tolson).

14. Ibid.

15. "Finds Disk, Sure It Came from Sky," *Chicago Daily News* (July 8, 1947) p. 4.

16. Project Blue Book files.

17. Kevin D. Randle, *The UFO Casebook* (New York: Warner Books, 1989).

18. Ed Ruppelt, *The Report on Unidentified Flying Objects* (New York: Ace Books, 1956).

19. Ruppelt, 1956.

20. Daniel S. Gillmor, ed., *Scientific Study of Unidentified Flying Objects* (New York: Bantam Books, 1969).

21. Ruppelt, 1956.

22. Ibid.

23. Ibid.

24. Ibid.

25. Gillmor, 1969.

26. Air Defense Command Regulation 24-2, January 1953.

27. Air Force Regulation 200-2, August 1953.

28. Ibid.

29. Ibid.

30. Clifford Stone, "The U.S. Air Force's Real, Official Investigation of UFO's" (Roswell, NM: The author, 1993).

31. Air Force Regulation 200-2, August 1953.

32. Stone, 1993.

33. "AFCIN Intelligence Team Personnel," November 3, 1961.

34. Ibid.

35. Ibid.

36. "All American Diplomatic and Consular Posts," July 26, 1973.

37. Stone, 1993.

38. Ibid.

39. Ibid.

40. Ibid.

41. Project Blue Book files, Kecksburg, PA, file, December 9, 1965.

42. Arthur Exon, personal interview conducted May 1990.

43. Stone, 1993.

44. Clifford Stone, personal interview conducted July 1993.

45. Letter to Senator Jeff Bingaman from Lieutenant Colonel John E. Madison, Jr.

46. Letter to Senator Jeff Bingaman from Colonel George M. Mattingley, Jr., dated April 14, 1993.

47. Letter to Robert Todd from Colonel Phillip E. Thompson, dated July 1, 1987.

Chapter 14: The Search for the Archaeologists

1. Date of Barnett's death confirmed by friends and relatives, including Alice Knight and Vern Maltais.

2. Charles Berlitz and William M. Moore, *The Roswell Incident* (New York: Berkley Books, 1988).

3. Tom Carey, personal interview conducted May 1993.

4. Various interviews with archaeologists, including Wesley Hurt, Dan McKnight, Albert Dittert, and Herbert Dick.

5. Personal interview conducted with an archaeologist, name withheld by request.

6. Personal interview conducted with an archaeologist, name withheld by request.

7. Kevin Randle and Donald R. Schmitt, "Missing Time," *IUR* (July/August 1992).

8. Mary Ann Gardner, personal interview conducted April 1990.

9. Information reflects that gathered by Schmitt as he attempted to discover the name of the dying cancer patient.

10. Tom Carey, personal interview conducted July 1993.

11. Fred Windorf, personal interview conducted May 1989.

12. Information provided to Mark Rodeghier by J. H. Kelly.

13. Letter to Tom Carey from Megan Lehmer.

14. Iris Foster, personal interview conducted February 1990.

15. Peggy Sparks, personal interview conducted December 1990.

16. Tom Carey, personal interview conducted April 1993.

17. Verified by checks with various institutions and individuals.

18. C. Bertram Schultz, personal interview conducted May 1993.

19. C. Bertram Schultz, personal interview conducted October 1992.

20. W. Curry Holden, personal interview conducted November 1992.

21. J. H. Kelly, personal interview conducted April 1993.

22. Records reviewed at the Southwest Collections, Texas Tech Lubbock, Texas.

23. C. Bertram Schultz, personal interview conducted May 1993.

24. Donna Wilcox, personal interview conducted June 1993.

25. Review of the field notes conducted by Randle, May 1993.

26. Program for the conference found in the Holden Collection, Texas Tech.

27. Tom Carey, personal interview conducted July 1993.

28. George Agogino, personal interview conducted September 1993.

Bibliography

ABNEY, David L. "Expert Testimony and Eyewitness Identification." *Case and Comment* (March–April 1986).

"Air Defense Command Briefing" (January 1953).

ALBERTS, Don E., and PUTNAM, Allan E. *A History of Kirtland Air Force Base 1928–1982*. Albuquerque, NM: 1606th Air Base Wing, 1985.

ANDERSON, Ted. Alleged diary for July 1947.

"ATIC UFO Briefing" (April 1952).

BAKER, Raymond D. *Historical Highlights of Andrews AFB 1942–1989*. Andrews AFB, MD: 1776th Air Base Wing, 1990.

BARKER, Gray. "America's Captured Flying Saucers—The Cover-up of the Century." *UFO Report* (May 1977).

———. "Archives Reveal More Crashed Saucers." *Gray Barker's Newsletter* (March 1982).

BARNETT, Ruth. Personal diary, 1947.

BAXTER, J., and ATKINS, T. *The Fire Came By*. Garden City, NY: Doubleday, 1976.

BECKLEY, Timothy Green. *MJ-12 and the Riddle of Hangar 18*. New Brunswick, NJ: Inner Light Publications, 1989.

BERLITZ, Charles, and MOORE, William L. *The Roswell Incident*. New York: Berkley Books, 1988.

BINDER, Otto. *What We Really Know About Flying Saucers*. Greenwich, CT: Fawcett Gold Medal Books, 1967.

BLOECHER, Ted. *Report on the UFO Wave of 1947*. Washington, DC: author, 1967.

BLUM, Howard. *Out There: The Government's Secret Quest for Extraterrestrials*. New York: Simon and Schuster, 1991.

BLUM, Ralph, with BLUM, Judy. *Beyond Earth: Man's Contact with UFOs*. New York: Bantam Books, 1974.

BRACEWELL, R. N. *The Galactic Club: Intelligent Life in Outer Space*. San Francisco, CA: W.H. Freeman, 1975.

232

BREW, John Otis, and DANSON, E. B. "The 1947 Reconnaissance and the Proposed Upper Gila Expedition of the Peabody Museum of Harvard University." *El Palacio* (July 1948): 211–222.

"Briefing to General Garland" (July 1967).

BRITTON, Jack, and WASHINGTON, George, Jr. *Military Shoulder Patches of the United States Armed Forces*. Tulsa, OK: M.C.N. Press, 1985.

BROWN, Eunice H. *White Sands History*. White Sands, NM: Public Affairs Office, 1959.

BROWN, Fred R. *National Security Management*. Washington, DC: Industrial College of the Armed Forces, 1972.

BRUNVAND, Jan Harold. *The Choking Doberman and Other "New" Urban Legends*. New York: W.W. Norton & Co., 1984.

BUCKHOUT, R. "Eyewitness Testimony." *Scientific American* (December 1974).

BUSKIRK, Winfred. *The Western Apache: Living in the Land Before 1950*. Norman, OK: University of Oklahoma, 1986.

CAHN, J. P. "The Flying Saucers and the Mysterious Little Men." *True* (September 1952).

———. "Flying Saucer Swindlers." *True* (August 1956).

CANADEO, Anne. *UFO's: The Fact or Fiction Files*. New York: Walker, 1990.

CANNON, Martin. "The Amazing Story of John Lear." *UFO Universe* (March 1990): 8.

CAREY, Thomas J. "The Search for the Archaeologists." *International UFO Reporter* (November/December 1991).

CARPENTER, John S. "Gerald Anderson: Truth vs. Fiction." *The MUFON UFO Journal* (September 1991): 3–7.

———. "Gerald Anderson: Disturbing Revelations." *The MUFON UFO Journal* (March 1993): 6–9.

CAMERON, Grant, and CRAIN, T. Scott, Jr. *UFOs, MJ-12 and the Government*. Seguin, TX: Mutual UFO Network, 1991.

CATES, Cliff. *Air Force Collecting*. Tulsa, OK: M.C.N. Press 1982.

CATOE, Lynn E. *UFOs and Related Subjects: An Annotated Bibliography*. Washington, DC: Government Printing Office, 1969.

CITIZENS AGAINST UFO SECRECY. "MJ-12: Myth or Reality?" *Just Cause* (December 1985).

———. "Confirmation of MJ-12?" *Just Cause* (June 1987).

———. "The MJ-12 Fiasco." *Just Cause* (September 1987).

———. "More On MJ-12." *Just Cause* (March 1989).

———. "MJ-12 Update." *Just Cause* (June 1989).

———. "Conversation with Dr. Sarbacher." *Just Cause* (September 1985).

CLARK, Jerome. *UFOs in the 1980s: The UFO Encyclopedia,* Vol. 1. Detroit, MI: Apogee Books, 1990.

———. *The Emergence of a Phenomenon: UFOs from the Beginning Through 1959—The UFO Encyclopedia,* Vol. 2. Detroit, MI: Omnigraphics, 1992.

———. "UFO Reporters: Outside the Inside." *Fate* (December 1990).

"Committee on Science and Astronautics" (1961).

COHEN, Daniel. *Encyclopedia of the Strange.* New York: Avon, 1987.

———. *UFOs—The Third Wave.* New York: M. Evans, 1988.

COOPER, Vicki. "The Roswell Case Revived: Was It An Alien Saucer." *UFO* (January/February 1991): 25–29.

CREIGHTON, Gordon. "Top U.S. Scientist Admits Crashed UFOs." *Flying Saucer Review* (October 1985).

———. "Close Encounters of an Unthinkable and Inadmissible Kind." *Flying Saucer Review* (July/August 1979).

———. "Further Evidence of Retrievals." *Flying Saucer Review* (January 1980).

———. "Continuing Evidence of Retrievals of the Third Kind." *Flying Saucer Review* (January/February 1982).

DAVIDSON, Leon, ed. *Flying Saucers: An Analysis of Air Force Project Blue Book Special Report No. 14.* Clarksburg, VA: Saucerian Press, 1971.

DENNETT, Preston. "Project Redlight: Are We Flying the Saucers Too?" *UFO Universe* (May 1990): 39.

DIXON, Robert T. *Dynamic Astronomy.* Englewood Cliffs, NJ: Prentice-Hall, Inc., 1971.

DOBBS, D. L. "Crashed Saucers—The Mystery Continues." *UFO Report* (September 1979).

"DoD News Releases And Fact Sheets" (1952–1968).

DRAKE, Frank. "How Can We Detect Radio Transmissions from Distant Planetary Systems?" *Sky and Telescope* (January 1960): 140–143.

EBERHART, George M., ed. *The Roswell Report: A Historical Perspective.* Chicago, IL: CUFOS, 1991.

ECKER, Don. "MJ-12 'Suspected Forgery,' Air Force Says." *UFO,* Vol. 8, No. 3 (1993): 5.

EDITORS OF LOOK. "Flying Saucers." *Look* (1966).

EDWARDS, Frank. *Flying Saucers—Here and Now!* New York: Bantam Books, 1968.

———. *Flying Saucers—Serious Business.* New York: Bantam Books, 1966.

———. *Strange World.* New York: Bantam Books, 1969.

Eighth Air Force Staff Directory, Texas (June 1947).

Fact Sheet, "Office of Naval Research 1952 Greenland Cosmic Ray Scientific Expedition" (October 16, 1952).

FALK, Stanley L., and BAUER, Theodore W. *The National Security Structure*. Washington, DC: Industrial College of the Armed Forces, 1972.

FAWCETT, Lawrence, and GREENWOOD, Barry J. *Clear Intent: The Government Cover-up of the UFO Experience*. Englewood Cliffs, NJ: Prentice-Hall, 1984.

Final Report, "Project Twinkle" (November 1951).

FINNEY, Ben R., and JONES, Eric M. *Interstellar Migration and the Human Experience*. California: University of California Press, 1985.

First Status Report, Project STORK (Preliminary to Special Report No. 14, April 1952).

FITZSIMONS, Bernard, ed. *The Illustrated Encyclopedia of 20th Century Weapons and Warfare*. New York: Columbia House, 1969.

Flint (Michigan) City Directories 1945–1950.

"Flying Saucers Again." *Newsweek* (April 17, 1950): 29.

FORD, Brian. *German Secret Weapons: Blueprint for Mars*. New York: Ballantine Books, 1969.

FORWARD, Robert L. "Roundtrip Interstellar Travel Using Laser-Pushed Lightsails," *Journal of Spacecraft* (1984).

FOWLER, Raymond E. *Casebook of a UFO Investigator*. Englewood Cliffs, NJ: Prentice-Hall, 1981.

———. "What About Crashed UFOs?" *Official UFO* (April 1976).

FULLER, John G. *The Interrupted Journey*. New York: Dial Press, 1966.

Genesce County (Michigan) Telephone Directories 1945–1950.

GILLMOR, Daniel S., ed. *Scientific Study of Unidentified Flying Objects*. New York: Bantam Books, 1969.

GOLDSMITH, Donald. *Nemesis*. New York: Berkley Books, 1985.

———. *The Quest for Extraterrestrial Life*. Mill Valley, CA: University Science Books, 1980.

GOOD, Timothy. *Above Top Secret*. New York: Morrow, 1988.

———. *Alien Contact*. New York: Morrow, 1993.

HALL, Richard. *Uninvited Guests*. Santa Fe, NM: Aurora Press, 1988.

———, ed. *The UFO Evidence*. Washington, DC: NICAP, 1964.

———. "Crashed Discs—Maybe," *International UFO Reporter*, Vol. 10, No. 4 (July/August 1985).

———. "MJ-12: Still Holding Its Own Through Thickets of Debate." *UFO* (January/February 1991): 30–32.

HAUGLAND, Vern. "AF Denies Recovering Portions of 'Saucers.' " *Albuquerque New Mexican* (March 23, 1954).

HAZARD, Catherine. "Did the Air Force Hush Up a Flying Saucer Crash?" *Woman's World* (February 27, 1990): 10.

"History of the Eighth Air Force, Fort Worth, Texas" (microfilm). Air Force Archives, Maxwell Air Force Base, AL.

"History of the 509th Bomb Group, Roswell, New Mexico" (microfilm). Air Force Archives, Maxwell Air Force Base, AL.

HOGG, Ivan U., and KING, J. B. *German and Allied Secret Weapons of World War II.* London: Chartwell Books, 1974.

HURT, Wesley R., and McKNIGHT, Daniel. "Archaeology of the San Augustine Plains: A Preliminary Report." *American Antiquity* (January 1949): 172–194.

HYNEK, J. Allen. *The UFO Experience: A Scientific Inquiry.* Chicago: Henry Regency, 1972.

JACOBS, David M. *The UFO Controversy in America.* New York: Signet, 1975.

JONES, Willliam E., and MINSHALL, Rebecca D. "Aztec, New Mexico—A Crash Story Reexamined." *International UFO Reporter* (September/October 1991): 11.

JUNG, Carl G. *Flying Saucers: A Modern Myth of Things Seen in the Sky.* New York: Harcourt, Brace, 1959.

KEEL, John. "Now It's No Secret: The Japanese 'Fugo Balloon.' " *UFO* (January/February 1991): 33–35.

KEYHOE, Donald E. *Aliens From Space.* New York: Signet, 1974.

KLASS, Philip J. *UFOs Explained.* New York: Random House, 1974.

———. "Crash of the Crashed Saucer Claim." *The Skeptical Enquirer,* Vol. 10 (1986).

———. *The Public Deceived.* Buffalo, NY: Prometheus Books, 1983.

KNAACK, Marcelle. *Encyclopedia of U.S. Air Force Aircraft and Missile Systems.* Washington, DC: Office of Air Force History, 1988.

KOZEMCHAK, Dan. "USS *Antietam* in Research Role." *Naval Aviation News* (November 1961): 28.

LANG, Daniel. *The Man in the Thick Lead Suit.* New York: Oxford University Press, 1954.

LA PAZ, Lincoln, and ROSENFELD, Albert. "Japan's Balloon Invasion of America." *Collier's* (January 17, 1953): 9.

LAURENCE, J. R., and PERRY, C. *Hypnosis, Will, and Memory: A Psycho-legal History.* New York: Guilford, 1988.

Library of Congress Legislative Reference Service. "Facts About UFOs" (May 1966.)

LOFTUS, Elizabeth R. *Eye-Witness Testimony*. Cambridge, MA: Harvard University Press, 1979.

LORE, Gordon, and DENEAULT, Harold H. *Mysteries of the Skies: UFOs in Perspective*. Englewood Cliff, NJ: Prentice-Hall, 1968.

LORENZEN, Coral, and LORENZEN, Jim. *Abducted!* New York: Berkley Medallion Books, 1977.

———. *Encounters with UFO Occupants*. New York: Berkley Medallion Books, 1976.

———. *Flying Saucer Occupants*. New York: Signet, 1967.

———. *Flying Saucers: The Startling Evidence of the Invasion from Outer Space*. New York: Signet, 1966.

LUDWIG, A. M. *The Importance of Lying*. Springfield, IL: C.C. Thomas, 1965.

MACCABEE, Bruce. "Hiding the Hardware." *International UFO Reporter* (September/October 1991): 4.

———. "What the Admiral Knew." *International UFO Reporter* (November/December 1986).

MCCLELLAN, Mike. "The Flying Saucer Crash of 1948 Is a Hoax." *Offical UFO* (October 1975).

"McClellan Sub-Committee Hearings" (March 1958).

"McCormack Sub-Committee Briefing" (August 1958).

MCDONOUGH, Thomas R. *The Search for Extraterrestrial Intelligence*. New York: Wiley, 1987.

MENZEL, Donald H., and BOYD, Lyle G. *The World of Flying Saucers*. Garden City, NY: Doubleday, 1963.

MENZEL, Donald H., and TAVES, Ernest H. *The UFO Enigma*. Garden City, NY: Doubleday, 1977.

MICHEL, Aime. *The Truth about Flying Saucers*. New York: Pyramid Books, 1967.

MOORE, William L., and FRIEDMAN, Stanton. "MJ-12 and Phil Klass: What Are the Facts?" *MUFON Symposium Proceedings*. Seguin, TX: Mutual UFO Network, 1988.

MOORE, William L., and SHANDERA, Jaime H. *The MJ-12 Documents: An Analytical Report*. Burbank, CA: Fair Witness Project, 1991.

MUELLER, Robert. *Air Force Bases*. Vol. 1, *Active Air Force Bases Within the United States of America on 17 September 1982*. Washington, DC: Office of Air Force History, 1989.

National Security Agency. *Presidential Documents*. Washington, DC: Executive Order 12356, 1982.

Naval Research Newsletter. "Research with High-Altitude Balloons."

NICKELL, Joe. "The Hangar 18 Tales" *Common Ground* (June 1984).

NICKELL, Joe, and FISCHER, John F. "The Crash-Saucer Forgeries," *International UFO Reporter*, Vol. 15, No. 2 (March/April 1990): 4–12.

NORTHROP, Stuart A. *Minerals of New Mexico*. Albuquerque, NM: University of New Mexico, 1959.

O'BRIEN, Mike. "New Witness To San Agustin Crash." *The MUFON Journal* (March 1991): 3–9.

ORNE, M., SOSKIS, D. A., DINGES, D. F., and ORNE, E. "Hypnotically Refreshed Testimony: Enhanced Memory or Tampering with Evidence?" *National Institute of Justice: Issues and Practices in Criminal Justice*. Washington, DC: U.S. Government Printing Office, 1985.

PALMER, Ray, and ARNOLD, Kenneth. *The Coming of the Saucers*. Amherst, MA: Amherst Press, 1952.

PAPAGIANNIS, Michael D., ed. *The Search for Extraterrestrial Life: Recent Developments*. Boston, MA: D. Reidel, 1985.

PEACOCK, Lindsay T. *Strategic Air Command*. London: Arms & Armour Press, Ltd., 1988.

PEEBLES, Curtis. *The Moby Dick Project*. Washington, DC: Smithsonian Institution Press, 1991.

PETTINATI, H. M., ed. *Hypnosis and Memory*. New York: Guilford, 1988.

"Press Conference—General Samford" (1952).

PRICE, Alfred. *Luftwaffe*. New York: Ballantine, 1969.

"Project Blue Book" (microfilm). National Archives, Washington, DC.

RAAF Base Phone Book, Roswell, New Mexico (August 1947).

RAAF Yearbook, Roswell, New Mexico (1947).

RANDLE, Kevin D. "The Flight of the Great Airship." *True's Flying Saucers and UFOs Quarterly* (spring 1977).

———. "Mysterious Clues Left Behind by UFOs." *Saga's UFO Annual* (summer 1972).

———. *The October Scenario*. Iowa City, IA: Middle Coast Publishing, 1988.

———. "The Pentagon's Secret Air War Against UFOs." *Saga* (March 1976).

———. *The UFO Casebook*. New York: Warner, 1989.

RANDLE, Kevin D., and CORNETT, Robert Charles. "Project Blue Book Cover-up: Pentagon Suppressed UFO Data." *UFO Report*, Vol. 2, No. 5 (fall 1975).

RANDLES, Jenny. *The UFO Conspiracy*. New York: Javelin, 1987.

Register of the Army of the United States. Washington, DC: United States Army.

"Rocket and Missile Firings." White Sands Proving Grounds (January–July 1947).

RODEGHIER, Mark. "Roswell, 1989." *International UFO Reporter* (September/October 1989): 4.

ROSIGNOLI, Guido. *The Illustrated Encyclopedia of Military Insignia of the 20th Century*. Secaucus, NJ: Chartwell Books, 1986.

RUPPELT, Edward J. *The Report on Unidentified Flying Objects*. New York: Ace, 1956.

RUSSELL, Eric. "Phantom Balloons Over North America." *Modern Aviation* (February 1953).

SAGAN, Carl, and PAGE, Thornton, eds. *UFO's: Scientific Debate*. New York: Norton, 1974.

SANDRESON, Ivan T. *Uninvited Visitors*. New York: Cowles Communications, 1967.

———. *Invisible Residents*. New York: World Publishing, 1970.

SCHAFFNER, Ron. "Roswell: A Federal Case?" *UFO Brigantia* (summer 1989).

SCHEFLIN, A. W., and SHAPIRO, L. *Trance on Trial*. New York: Guilford, 1989.

SCULLY, Frank. *Behind the Flying Saucers*. New York: Henry Holt, 1950.

———. "Scully's Scrapbook." *Variety* (October 12, 1949): 61.

SHANDERA, Jaime. "New Revelation about the Roswell Wreckage: A General Speaks Up." *The MUFON Journal* (January 1991).

SHEAFFER, Robert. *The UFO Verdict*. Buffalo, NY: Prometheus Books, 1981.

SHKLOVSKY, I. S., and SAGAN, Carl. *Intelligent Life in the Universe*. New York: Dell, 1968.

SIMMONS, H. M. "Once Upon a Time in the West." *Magonia* (August 1985).

SNIDER, L. Britt. "What Are We Doing About Espionage?" *Defense* (November 1985).

Special Report No. 14 (Project Blue Book, 1955).

SPENCER, John. *The UFO Encyclopedia*. New York: Avon, 1993.

SPENCER, John, and EVANS, Hilary. *Phenomenon*. New York: Avon, 1988.

Status Reports. "Grudge—Blue Book, Nos. 1–12.".

STEIGER, Brad. *Project Blue Book*. New York: Ballantine, 1976.

———. *Strangers from the Skies*. New York: Award Books, 1966.

STEINMAN, William S., and STEVENS, Wendelle C. *UFO Crash at Aztec*. Boulder, CO: authors, 1986.

STEVENSON, William. *Intrepid's Last Case*. New York: Villard Books, 1988.

STONE, Clifford E. *UFO's: Let the Evidence Speak for Itself*. Roswell, NM: author, 1991.

STORY, Ronald D., ed. *The Encyclopedia of UFOs*. Garden City, NY: Doubleday, 1980.

STRINGFIELD, Leonard H. *Situation Red: The UFO Siege!* Garden City, NY: Doubleday, 1977.

———. *UFO Crash/Retrieval Syndrome: Status Report II*. Seguin, TX: Mutual UFO Network, 1980.

———. *UFO Crash/Retrievals: Amassing the Evidence: Status Report III*. Cincinnati, OH: author, 1982.

———. *UFO Crash/Retrievals: The Inner Sanctum: Status Report VI*. Cincinnati, OH: author, 1991.

STURROCK, P. A. "UFOs—A Scientific Debate." *Science* 180 (1973): 593.

SULLIVAN, Walter. *We Are Not Alone.* New York: Signet, 1966.

SUMNER, Donald A. "Skyhook Churchill 1966." *Naval Reserve Reviews* (January 1967): 29.

SUTHERLY, Curt. "Inside Story of the New Hampshire UFO Crash." *UFO Report* (July 1977).

TAYLOR, John W. R. *Combat Aircraft of the World.* New York: G.P. Putnam's Sons, 1969.

Tech Bulletin. "Army Ordnance Department Guided Missile Program" (January 1948).

Technical Report. "Unidentified Aerial Objects, Project SIGN" (February 1949).

Technical Report. "Unidentified Flying Objects, Project GRUDGE" (August 1949).

TODD, Robert G., "MJ-12 Rebuttal." *MUFON Journal* (January 1990): 17.

TODD, Robert G., RODEGHIER, Mark, GREENWOOD, Barry, and MACCABEE, Bruce. "A Forum on MJ-12." *International UFO Reporter* (May/June 1990): 15.

U.S. CONGRESS, Committee on Science and Astronautics. *Symposium on Unidentified Flying Objects.* Hearings, July 29, 1968. Washington, DC: U.S. Government Printing Office, 1968.

U.S. CONGRESS, House Committee on Armed Forces. *Unidentified Flying Objects.* Hearings, April 5, 1966. Washington, DC: U.S. Government Printing Office, 1968.

VALLEE, Jacques. *Anatomy of a Phenomenon.* New York: Ace, 1966.

———. *Challenge to Science.* New York: Ace, 1966.

———. *Revelation.* New York: Ballantine, 1991.

"Visitors from Venus." *Time* (January 9, 1950): 49.

WALKER, Lois E., and WICKAM, Shelby E. *From Huffman Prairie to the Moon.* Dayton, OH: 2750th Air Base Wing, Wright-Patterson AFB.

WAR DEPARTMENT. *Meteorological Balloons* (army technical manual). Washington, DC: Government Printing Office, 1944.

WATKINS, John G. "Hypnotic Hyermnesia and Forensic Hypnosis: A Cross-examination." *American Journal of Clinical Hypnosis,* 32.

WEBBER, Bert. *Retaliation: Japanese Attacks and Allied Countermeasures on the Pacific Coast in World War II.* Corvallis, OR: Oregon State University Press, 1975.

WILBUR, W. H. "Those Japanese Balloons." *Reader's Digest* (August 1950).

WILCOX, Inez. Personal writings 1947–1952.

WILKINS, Harold T. *Flying Saucers on the Attack.* New York: Citadel Press, 1954.

———. *Flying Saucers Uncensored.* New York: Pyramid Books, 1967.

WILSON, Colin. *Mysteries.* New York: Perigee Books, 1978.

WISE, David, and ROSS, Thomas B. *The Invisible Government.* New York: 1964.

ZEIDMAN, Jennie. "I Remember Blue Book." *International UFO Reporter* (March/April 1991): 7.

Periodicals

The following newspapers and periodicals were used as research sources for this work:

Alamogordo News

Albuquerque Journal

Albuquerque Tribune

Ann Arbor News

Arizona Republican

Atchison Globe

Beaver County Times

Beaver Falls News-Tribune

Boston Advertiser

Bozeman Daily Chronicle

Burlington Hawk-Eye

Carlsbad Current-Angus

Cedar Rapids Gazette

Cheyenne Tribune

Chicago Daily News

Chicago Daily Times

Chicago Herald American

Chicago Sun

Circleville Herald

Clinton Herald

Dalhart Texan

Dallas Morning News

Dallas Times Herald

Dayton Daily News

Decatur Evening Republican

Denver Post

Deseret News and Telegram

Des Moines Register

Detroit Evening News

Detroit Free Press

El Paso Herald Post

El Paso Times

Erie Daily Times

Eureka Reporter

Flint Journal

Fort Worth Star Telegram

Greenburg Tribune-Review

Harrisburg Evening News

Harrisburg Patriot

Houston Chronicle

Las Vegas Review-Journal

Las Vegas Sun

Latrobe Bulletin

Lebanon Daily News

Lincoln Daily State Journal

Livonia Observer & City Post

London Times

Lorain Journal

Los Angeles Herald Express

Los Angeles Times

Louisville Courier-Journal

Lubbock Avalanche-Journal

Midland Reporter Telegram

Nashville American

Nebraska Nugget

Nephi Times-News

Nevada State Journal

New York Herald Tribune

New York Times, The

Odessa American

Omaha Daily Bee

Omaha World-Herald

Oregonian

Oregon Journal

Palm Beach Post

Phoenix Gazette

Pittsburgh Post-Gazette

Pittsburgh Press

Reno Evening Gazette

Rocky Mountain News

Roswell Daily Record

Roswell Morning Dispatch

Salt Lake Tribune
San Francisco Call
San Francisco Chronicle
St. Joseph Daily Herald
St. Paul Pioneer Press
Sterling Gazette

Syracuse Herald-American
Syracuse Post Standard
Toledo Blade
Toronto Daily Star
Washington Post
Waterloo Courier

Organizations:

Literally dozens of organizations and institutions provided research assistance for this work. Although none of them subscribed to the theory of extraterrestrial intervention, all were willing to provide what assistance they could.

Air Force Archives, Maxwell Air Force Base, AL
Albuquerque High School, Albuquerque, NM
Albuquerque Public Library, Albuquerque, NM
Albuquerque Public School System, Albuquerque, NM
Arizona State Museum, Tempe, AZ
Bettmann Photo Archives, New York, NY
Brigham Young University, Provo, UT
Bureau of Land Management (BLM), Roswell, NM
Bureau of Mines, Socorro, NM
Carswell Air Force Base, Fort Worth, TX
Cedar Rapids Public Library, Cedar Rapids, IA
Clark County Public Library, Las Vegas, NV
Clark County Sheriff's Office, Las Vegas, NV
Dallas Public Library, Dallas, TX
Dayton and Montgomery County Library, Dayton, OH
Department of the Air Force, Washington, DC
Department of the Army, Washington, DC
Department of Defense, Washington, DC
Department of the Navy, Washington, DC
Department of State, Washington, DC
Ector County Public Library, Odessa, TX
Eisenhower Center, Abilene, KS
El Paso Public Library, El Paso, TX
Federal Bureau of Investigation, Washington, DC
Flint Public Library, Flint, MI
Forest Service, Magdalena Ranger District, Magdalena, NM
Highland High School, Albuquerque, NM
Holloman Air Force Base, NM
Institute of Meteorics, Albuquerque, NM
International UFO Museum and Research Center, Roswell, NM
Iowa City Public Library, Iowa City, IA

J. Allen Hynek Center for UFO Studies, Chicago, IL
KBIM-TV, Roswell, NM
Kirtland Air Force Base, NM
Kirtland Air Force Base East (Sandia), Public Affairs Office, NM
KOB-TV, Albuquerque, NM
KOBR-TV, Roswell, NM
Laboratory of Anthropology, Santa Fe, NM
Los Alamos Historical Museum, Los Alamos, NM
Los Alamos Public Affairs Office, Los Alamos, NM
Mama's Minerals, Albuquerque, NM
Midland County Public Library, Midland, TX
Museum of New Mexico, Santa Fe, NM
National Aeronautics and Space Administration, Houston, TX
National Archives, Washington, DC
National Personnel Records Center (Army), Saint Louis, MO
National Transportation and Safety Board, Washington, DC
New Mexico Institute of Mining and Technology, Socorro, NM
Offutt Air Force Base, Omaha, NE
Operational Archives—Aviation Historical Branch, Washington, DC
Pease Air Force Base, NH
Roswell Chamber of Commerce, Roswell, NM
Roswell Public Library, Roswell, NM
Smithsonian Institution, Washington, DC
Socorro Chamber of Commerce, Socorro, NM
Southern Methodist University, Dallas, TX
Southwest Collections, Texas Tech, Lubbock, TX
Southwestern Minerals, Albuquerque, NM
Texas State Archives, Austin, TX
Texas Tech University, Lubbock, TX
Truman Presidential Library, Independence, MO
UFO Enigma Museum, Roswell, NM
United States Department of Agriculture, Washington, DC
University of Colorado, Boulder, CO
University of Arizona, Tucson, AR
University of Iowa, Department of Anthropology, Iowa City, IA
University of New Mexico, Albuquerque, NM
University of Pennsylvania, Philadelphia, PN
University of Texas—Arlington, Arlington, TX
University of Texas of the Periam Basin, Odessa, TX
U.S. Army Center for Military History, Washington, DC
U.S. Army Intelligence and Security Command, Fort Meade, MD
U.S. Army Materiel Command, Alexandria, VA
U.S. Army Military History Institute, Carlisle Barracks, PA

U.S. Army Missile Command, Redstone Arsenal, AL
U.S. Army Ordnance Museum, Aberdeen Proving Ground, MD
White Sands Missile Range, NM
Wright-Patterson Air Force Base, Dayton, OH

Index